UNDERSTANDING ORGANIZATIONS THROUGH

LANGUAGE

UNDERSTANDING ORGANIZATIONS THROUGH LANGUAGE

SUSANNE TIETZE, LAURIE COHEN AND GILL MUSSON

SAGE Publications
London • Thousand Oaks • New Delhi

SAGE Publications Ltd
6 Bonhill Street
London EC2A 4PU

SAGE Publications Inc.
2455 Teller Road
Thousand Oaks, California 91320

SAGE Publications India Pvt Ltd
B-42, Panchsheel Enclave
Post Box 4109
New Delhi 100 017

British Library Cataloguing in Publication data

A catalogue record for this book is available from the British Library

ISBN 0 7619 6718 4
ISBN 0 7619 6719 2 (pbk)

Library of Congress Control Number is available

Typeset by C&M Digitals (P) Ltd., Chennai, India
Printed in India at Gopsons Papers Ltd., Noida

Contents

Acknowledgement

This book arose out of a need to develop teaching material for use on language and organization courses. To a large extent, the approach we have taken in this text has been directed by the responses and feedback from our students. We thank them for their keen involvement.

Introduction

This is a book about language and meaning making. We have written it because we believe that an understanding of how language works is essential to an understanding of organizational processes. This is as such not a radically new position; rather, the centrality of language in creating and reflecting organizational realities has been firmly established amongst many management and organization theorists.

A recent contribution, for example, is a book on the language of organizations edited by Westwood and Linstead (2001). Its essays explore such topics as power, knowledge, narrative, meaning, rhetoric, change and discourse. Similar themes are pursued in this book, though its emphasis is on providing a source for the novice reader, as well as the teacher and/or scholar, by providing a context to the themes, examples and exercises derived from our teaching practice and research projects.

Most management or business teaching curricular or training syllabuses still omit explicit discussions on **how** language works and **why** it is central to organizational meaning making processes. In writing this book we hope to address this gap by demonstrating the relevance of language to all organizational processes and to everyone who has an interest in understanding organizations better, be it as researcher, consultant, student, teacher, manager or employee.

An English saying goes like this:

Sticks and stones can break my bones, but words can never hurt me.
Do you agree?

Anticipating one of the book's major tenets, that the meaning of an **object** is made by what it is not (see Chapter 2), we wish to draw attention to what this book is not: it is not another textbook on organizational behaviour/theory, summarizing and presenting the traditional store of knowledge from the field of organization studies. Nor is it a skills-based book, promising to reveal 'the 10 definite steps to become an efficient communicator'. Indeed, we are quite sceptical about these approaches and found much to agree with in Deborah Cameron's book (2000) *Good to Talk?*. Cameron takes issue with the current commodification of talk, as exemplified in the obsession with communication and the plethora of workshops, seminars and training programmes which provide value laden prescriptions aiming to make their participants into more effective, more efficient communicators (with a higher market value).

We do not attempt – nor wish – to equip anyone with a set of mechanical rules for speaking or listening. In focusing on **meaning** (and interpretation) we endeavour to draw attention to unstable, dynamic and complex processes. At best, we hope to instil a sense of awareness and choice in the readers of this book. We agree with Cameron (2000: 180) that: "A competent speaker is one who understands the 'grammar of consequences' [how her choices will be interpreted – the authors] and can judge which of the available choices will come closest to producing the desired interpretation in a particular set of circumstances."

Handle with care!

This is *not* a book about organizational communication that flows upwards, downwards and laterally within organizations in a neat container – **the channel**. Therefore you will *not* find instructions how to direct your **message flow** more effectively or how to avoid **breakdown in communication**; you will *not* receive advice on optimum frequency of communication; on how to process information or on how to become an effective communicator. The assumptions entailed in this kind of understanding of communication are simplistic and functional: they view communication as a thing and the essence of communication as being located in the transmission and the channel – not in the **meaning** and **meaning making processes**, which is our perspective.

We attempt to deal with complexity and change. We address themes such as power, bias, multiple perspectives, plurality and contradiction. There are no easy or quick remedies for solving organizational problems. This stance requires the reader to be patient, maybe even to accept degrees of frustration; though we believe it rewards through insightful discovery and understanding.

In this book we use a particular set of ideas that originate from semiology (the study of meaning). We apply these ideas to social and organizational settings to illuminate the processes of how meaning is made and how it is established as truthful and normal. From the readers' point of view exploring these processes might entail gaining a better understanding of their own involvement in meaning making and a better appreciation of the choices they have as students, researchers, managers, consultants and citizens.

How to work with this book

We do not presume that the reader has any prior knowledge about the topics and themes of the book. Therefore, in each chapter we provide definitions and explanations of the relevant basic concepts and ideas, as well as the theoretical themes, and we ground them in current literature and theoretical debates. Linkages between themes are indicated through cross-references, in particular where themes such as power are discussed within different chapters. Furthermore, each chapter provides applications and examples, together with case studies, tasks and activities. These draw on academic literature, our own research and on our own observations, reflections and experience, and examples taken from fiction, film and newspapers and the world wide web. In choosing this approach we endeavour to bring the theoretical themes alive and to make their study enjoyable. We found this varied approach helpful in leading and facilitating the language workshops and courses that we have run and continue to run in our respective institutions (see Musson and Cohen, 1999, for a more detailed discussion). We have found that edification and entertainment are not mutually exclusive entities, but inform and nourish each other.

At the end of each chapter we provide a summary and some recommended readings. Recommended readings present a selection of sources that we have found useful and that helped us to gain insight into particular ideas or concepts. Some of these are seminal classical texts; others are more obscure and less well known, but we found them helpful. We have selected them on the basis of whether they furthered understanding in pedagogical and/or academic terms, or just because we found them interesting. References at the end of the book list in alphabetical order all the sources that have been used.

As you, the reader, will have noticed, we choose to refer to us, the authors, as *we*. *We* is the collective voice of three individuals, who come from different national and social backgrounds and whose lives and professional development followed different twists and turns. However, we share a love and enthusiasm for all things linguistic, as well as the belief that language matters in defining who we are. We will address *you*, the reader, as either reader or readership or use personal pronouns when inviting you to do an exercise or to reflect about a given theme.

We have used the plural forms when referring to groups of people, attempting to avoid the clumsiness of s/he, her/him, but have, if this was not possible or would have detracted from the point we are trying to make, privileged the female voice.

Nevertheless, a personal introduction

We wrote this book because of our shared enthusiasm for language, our shared professional and subject backgrounds and our shared concern about organizational processes that frequently seem to be unjust, obscure, messy or ineffective or even dangerous. We also found that understanding processes of meaning making helped us to orientate ourselves in our individual, professional and private lives.

(Continued)

Gill: All my life I have lived and worked within a forty-mile radius of the English town in which I was born. But from a very early age I have moved between cultures, and thereby encountered and learned different 'languages'. My background as a working class grammar school girl from a mining village, the only child of six siblings that enjoyed/endured that particular kind of education, necessitated 'translating' between these two cultures from the age of eleven, often painfully. A clear and vivid memory is enough to demonstrate my point. It was the end of the first chemistry lesson (Chemistry! What's chemistry? What's a Bunsen burner?) at the grammar school, and I asked one of my schoolmates to help me **siden** the equipment from our table, a verb which was used every day in my home instead of **clear**. The confusion, embarrassment and amusement that this caused is an enduring reminder of the misunderstanding and humiliation that can occur when you speak the same national language, but use a different dialect. Linguistic confusion, then, came to symbolise for me the strange new world that confused, frightened and at times frustrated me, and I left at sixteen. I returned to education many years later, taking a first degree in communication studies, resurrecting my dormant interest in language, culture and meaning making (and learning yet another new 'language' of academe). This interest was fuelled when I did my PhD in social and occupational psychology, where language seemed to be ignored (then) except as a mirror of an objective reality. I have been able to follow my fascination with language, culture and meaning making through into the organizational arena during my subsequent work in business and management schools.

Laurie: My interest in language and meaning making is both personal and academic. I am American and have been living and working in the UK for nearly 20 years. Given our seemingly common language, I expected that after a little while the strangeness of those early days would fade and gradually disappear. This didn't happen. Instead, I am struck by how often I still find myself translating between my two worlds, slipping and sliding between the curious gaze of the tourist and the nonchalant confidence of the local. On the academic side, with a first degree in English literature and French, and a Masters in communication studies, I have long been fascinated by the relationship between language and culture, and between authors, texts and readers. Moving to a business school to do my PhD, I was (and still am) keen to understand more about how these relationships are played out in organizational settings.

Susanne: I am by national background German and came to live and work in the United Kingdom in the early 1990s. Having been socialised – indoctrinated? – in the traditions of German idealism and its methods of *verstehen* (to understand), I found myself in a prolonged state of linguistic confusion during the first years of my employment as a lecturer in a

British Business School. Despite a technical proficiency in the English language, and despite being technically able to do my job, the vocabulary and practices of **customer and client**, **customised courses**, **market demands** and so on troubled, irritated and confused me. I remember that a senior manager of the school once told me that I as a linguist needed to define my "added value" to the school – an invitation that I responded to with a helpless and hostile silence. Eventually, the experience of puzzlement, strangeness and frequent feelings of powerlessness led to the writing of a PhD thesis, which was a theoretical and empirical attempt at resolving this linguistic confusion. Analysing organizational images, discourses, stories and symbols within the traditions of semiology helped me to understand better my own involvement, role and practice in organizational and social worlds and, consequently, began to inform the choices I made.

A brief overview of the book

The first chapter lays the foundations for the other chapters in so far as it summarizes our understanding of how language reflects and constitutes social realities. The second chapter explains and describes semiological ideas about relationships within and between signs and how meaning is forged in these relationship-building processes. In this regard Chapter 2 has a theoretical slant, since it introduces the conceptual lenses we will wear throughout the book. The other chapters are mainly self-contained; that is they can be read on their own, with the cross-referencing system indicating linkages between the chapters and their themes.

Chapter 1, *Spinning webs of meaning: language and social reality* explains the bedrock of our position regarding the role of language in the shaping of social realities. It entails reflections on the interpretive approach to analysing organizations and focuses, in particular, on the role of language.

Chapter 2, *A semiological approach to meaning making*, introduces the ideas and terminology of semiology, and demonstrates how it is conducive to understanding the processes of decoding and encoding, which are played out in cultural contexts. Meaning is shown to be systematic and changeable.

Chapter 3, *Understanding organizations through metaphor*, focuses on one particular device through which meaning is generated, changed and challenged: the metaphorical process. Metaphors are discussed from an applied perspective and from an empirical perspective.

Chapter 4, *Understanding organizations through stories and narratives*, introduces the concept of stories and narrative as depositories of meaning in an increasingly fragmented and diverse (organizational) world. Stories are viewed as the medium, as well as the target of research on the one hand, and as a means of organizational control on the other hand.

Chapter 5, *Understanding organizations through discourse*, reviews meaning making as positioned in wider contexts, focusing on the notions of **genre** and **frame** to investigate the notion of meaning making. The issues of power and influence are addressed in this chapter.

Chapter 6, *Language, culture, meaning*, examines the connection between language and culture (linguistic determinism and linguistic relativity) and focuses on the issue of meaning making within different cultural contexts; English as the lingua franca of business; non-verbal meaning making; and ethnocentrism as the main barrier to the exchange of meaning. The focus of this chapter is on intercultural communication as it occurs in encounters between groups from different cultural backgrounds.

Chapter 7, *Gender and language*, looks at the processes of gendering and how gender and language intersect in organizational contexts.

Chapter 8, *Leadership and language* defines leadership as a social function, subject to the exercise of hegemonic processes. Leadership is considered as a process of generating new meaning. The rhetorical devices used by leaders are discussed.

Chapter 9, *Meaning making in the electronic age*, reviews emergent new forms of communication from a semiological perspective. It discusses how metaphorical, written and non-verbal codes continue to play an informative part in the shaping of virtual worlds.

Conclusion: This entails a brief reflection and points to possible future fields of enquiry.

CHAPTER ONE

Spinning Webs of Meaning: Language and Social Reality

This chapter describes the basic assumptions we, the authors, make about social reality and the processes through which it is constructed. It focuses on the role of language in the processes of bestowing meaning to the social world: an interpretive perspective is explained and espoused. Within this approach the willingness to examine one's own beliefs and assumptions is recognised as crucial to the development of genuine dialogue between different social groups.

Objectives

In this chapter we will:

- introduce the notion of social construction;
- explain the central role of language to the processes of meaning making;
- explain the interpretive perspective on social life; and
- introduce the notion of dialogue as the key aspect to understanding other worlds of meaning.

Words and signs are around us during every waking minute, and even in our dreams signs and symbols make up the journeys of our sleeping hours. We cannot escape words, we cannot but communicate. Language and communication are essential to what makes us human. How we talk, which language we use, and how we can express ourselves is intrinsically tied in with our concepts of identity and our sense of self. For example, everyone who has ever learned and practised a foreign language will appreciate that it is difficult to express one's true self when struggling to articulate in a foreign language. The power of language in expressing one's identity is vividly illustrated in a moving story told by a former colleague about one of her PhD students, a young man from Malaysia. Although their supervision sessions were conducted in English, the student always brought his wife with him, who did not speak any English at all. So she sat there looking at the floor, a mute presence, usually ignored. One day there was a knock at the colleague's office door. It was the PhD student's wife, all by herself. She took our colleague by the hand and led her across the campus, to the music department and into a beautiful room with a grand piano. She motioned for our colleague to sit down. She herself sat down at the piano and proceeded to play the first movement of Rachmaninov's Second Concerto.

To us, this story reveals the need to express who we are. Normally, we do this through talking (language), or through dressing in a particular way (using symbols) and socialising with particular people, as behaviour and practices carry a symbolic function too. However, the 'mute' woman in our story was on foreign territory, an alien to the academic world and its emphasis on intellect as a prime feature of worthiness and standing. Her piano playing was a symbolic gesture that carried the following message: "I am a human being, too, with my own amazing talents and unique gifts. This is an expression of my humanity."

The ethnographer and management researcher Tony Watson (2001b: 19–20) muses about the difference between humans and hedgehogs:

> Humans [unlike hedgehogs] do not have guidelines for behaviour and interaction with others 'wired into' their brains. Humans have continually to 'work on' their humanness. They have to achieve humanness. They have to think about what it is to be female or male, a parent, a teenager, an ageing individual, a husband, wife, lover, friend, enemy, brother, sister, manager. We have an awful lot we need to make sense of to survive mentally. And we could not handle alone all these sources of anxiety. Our capacity for culture, language and concepts partly creates these problems. It makes possible, through the provision of the very words for example, the question 'Who am I?', or the question, 'Why should I follow this managerial instruction?'. But it also assists us with handling them.

We see language as both the medium through which, as well as the context within which, these fundamental processes of identity are forged. We propose to investigate these processes to see how meaning is bestowed on things, people, actions and practices through and in language.

An evening amongst friends ...

The evening progressed like so many evenings we had spent together. We talked, mostly about the same things, going back and forth over the same subjects until they were worn and soft with use. I sometimes think it was like we were weaving a cloth of our talk, all the strands of our lives threading back and forth, up and down, making a dense, intricate sort of pattern that we repeated and repeated until we could understand it. We never got bored of it, we were so easy with each other, wrapped up in these conversations that had gone on for years. (Denby, 2001: 46)

This is a short extract from the novel *Corazon* by Joolz Denby. Have you similar experiences? What part do they play in your life?

The novel is about a woman drawn into a new age religious cult – but it also provides interesting insights about words, meanings and misunderstandings. Potential readers be warned, there are some gruesome scenes and no happy ending.

Words and the meaning we attach to them are the fabric of life. How – and why – meanings are attached to words and phrases is the subject of this book. This includes consideration of how the meanings of words are changed and how words can carry different meanings. For example, much of the language of advertising uses words taken from religious or spiritual contexts. *Zen, uplifting, harmony, inner peace, soulful* are frequently cited to sell bubble baths, yoghurt or furniture. Whether these words carry both old and new meanings simultaneously, or simply have become **polysemic** (carrying different meanings), or have become empty slogans, is subject to debate. In this book we concern ourselves mainly with explaining the very processes of meaning making and how meanings change.

The anthropologist Clifford Geertz describes humans as being essentially defined by systems of meaning: "Man is an animal suspended in webs of significance he himself has spun .... and culture is those webs" (1973: 5). We agree with this metaphor as it views humans as being both actively making/spinning their worlds and bestowing meaning onto them as well as being passively suspended in the thus created worlds. Watson (2001b: 27) develops the idea of the basic two-sidedness of social life in so far as there is the side in which individuals can be seen to initiate, choose and shape their world, and the side in which they can be seen as being constrained and shaped by influences external to themselves. He writes:

Human initiative ('agency') is not simply constrained by the circumstances in which it occurs ('structure'), it may equally be enabled. The structures and circumstances in which humans find themselves partly shape what they think and do, yet humans also shape those thoughts and circumstances (the extent to which they are able to do this varying with the power associated with the position in which they find themselves).

We argue that language is central to these processes of **weaving, shaping** and **influencing**. Therefore, at the core of this book lies the view that sharing and negotiating meaning is fundamental to social/organizational life. These processes can be illuminated and investigated through a semiological analysis (see Chapter 2).

A case study

Judith is fifty-five years old, and is the owner/manager of a nursing home. As a nurse, she worked as a night sister in a large teaching hospital in a northern city in the UK for 20 years. She has been in business for herself for three years.

Judith sees nursing as her vocation. She completed her professional training within the UK NHS (National Health Service), and anticipated lifelong employment within that organization. She spoke of her early days in the NHS as challenging, but rewarding; at that time she strongly believed in what the NHS was trying to do. She said that she had "NHS values", that she belonged there. To Judith, what is most important is providing high-quality, personal attention for her patients, and she explained how she felt this approach used to be at the heart of NHS policy and practice.

In the last few years of her employment within the NHS, Judith became increasingly disillusioned. She explained how she felt that the Health Service was changing, becoming less caring and more business-like, and she found herself increasingly at odds with the organization and its direction. She profoundly disagreed with the radical shift in NHS policy, and felt that within her hospital she could no longer practice the highest quality nursing, the sort of nursing that she was trained for. She said she felt constrained and disabled by the new regime. What Judith found especially difficult was trying to reconcile her commitment to patients with the new emphasis on financial control, efficiency and accountability to managers. After 20 years Judith decided to resign.

As a demoralized night sister, Judith had a vision of the high-quality, one-to-one care she would be able to offer to the elderly residents in her future nursing home. After having purchased the home, inheriting, of course, its residents and their families, Judith continued to work in the NHS for three months. During these months she worked night and day, stopping only occasionally to "cat-nap on the floor, under the buzzers so that if anyone needed me I could hear". She describes those early days as "your worst nightmare. Because I didn't have a clue how to run the place …. It was horrific … If anyone had asked me after three months, I would've said that I'd have made the most awful mistake of my life". She felt "totally and utterly out of control."

Apart from the problem of doing two jobs, there were aspects of the venture that Judith had not considered. She was unprepared to deal with personnel issues, operational matters such as the on-going maintenance of the building, food preparation and laundry; and the social dimension of business life, which involved extensive networking with families, doctors and outside agencies. "Everything about it was new … I mean, I didn't know what the daily routine was, how they got people out of bed, who did what … I'd met these people once, for an hour on the Saturday, and then Monday morning at eight o'clock it was mine". At the time, Judith was overwhelmed by what she saw as these new and ever-increasing demands on her time, energy and personal resources – she was having to do things far beyond the role of a nurse.

Judith explained how as time went on she regained her sense of control and self-confidence. She described her home as happy and caring, and felt she offered her residents and their families high-quality provision. She had the respect and support of her staff and had established very positive working relationships with professionals and agencies outside the home.

Although Judith had become a successful owner/manager of a small business, she spoke with utmost pride and passion about "giving one-to-one care", "not minding night work" and "getting my hands dirty." When asked directly, she acknowledged that she had certain management skills, but said that she saw herself "first and foremost as a nurse."

- To what extent is Judith suspended in webs of meanings not of her own making?
- To what extent is she spinning her own webs of meaning and in doing so changing the structure of the web?
- Can you think of examples from your experience?

Interpretive understanding

Our view of organizational life is a processual one; that is to say we see organizations not as static entities, but as dynamic processes, constantly constructed and reconstructed through activities and practices, being woven in and through language and talk. Hence, we cannot claim to offer our readership a guide to finding out how things really are in their respective organizations. Indeed, any reader with such hopes will be bitterly disappointed. However, what we do offer is a particular framework (semiology) through which readers can attempt to understand how 'things' come to be imbued with particular meanings, that is, how meaning is made. We see language at the core of such processes and agree with Boden when she says that language, "is the lifeblood of all organizations and, as such, it both shapes and is shaped by the structure of the organization itself" (1994: 8). By this, we do not mean that language is simply a mirror of an objectively existing reality – an unchanging and unchangeable "web" so to speak – rather, that it both creates and reflects organizational realities. Language is not a "mere messenger from the kingdom of reality" (Gergen, 1999: 11), but to use language is to engage in a social process of constructing particular realities.

Whenever we talk, we are partaking in the process of constructing a particular social reality.

The meaning of words?

Words such as empowerment, leadership, performance, knowledge, global, flexibility, excellence are examples of expressions that are frequently used in organizational contexts. You might wish to supplement this list with others, some of which may be more specific to your organization.

- Do these words carry any particular meanings within your unit/ department/work group? Do they carry different meanings outside these contexts?
- Have these words been used for a long time? If yes, has their meaning changed over time? If no, how have they been introduced?
- Who uses these words: *when*, *where* – and *why?*

Based on the above exercise you might have found that these words do not carry simple or absolute meanings and that there is no one-way relation between the word and the organizational reality 'out there'. You might also have found that some words are quite powerful and persuasive. This might be a function of who uses them (for example, a hierarchically senior person, someone you respect), but equally their power might lie in their very normality. Who, for example, would seriously argue with the logic and necessity of 'being a global player' or 'providing value for money' or 'relationship marketing'? How and why meaning is sometimes not only shaped, but manipulated and changed, so as to legitimise particular purposes and actions over others, forms part of the discussion of this book.

However, we do not mean that these words are not capable of capturing particular social phenomena or articulating something relevant about organizational processes, or stimulating reflection and critique on them. Rather, we point to the meaning of the words being unstable, dependent on context and perspective.

In doing this exercise you will have worked from an interpretive perspective. This means that you have studied the meaning of these words, the way they are made sense of in your organization. If you have investigated themes of power and persuasion you will have included some critical reflections about the constitution of social reality.

The interpretive approach

The **interpretive approach** stresses the centrality of meaning in social actions. Social reality is constituted through the words, symbols and actions that people invoke. Language use, as well as the meanings enacted from verbal and non-verbal messages, creates and sustains social reality.
(Adapted from Putnam, 1982; 1983)

This definition of the interpretive approach sums up the perspective and position of this book. We will not reiterate in each chapter that we make certain assumptions about the nature of social reality, that we view **meaning** and **meaning making** as ongoing intersubjective processes, that we view organizational actors as both agents of and subject to structures and external influences. We consider meaning as social rather than idiosyncratic. Thus, at this very moment of reading this text, you the reader are part of the meaning making process – the audience always is.

What's different?

The notion of **différance** is drawn from the work of Derrida (1978), a French philosopher. It indicates first, that the meaning of something, for example, *masculinity* or *health* is not inherent within, but lies in terms of its **différance** from other things – in this case, *femininity* and *illness*. But **différance** also indicates the idea of **deferral** – that the value of something is always modified by what comes after it (like words in a sentence, for example). Derrida used this idea of **deferral** to show how signs carry what he called *traces* of other signs, in the meaning making process (see Chapter 2 on Semiotics for more about signs and how they function).

The investigation of these social processes also entails looking at how meaning comes to be considered legitimate and how it informs action. The content of this book, therefore, goes beyond a purely 'textual' analysis of words and sentences, but also includes: the social and cultural contexts within which meaning is made; the relationship between talk and action; and the role of power and ideology in shaping worlds of meaning. Here we are referring to ideology as mobilising meanings to further the interests of certain groups.

Our main concern is to enable readers to understand better the processes of construction of (their) organizational realities. It is possible that on the basis of better understanding, critical questions may be asked, taken-for-granteds may be queried, the normal may begin to appear strange or fabricated. These reflections may well be part of a process of individual or organizational change. However, we are wary about any exaggerated claims about the potential of this book to have an emancipatory effect. Rather, we hope to raise questions, offer illustrations and examples and put forward arguments to convince the readers that a working knowledge of semiology can be quite a useful thing!

Thus, we invite the reader to suspend, even if it is only momentarily, their own taken-for-granteds, the assumptions they make about what it means to be *a manager, a student, a reader*, what it means to *behave professionally, become a global player* or provide *value for money*. Rather we should like the reader to investigate how these meanings came about.

Redescribing worlds

The liberal philosopher Richard Rorty (1989) proposes that the *ironist* is someone who is able to redescribe her own world and identity in new words, reaping the potential for regeneration, whilst being simultaneously never quite sure of herself, never being able to deny the fragility inherent in redescriptions.

"The opposite of irony is common sense." (Richard Rorty)

All human beings carry about a set of words, which they employ to justify their actions, their beliefs and their lives. These are the words in which we formulate praise of our friends and contempt for our enemies, our long-term projects, our deepest self-doubts and our highest hopes. They are the words in which we tell, sometimes prospectively and sometimes retrospectively, the story of our lives. I shall call these words a person's 'final vocabulary' (...) A small part of a final vocabulary is made up of thin, flexible, and ubiquitous terms such as 'true,' 'good,' 'right' and 'beautiful.' The larger part contains thicker, more rigid and more parochial terms, for example 'Christ,' 'England,' 'professional standards,' 'decency,' 'kindness,' 'the Revolution,' 'the Church,' 'progressive,' 'rigorous,' 'creative.' The more parochial terms do most of the work.

Rorty continues to define **the ironist** as someone, who:

- has radical and continuing doubts about the final vocabulary she uses, because she has been impressed by other vocabularies, vocabularies as taken as final by people or books she has encountered;
- realizes that arguments phrased in her present vocabulary can neither underwrite nor dissolve these doubts; and
- does not think that her vocabulary is closer to reality than others, that it is in touch with a power not herself.

Ironists realize that anything can be made to look good or bad by being redescribed. They are never quite able to take themselves seriously because they are always aware that the terms in which they describe themselves are subject to change, always aware of the contingencies and fragility of their final vocabularies, and thus of their selves. (Rorty 1989: 73–74)

The invitation to investigate organizational worlds of meaning and how they are constituted is likely to entail some reflection on their historical and socio-political contingencies, as well as situational expediencies. Only within these contexts can we understand their meaning. The meanings are changeable and relative; they are not permanent and absolute. Sometimes it is argued that this approach leads to a position of nihilism, where everything is as significant and thus as insignificant as everything else and no moral assessment is possible. We do not subscribe to this. Rather, we view our position as one that invites and appreciates dialogue and conversation.

Conversation, dialogue and the single voice

The constructionist may recognize the legitimacy of the competing value investments, each within its own tradition. The constructionist may even share in one or more traditions. There is nothing about constructionism that argues against having values. However, there is also the recognition that strong commitments lend themselves to eradicating the other, to eliminating any voice antithetical to one's own. The end of this process of elimination is the single voice – the one and only word. The existence of the single voice is simultaneously the end of conversation, dialogue, negotiation – or in effect, the death of meaning itself. Thus, in hostile conflict we lurch toward the end of any values, ethics or politics. (Gergen 1999: 233)

Within one of the traditions that we, the authors, share that is, the tradition of organization studies, there is an emergent emphasis on conversation and dialogue (see Isaacs, 1993, 1999; Schein, 1993, 2000). Dialogue theory assumes that getting knowledgeable about one's own assumption is the first and foremost step to a richer understanding of the social world and social 'others'. Schein (2000: xxxx) puts it as follows: "If we are to gain any understanding of another group's assumptions, we must get into a communication mode that legitimates self-examination and acknowledges that perception and thought are anything but objective."

Dialogue: from Greek *dia* and *logos* = the flow of meaning
Dia = through
Logos = word; meaning; to gather together

Giving up one's own position as final, ultimate and absolute implies relaxing one's grip on certainty. Initially, this can be a confusing, even worrying enterprise. It can also open possibilities and break new grounds.

Recommended reading

Geertz's collection of essays (1973) *The Interpretation of Cultures* is a classic collection of texts, outlining the interpretive approach. Watson's (2001b) ethnography *In Search of Management: Culture, Chaos and Control in Managerial Work* is helpful in seeing the principles of reflective writing applied to an organizational setting.

Burrell and Morgan's (1979) *Sociological Paradigms and Organizational Analysis* on different research paradigms is the classic source to go to inform oneself on the assumptions that underlie the research process. It is referred to in most other discussions about research paradigms and approaches.

Linda Putnam's (1983) essay, "The Interpretive Perspective. An Alternative to Functionalism," in Linda L. Putnam and Michael E. Pacanowsky, *Communication and Organizations. An Interpretive Approach*, is a seminal piece of work about the interpretive approach from a communication perspective.

Gergen's work is generally informed by a social constructionist position. We suggest his 1999 *Invitation to Social Construction* as an approachable and informed text for both the novice and advanced reader. A similarly approachable introduction is Vivien Burr's (1995) *An Invitation to Social Constructionism*.

The works of Mats Alvesson and Hugh Willmott are mainly written from a critical-interpretive perspective. For a flavour of this approach we suggest dipping into their edited volume of essays, *Critical Management Studies* (1992).

The recent collection of essays by Clifford Geertz (2000), *Available Light. Anthropological Reflections on Philosophical Topics* contains one essay, "Anti-Anti-Relativism," that lays out the arguments for cultural relativism.

An easy read and introduction to different world views is the latest novel by David Lodge (2001), *Thinks*, in which ultra-realist and natural scientist Ralph Messenger meets the distinguished and bereaved novelist Helen Reed.

CHAPTER TWO

A Semiological Approach to Meaning Making

The previous chapter described communication as a social process and discussed the role of language in creating and sustaining our realities. In this chapter we focus more closely on the process of meaning making, and how it is that we come to understand – or misunderstand – each other. In other words, it is not the pen marks or the sounds themselves that are our main concern, but "what it is that makes marks on paper or sounds in the air into a *message*" (Fiske, 1982: 39).

Objectives

In this chapter we will:

● introduce semiology;
● consider the relationship between signs in a sign system;
● discuss the role of myth in cultural sense-making; and
● further develop the idea of meaning making as a dynamic social process.

Principles of meaning making

Swiss linguist Ferdinand de Saussure is widely regarded as the founder of semiology. Frustrated by the emphasis in traditional linguistics on the origins and development of language, he wanted to understand how language actually worked. In a series of lectures to students at the University of Geneva (posthumously written up by his students), Saussure introduced a whole new approach to the study of language. He called this new approach **semiology**, or the **science of signs and meanings**.

Ferdinand de Saussure

Saussure (1857–1913) is known as the founder of modern linguistics, reconceptualising the study of languge, and in so doing paving the way for the development of twentieth century linguistic theory. Saussure, like his contemporaries Sigmund Freud and Emile Durkheim, emphasised the essential difference between the physical and the social world, and in particular the central role of meaning making in human behaviour. Saussure sought to discover the underlying system upon which the process of meaning making is based.

Other important figures in semiology include Charles Sanders Pierce (1958), Claude Levi-Strauss (1969), Roland Barthes (1973) and Julia Kristeva (1979). In the UK semiology began to take hold as an important approach to media studies in the 1960s. However its application to organization theory came much later (Barley, 1983; Nippert-Eng, 1996; Phillips and Brown, 1998; Tietze, 1998; Tsoukas, 1999) and its impact has been less widespread.

Saussure's starting point was the idea that we human beings communicate through our use of symbols. To take some familiar everyday examples, in the UK the crown is a symbol of the monarchy, while in the United States, the eagle stands for democracy and freedom and in Germany the oak tree stands for strength, longevity and endurance. In all three cultures red roses symbolise passion and romance, diamonds enduring love, and gold bands represent marriage. While we might not all like these symbols, or agree with one another about whether they are good or bad, right or wrong, most of us probably will agree on what they are conventionally seen to represent within those cultures.

Turning to organizations, dress code often symbolises occupation and status. Thus, in a UK courtroom the wig and robe are symbols of the judge's power and authority, while a doctor's white coat represents medical expertise. However, while many of us will recognise these symbols, their meaning is not inevitable. Indeed, as judges in the United States and Germany never wear wigs, a German or an American might not see the wig as a symbol of power or authority, but as a symbol of *Britishness*. Similarly, the meaning of the crown or the eagle will depend on an individual's political orientation, and their social/cultural background. Furthermore, if the judge's wig was placed alongside other wigs and hairpieces, it would mean something different than it would alongside a robe and gavel.

These examples lead to a number of important points about the process of meaning making, as we outline in the box below.

The five basic principles of semiology

- First, we make meaning through our **shared** use of symbols – including language as a symbolic sign system.
- Second, what symbols mean is **not inevitable**. Rather, it is based on our socio-political and cultural agreement and usage.
- Third, meaning **cannot be divorced from context**.
- Fourth, meaning is **relational**. That is, we make sense of things (objects, words, actions) in relation to other things (Derrida's concept of **différance**).
- Fifth, we engage in these processes **largely subconsciously**.

Although in the above examples we used high profile symbols to illustrate these basic points, it is important to note that other more ordinary and everyday things work in just the same way. Indeed, everything around us carries meaning. As we sit and write this book we are aware that our offices, our desks, chairs, computers, bookshelves, pictures and posters, whiteboards etc. are not only functional, but are also invested with meaning. For example, in an academic's office, an empty bookshelf means something very different from an overflowing set of shelves, as does the size of the office and its aspect, and the photos and pictures that adorn the walls. We can examine what these symbols represent in relation to the points raised above. In this book, we will use the term **cultural text** to refer to these things, be they physical objects or spaces, written or spoken language, or behaviours. In other words a cultural text is anything that can be read for its meaning.

The meanings of flags

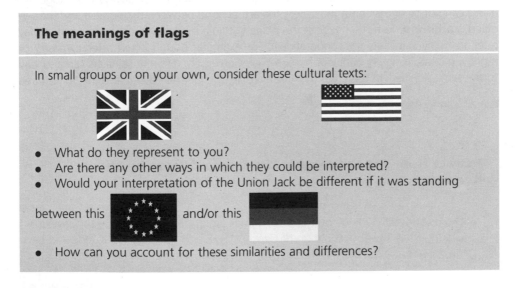

In small groups or on your own, consider these cultural texts:

- What do they represent to you?
- Are there any other ways in which they could be interpreted?
- Would your interpretation of the Union Jack be different if it was standing

between this   and/or this

- How can you account for these similarities and differences?

Introduction to semiology: the study of signs and meanings

Defined as "the relationship between a sign and its meaning" (Fiske and Hartley, 1978: 37), semiology has been theorised and applied in diverse ways. However, common to all is the centrality of the **sign**, a two-sided concept consisting (in Saussure's terms) of a **signifier** and a **signified**. The signifier refers to the material aspect, while the signified refers to the mental aspect. The sign *tree* could be analysed thus:

Signifier-   t-r-e-e

Signified-

Figure 2.1   What is a tree?

The key point here is that the signifier and the signified refer to different levels of meaning: the material level and the mental level, with the sign representing the combination of the two. In more everyday language, the signifier is frequently referred to as the level of **denotation** or literal meaning, while the signified refers to **connotation**, or interpretive meaning. Using the tree example, the denotation would be the word *tree*, while the connotation is the mental image which that word conjures up to the individual. Writing this chapter in the middle of an English Autumn, the connotation might be an orange-yellow beech, for example. Writing it in the middle of a Scandinavian forest in winter would be likely to connote a rather different interpretation of a tree.

Of course if we lived in Hawaii, the signified – or connotation of the signifier t-r-e-e – might be 🌴, or in the mountains 🌲. Thus, there is no inevitable or fixed relationship between the signifier and the signified. Although they always work together (there can not be one without the other), the actual bond between the signifier and the signified is **arbitrary**. To further explain this point, within a single language, one signifier may refer to many signifieds (or connotations). For example, dough could refer to pastry or money; gay could signify happy or homosexual. Conversely, different signifiers can also lead to the same signified. In this case, the Italian *arbole*, the German *baum* and the English *tree* can all lead to the same signified: 🌳.

Extract from *The Unbearable Lightness of Being* by Milan Kundera

Some context: Sabina and her lover Tomas emigrated from Prague to Geneva during the Soviet occupation of Czechoslovakia. In this extract, Kundera is talking about a bowler hat that Sabina and Tomas used to play around with.

> But let us return to the bowler hat:
>
> First, it was a vague reminder of her forgotten grandfather, the major of a small Bohemian town during the nineteenth century.
>
> Second, it was a memento of her father. After the funeral her brother appropriated all their parents' property, and she, refusing out of sovereign contempt to fight for her rights, announced sarcastically that she was taking the bowler hat as her sole inheritance.
>
> Third, it was a prop for her love games with Tomas.
>
> Fourth, it was a sign of her originality, which she consciously cultivated. She could not take much with her when she emigrated, and taking this bulky, impractical thing meant giving up other, more practical ones.
>
> Fifth, now that she was abroad, the hat was a sentimental object...
>
> The bowler hat was a motif in the musical composition that was Sabina's life. It returned again and again, each time with a different meaning, and all the meanings flowed through the bowler hat like water through a riverbed. I might call it Heraclitus' ('You can't step twice into the same river') riverbed: the bowler hat was a bed through which each time Sabina saw another river flow, another *semantic river*: each time the same object would give rise to a new meaning, though all former meanings would resonate. (1984: 88–9)

In a business setting the notion of meaning (that is, the relationship between the signifier and the signified) as essentially arbitrary is illustrated in Cohen's (1997) study of women who left jobs in organizations to set up their own businesses. In interviews with respondents, the word *independence* came up repeatedly. However, it soon became apparent that people's connotations of this signifier varied significantly. As one participant explained,

> We might all be using the word, but in a variety of ways, depending on our lives and situations. What I mean by independence has to do with being free, at last, from my old prison-like job, but for others it might have to do with flexibility and childcare.

Interestingly, none of these interpretations challenged the idea that independence is necessarily and always positive. In the literature on self-employment, the word *independence* is ubiquitous. However, possibly because it is such a normal and everyday term, it is rarely considered in detail. Rather, there seems to be an assumption that the meaning of the word is obvious – that we all understand it in the same way. But consensus around meaning was clearly not the case in Cohen's study.

Similarly, in her study of changes in National Health Service policy and practice, Musson (1995) found that key stakeholders (including general medical practitioners, nurses and health authority officials) agreed on the logic of a primary care led service, promoted by the government of the day. However, after numerous planning meetings it became clear to the observer that these health care professionals had different views about what the term **primary care** actually meant, and on what their respective roles within such a system might be. These varied between a service run primarily by the family doctors themselves, to one in which the nurses had a central role and equal status and power, to the hospital consultants' version of a service delivering, "all the other treatments that we can't or don't want to deliver." Furthermore, these basic differences in the future direction of the service had never been explored or discussed because everyone assumed that theirs was the right and only interpretation – that their webs of meaning were fundamentally true and exclusive. This outcome is more than simply interesting; these different versions of reality can clearly produce different concrete services but also, without exploration and explication of fundamental differences between the different stakeholders, the conflicts that have dogged the UK National Health Service might continue to create barriers to the delivery of better services (O'Cathain et al., 1998).

Changing meanings

In Chapter 1 you were asked to consider the meanings of a number of words, including empowerment, leadership, global, excellence and knowledge. Go back to this exercise, and try to explain it using the concepts of signifier/signified/sign, denotation and connotation.

This is not to suggest, though, that individuals have a free reign as to how signifiers are interpreted. As Saussure suggests:

> the individual has no power to alter a sign in any respect once it has become established in a linguistic community... the term [arbitrary] implies simply that the signal is ... arbitrary in relation to its signification, with which it has no natural connection in reality. (1974: 68–69)

The point here is that meaning making is not purely individualistic or idiosyncratic. Rather, it is a process and product of collectives. That is, meanings are generated and agreed within particular social and cultural contexts. Significantly, the process of establishing consensus happens on a subconscious level: in most cases we are not aware of our active involvement in meaning making.

Beyond language

As a linguist, Saussure was most interested in the linguistic sign. However, as it may already have become apparent, within semiology the term **sign** is not only used for language, but also for any other cultural text, including images, sounds, objects and artefacts and behaviours. Thus the rose, diamond, gold band, wig and white coat are all signs, incorporating both material and mental aspects. Returning to the wig example, the signifier would be the wig itself, while the signified refers to what it represents (status, power, Britishness). As regards actual practices and behaviours, the idea here is that what people *do* can be understood semiologically. In a business context, a semiological approach might be used to explore attendance at meetings, lunch-time rituals or the use of information systems, examining how these systems of signs are interpreted by individuals and groups.

Making meaning in funeral homes

In an organizational context, cultural texts such as buildings, grounds, office layout, decor and dress codes give us valuable clues about who and what is seen as important and unimportant, about power, prestige and the social arrangements embedded within those settings. Barley's (1983) research into funeral homes is an intriguing example. To enhance his interview data, Barley analyses funeral home environments semiologically to provide insights into that occupational world. He identifies three key sign systems: the homes' interior décor, other related settings (for example, hospitals and private houses) and the positioning of the corpses themselves (in particular, the way they are posed so as to appear 'lifelike'). Barley argues that this analysis illuminates aspects of the unique culture of funeral homes which other techniques do not yield. In his view, semiology helps to reveal the "interpretive structure that lends a culture its coherence" (1983: 39).

Meaning as relational

Within semiology, then, meaning making is seen as a dynamic process. Given this inherent dynamism and arbitrariness, on a practical level one might ask how signs work together to make sense. Semiologists argue that signs do not derive their meaning in isolation, but through their relationships with other signs in a given sign system (or code). Looking back to the judge's wig mentioned earlier, whereas alongside other hairpieces this wig might signify the olden days or old fashioned aristocracy, amongst gavels and robes it might connote the courtroom, legal profession and its traditions, or even justice. Saussure was very interested in the relationships between signs. He explained how we draw up categories for meaning making, arguing that the question, "What do we mean by sign x?" can only be answered in light of what we do *not* mean by that sign. Thus, the sign signifies by virtue of its difference from other signs: a tree is a tree because it is *not* a bush. In other words, in agreeing, albeit implicitly, that a certain signifier means *this*, we are also agreeing that it does not mean *that*. This concept of **difference** (see Introduction), of meaning as **relational**, is a fundamental principle of semiology.

The idea that we make meaning of a sign in terms of what it is not leads to a focus within semiology on the concept of **binary opposition**. Thus, we understand *good* in relation to *evil*, *thin* in relation to *fat*, *young* in relation to *old*. The identification of binary opposites is a common approach in semiological analysis, perhaps most explicitly and transparently in the context of advertising.

It's good to talk

In a paper presented to the Market Research Society's annual conference, Monty Alexander (1995), co-founder (with Virginia Valentine) of the innovative marketing agency *Semiotic Solutions*, discusses his firm's use of binary opposites in their work on the *BT* "**It's Good to Talk**" campaign. Central to their analysis was a distinction between **big talk** and **small talk**.

BIG TALK	SMALL TALK
important	unimportant
male	female
serious	trivial
official – proper	unofficial – improper

In helping *BT* to redefine its strategy, Alexander and Valentine sought to challenge these values: "In order to justify and legitimise female usage of the phone and to encourage greater usage of the phone by men – a campaign was needed which raised the status of small talk, by emphasising the emotional, rather than rational benefits of communication" (Alexander et al., 1995: 279). It is important to note that Alexander and Valentine did not question the concept of binary opposition itself. Rather, it was the values embedded within this particular set of oppositions which they sought to challenge. In "It's Good to Talk" the principle of binarism holds, but the values associated with big talk and small talk are reversed.

In a research context, the use of binary oppositions in sense-making was aptly illustrated in Cohen's (1997) research. In discussing their decisions to leave and their expectations of business ownership, respondents described self-employment in opposition to organizational employment. Whereas their organizations were typically characterised as rigid, inflexible and constraining, self-employment was seen as liberating and accommodating. Thus, business ownership *was* what organizations *were not*.

Finding binary opposites in advertising

Choose an advert that you find interesting or striking in some way. Can you analyse it in terms of binary opposites?

How sign systems work: paradigms and syntagms

Given semiology's emphasis on meaning making as systematic and relational, questions arise about how signs are organized. Semiologists often refer to the systems in which signs are positioned. Saussure suggests that signs are organized into codes in two ways:

paradigmatically and **syntagmatically**. These dimensions are often considered as two axes: the vertical axis is seen as paradigmatic and the horizontal axis as syntagmatic. Fiske (1982: 57) describes a paradigm as "a set of signs from which the one to be used is chosen." He uses a system of road signs as an example. The set of shapes: triangle, square, round, hexagon etc. forms a paradigm. In planning a road sign, the designer selects one from this collection. Fiske explains that the units in a paradigm must, first, have something in common that determines their membership; and second, they must be easily distinguished from one another. That is, they must have certain distinctive features that differentiate them from other signs in the paradigm. And these distinctive features always carry meaning. For example, let us consider as a paradigm this list of adjectives – *fat, chubby, well-built, solid, plump, obese*. While they clearly have features in common, they are also all distinct. There is a world of difference between "she is solid" and "she is obese" – and between "he is well-built" and "she is well-built." In choosing between these words, we are constructing certain meanings, meanings that have cultural value, and that make sense to us in terms of the words in the group which we did not select. As Fiske suggests: "Everytime we communicate we select from a paradigm. Where there is choice there is meaning, and the meaning of what was chosen is determined by the meaning of what was not" (1982: 58).

Once a sign has been chosen from a paradigm, it is combined with other kinds of signs (which have likewise been selected from other paradigms) to form a syntagm. The horizontal, syntagmatic axis, then, is the way in which the chosen signs are combined in a particular situation. Returning to Fiske's road signs, while the category of available shapes is the **paradigm**, a specific sign (say, a stop sign) is a **syntagm:** a specific combination of shape, symbol and colour.

Any sign system can be analysed in terms of paradigms and syntagms. In a wardrobe, the range of shirts is a paradigm (one could choose between T-shirts, dress shirts, camisoles, polo necks, vests etc.), while one's outfit on a particular day is a syntagm (including, for example, jeans, a T-shirt, cardigan and boots). In a restaurant, the choice of starters could be seen as a paradigm, while the whole order given to the waiter is the syntagm. In music the harmony is the paradigm, and the melody the syntagm. At first glance this approach might appear terminology-bound and unwieldy. However, semiologists see these two fundamental organising principles as central to meaning making.

Using semiology to understand physical environments

In her study of a university re-location, Tietze (1998) considers the two campuses (one situated in the city centre and the other in the suburbs) as cultural texts. These texts consist of a variety of signs, including: buildings, offices, classrooms, furnishings, pictures and photographs, curtains, lighting, parking facilities, plants and flowers, landscaping etc. While a paradigmatic analysis might examine one of these categories, a syntagmatic analysis would look at the ways in which these different signs were combined, and consider the meanings behind particular combinations. Through such an approach, Tietze developed a close and detailed understanding of the cultural context in which the organizational change was enacted.

• Consider two contrasting offices with which you are familiar, and analyse them semiologically, using the concepts of **paradigm** and **syntagm**.

Semiology and myth

Semiology can be divided into three interrelated areas (Schirato and Yell, 2000). The first is the sign itself, while the second is the relationship between signs in particular sign systems. It was these aspects which most interested Saussure. The third area considers the relationship between signs and their wider social context: that is, the ways in which meaning systems are played out in social practice. This dimension of semiology, the interaction between the text and its users, has been of particular interest to organization theorists.

In the 1970s, the work of French cultural theorist Roland Barthes made a significant contribution to our understandings of the social and cultural dimension of meaning making. In *Mythologies* (1973) Barthes constructed a systematic model within which the negotiation of meaning takes place. Barthes refined and further developed Saussure's concepts of denotation and connotation, drawing on systems of cultural values. It has become a classic text in the field of cultural studies.

Barthes, like other semiologists, made a distinction between **denotative** and **connotative** meaning: whereas denotation is relatively stable, connotation is fluid and changeable. But Barthes also describes a third level that he refers to as **myth** (using this term in the traditional sense of stories through which a culture explains some aspect of its reality). Early myths were concerned with questions of good and evil, love, nature and disease. However, Barthes' work focused on more recent myths which dealt with issues such as masculinity and femininity, ethnicity, work and family, and was concerned with the ways in which signs both reflect and reproduce these cultural myths. Barthes argues that myths are social products, reflecting dominant and subordinate social interests. For example, feminist critics believe that myths in Western society of women as naturally nurturing and therefore having primary responsibility for childcare have served to reinforce dominant male interests.

From this perspective, the real power of myth is that it renders the semiological workings behind these relationships invisible. Myth, then, is not seen as a constructed social process, but as a social fact. In *Mythologies*, Barthes considers the cultural myths (and underlying social relationships) associated with signs as diverse as wrestling, cruises, toys, Greta Garbo's face, wine and milk, ornamental cookery and striptease. In doing so, he exposes the everyday assumptions and ideas underpinning much of what we think, say and do, and which we have come to accept as facts.

Denotation, connotation and myth

Daniel Chandler (2001) uses this picture of Marilyn Monroe to illustrate the denotative, connotative and mythic levels of meaning making:

He suggests that at the denotative level, it is a photo of the film star Marilyn Monroe. At the connotative level, it is associated with glamour, sexuality and beauty – maybe also with drug-taking and death. At the level of myth this sign represents Hollywood, "the dream factory that produces glamour in the form of the stars it constructs, but also the dream machine that can crush them – all with a view to profit and expediency" (Hayward, 1996: 310, cited in Chandler, 2001).

Consider these signs on the level of denotation, connotation and myth:

- Mother Theresa
- a stethoscope
- Richard Branson
- beef
- *Marlboro* cigarettes
- *The Body Shop*

Barthes takes the concept of socially constructed reality as his starting point, and seeks to reveal the hidden ideological scaffolding on which it is based. Critics have taken issue with the obscurity of Barthes' language, and the difficulty in differentiating between his levels of signification. However, in his emphasis on the relationship between language and culture, the invisibility of meaning making, and the role of myth in power relationships, his work can provide valuable insights into the construction and reconstruction of organizational culture.

The Brent Spar debacle: a modern re-working of David and Goliath

In his article on the Brent Spar debacle, Tsoukas (1999) considers the myths and counter-myths associated with *Greenpeace* and *Shell*. Investigating the dispute about the disposal of the oil rig, he analyses the (symbolic) process by which *Greenpeace* tapped into the public's deep anxieties about pollution and environmental despoliation and into our cultural inclination to support the underdog, that is, the seemingly powerless *Greenpeace* (which he likens to the mythical David) in the face of the giant *Shell* (referred to as Goliath). Tsoukas explains how in doing so, *Greenpeace* managed to generate widespread public support, seizing the ideological agenda, and forcing *Shell* to abandon plans to dispose of Brent Spar in the North Sea.

Alexander (1996) of *Semiotic Solutions* illustrates how these ideas can be applied to marketing. He starts with Levi Strauss' suggestion that "the purpose of myth is to provide a logical model capable of overcoming a contradiction" and discusses the centrality of this concept in market analysis and research.

Translating this [Levi Strauss'] definition into modern marketing language means that a *brand's* myth is the belief by consumers that the brand offers them a way of resolving a problem or situation that hitherto represented some kind of contradiction. Or, from the perspective of the marketer, that the brand holds the power to reconcile a cultural opposition. (1996: 111)

These contradictions, then, are the spaces in which marketers can position their products. In his paper, Alexander applies the concept of brand myth to *Persil* washing powder and *Marks and Spencer's* original launch of their ready-prepared meals. In the former, the *Persil Mum* is seen to reconcile the cultural opposition between the detachment of a high-tech washing agent and the caring mother. In the case of *M&S*, prepared meals were presented as overcoming the cultural contradictions between real food as good and commercially made food as bad. It is interesting to note that 30 years after this launch, as quality prepared foods have become established supermarket products, this myth seems outdated, and the original positioning of the *M&S* line has lost much of its uniqueness – and its power.

Organizations and myth

Make a list of companies which you feel have a particularly strong public image. When we did this, the companies that came to mind included: *The Body Shop*, *Virgin*, *Tommy Hilfiger*, *Morgan Cars* and *IKEA*.

- Consider the myths underpinning these images.
- Do these myths continue to hold cultural power? If not, why not?

Making semiology social

Myths are collective stories – reproduced and sustained through shared understandings and experiences. Central to the working of myth is the idea of meaning as fundamentally social, belonging to and emerging from the collective. Having said that signs are dynamic and vary from person to person, it must not be assumed that meaning making is just haphazard, that people make sense in random ways. Rather, semiology sees language and meaning making as essentially **social processes**:

in order to have a language [or any other meaning system], there must be a *community* of speakers. Contrary to what may appear to be the case, a language never exists even for a moment except as a social fact, for it is a semiological phenomenon. Its social nature is one of its internal characteristics. (Saussure, 1974: 77)

Thus communities and organizations of all sorts (including families and friendship groups in addition to more formal types of organizations) construct new vocabularies and terminologies which are seen by group members as obvious and unambiguous, but which may be understood very differently by the outside world. Put simply, language does not exist in a vacuum, or within an individual. Instead, words and meanings always exist previously in other people's mouths, in other concrete contexts, serving other people's intentions. That is, speakers always invoke particular social languages that both shape and are shaped by what the speaker can and does say. Different social languages come to be accepted as suited to particular contexts and speech communities.

Ventriloquation

The concept of **ventriloquation** is useful here. It refers to the ways in which people, as they move between social groups, take the language and speech patterns from one socio-cultural setting and adapt it for use in another.

In their study of public sector science institutes, Cohen et al. (1999a) found that where the term **mission statements** was seen as important and useful by institute directors and senior management, to scientists it was derided as a symbol of increasing management control. Although further discussion revealed that managers and scientists were frequently talking about the same processes, to be seen as acceptable by scientists, managers had to ventriloquate through scientific rather than management terms.

This emphasis on the social dimension of meaning making is sometimes referred to as **social semiotics**, and was principally developed by theorists in Britain and Australia (see, for example, Halliday, 1978; Hodge and Kress, 1988, 1993; Kress, 1985):

> We see communication essentially as a process, not as a disembodied set of meanings or texts. Meaning is produced and reproduced under specific social conditions, through specific material forms and agencies. It exists in relation to concrete subjects and objects and is inexplicable except in terms of this web of relationships. (Hodge and Kress, 1988: viii)

In the view of Hodge and Kress, linguists should not restrict their gaze to abstract linguistic systems. Instead, their prime concern must be the ways in which these systems are enacted socially, in everyday life. In so far as society consists of certain structures, reflecting patterns and relations of domination, subordination and resistance, so these patterns are reflected, negotiated and reconstituted through the processes of meaning making (these issues are further developed in the chapters on discourse and gender). Central to Hodge and Kress' analysis is the concept of **ideology**, which they define as "a level of social meaning with distinctive functions, orientations and content for a social class or group" (1988: 3).

Langue and parole

Saussure made a distinction between **langue**, language as an abstract, structural system and **parole**, actual speech. Saussure focused almost exclusively on langue: "The linguist must take the study of linguistic structure as his primary concern, and

(Continued)

relate all other manifestations of language to it" (1974: 9). In contrast, though, social semiologists do not make this rigid distinction. Instead, they argue that: "Meaning systems are never closed or finite, but always open, dynamic and changing, as we recreate the system of possible meanings continuously through our communication practices" (Schirato and Yell, 2000: 107).

In our view, social semiotics leads to a much more dynamic view of meaning making than that which is proposed by more traditional semiological approaches. Indeed, a key principle within social semiology is that of meaning making as a negotiated process, central to which are struggles over power and legitimacy.

Social semiologists are principally concerned with the concept of language as a social phenomenon, and in particular "social, political forces and processes as they act through and on texts and forms of discourse" (Hodge and Kress, 1988: vii). Here, signs are seen to both reflect and constitute the context in which they operate. This approach is illustrated in Musson's (1995) previously cited research into the National Health Service. In this study, she examines the change in healthcare policy towards a primary care led service, and investigates the process through which multi-disciplinary healthcare teams redefined the term **primary care** according to their particular occupational and organizational contexts, restructuring their working practices around this new definition. However, Musson argues that the process was not one way, that it was not simply a case of healthcare professionals responding to government-imposed change. Rather, she found that these new meanings and working practices then became the realities upon which further policy changes were enacted.

Activity: consider a change initiative in an organization you know well

- Identify the key terms associated with this change.
- Who first started using these words? Where do you think they came from?
- How were they introduced to other organizational members?
- How were they received?
- To what extent were any diverse or contradictory meanings heard by more senior members?

Summary

In this chapter, we focused on semiology and explored its relevance to organization studies. We began by introducing key semiological concepts and relationships: signifier, signified and sign; denotation and connotation – and how they work to create meaning. A key point was the notion of the relationship between the signifier and the signified as inevitable, but essentially arbitrary. While Saussure was primarily interested in linguistic systems, the chapter also explored other kinds of cultural texts, and illustrated how they have been used in organizational research. Moving on, we considered the view that within semiology signs do not derive their meanings in isolation, but through their relationship with other signs in sign systems. This point was developed through our discussion of the use of binary oppositions, and of paradigmatic and syntagmatic analyses. In the next section, we considered a third level of semiological analysis – that of myth. We discussed myths as social products, working to create particular views of reality. In the final section, we discussed social semiologists' emphasis on the concept of meaning making as a fundamentally social process.

Underpinning the chapter is an emphasis on the idea that everything around us – language, artefacts, even behaviour – is a sign, generating cultural meaning. However, in most cases, this process goes on at the subconscious level. The purpose of this chapter was to increase the reader's awareness of these processes and to demonstrate the value of semiology in illuminating the symbolic nature of organizational life.

Recommended reading

Some key texts in this area are Saussure's (1974) *Course in General Linguistics* and for a more accessible interpretation of Saussure's *Course,* Culler's (1986) *Saussure* in the Fontana Modern Masters series. In addition, Fiske's (1982) *Introduction to Communication Studies* and Cobley and Jansz' (1997) *Semiotics for Beginners* both provide illuminating introductions to the field, while Schirato and Yell's chapter 'Signs and meaning' in their (2000) *Communication and Culture* offers a more critical analysis.

As regards the use of semiology in organization studies, Jackson and Carter's (2000) 'Semiotics' chapter in their innovative *Rethinking Organizational Behaviour* is an excellent starting point. Their chapter outlines the key principles of semiology and examines the relevance of these for understanding organizational processes and practices.

In addition to these more general texts, there is a whole range of books and articles which explore specific applications of semiology. Barthes (1993/1st edition 1957) *Mythologies* is a classic. In addition to the highly theoretical essay, 'Myth Today', his chapters cover such diverse cultural phenomena as wrestling, steak and chips, striptease and plastic. For a fascinating analysis of advertising, see Williamson's (1978) *Decoding Advertisements*.

For more specific reference to organizations, see Barley's (1983) insightful analysis of funeral homes and Tsoukas' (1999) examination of the *Greenpeace/Shell* debacle in the North Sea.

Finally, Chandler's excellent website: http://www.aber.ac.uk/~dgc/semiotic.html offers a wealth of useful, accessible information.

CHAPTER THREE

Understanding Organizations Through Metaphor

The previous chapter provided an overview of semiology and how it can be applied to organizations. This chapter explores the function and role of metaphor. There is a continuing interest in this figure of speech and discussions of aspects of metaphor are now included in textbooks such as Hatch (1997); Jackson and Carter (2000); Mullins (1999) and Rollinson et al. (1998). This chapter aims to provide a more comprehensive overview of metaphor, its conceptual basis and in particular the problems and dilemmas associated with understanding organizations through metaphor.

First, a definition of metaphor is given, followed by a discussion of how metaphors are used and what they mean. Then metaphors are discussed with a view to their reframing potential, enabling people to see the world anew. This section includes an introduction to Gareth Morgan's work, a discussion of the debate and a criticism of reframing approaches. Finally the chapter introduces some works of organizational scholars that hunted metaphors – and other tropes – as they found them used by organizational members. The contribution to organizational analysis of these approaches is discussed to assist our understanding of organizational meaning making.

Objectives

In this chapter we will:

- introduce and define metaphor;
- establish the key functions of metaphor;
- discuss and explain metaphor as reframing; and
- discuss and explain the notion of metaphors-in-use.

Metaphor transfers meaning

Its etymological roots are in the Greek: meta (trans) + pherein (to carry)

Metaphors are particular figures of speech. Figures of speech are also referred to as **tropes**, from the Greek word for **figure**. Figures of speech play with meaning in so far as the borrowed sign, taken in its figurative sense, is substituted for an absent word, that carries the 'proper' meaning. For example, describing a group of managers as a pack of wolves is using the figure of metaphor. It links two previously unconnected signs or subject domains; in doing so we can explain the appearance and behaviour of this group in terms of our knowledge of animal behaviour.

We might try to convey to a friend how a particular organization functions. As part of our explanation we might start to compare it to a machine (it runs smoothly; it runs like clockwork). In using these expressions we are indeed using metaphorical language. It is not literal language – organizations are not machines – rather some features that are attributed to machines are used to describe and explain certain features of an organization. The subject domain *organization* is linked to the subject domain *machine* and in doing so the previously unknown or less well known (the organization) becomes more familiar.

Metaphors highlight and obscure

The use of metaphor can make us see the world in a particular way by emphasising certain aspects of signs/subject domains, but it also hides other features. Describing organizations as machines might obscure other aspects of the organization that are not machine-like. We can therefore say that every metaphor contains an element of **tension** or **incongruity**. This is because they are suspended between **similarity** (some aspects of an organization are indeed similar to those of a machine) and **difference** (some aspects of an organization are different from those of a machine). Of course, the organization/machine metaphor is an example of a well-established way of seeing organizations. It could be argued that it has been the most dominant metaphor of the previous century. It entails no surprises and linking the two subject areas generates little genuine insight. Much of the work done in the field of organization theory can be understood as an attempt to move away from the 'machine imagery' and to develop different understanding of organizations. Gareth Morgan's work (1986, 1993) is a seminal contribution in this area and will be discussed later.

The machine metaphor

- What does the machine metaphor explain or reveal about organizations?
- What does it hide or obscure?

Some features of metaphor

The most often discussed feature of metaphor is its **generative function**, its inherent potential to create new ways of seeing the world. However, the very creation of new connections is always accompanied by constraining a particular view, because attention becomes focused on specific features at the expense of others. For example, describing an organization as an iceberg draws attention to the fact that only 10 per cent of an iceberg is visible and 90 per cent is covered by water. By using the iceberg metaphor, we are invited to concentrate our attention on the hidden parts of organizations, such as the emotional and political aspects of decision making. However, this metaphor also limits our understanding of the organization in so far that our analysis becomes focused on one aspect at the expense of other aspects. Within the logic of the metaphor, we are less likely to concentrate our thinking on the map of the polar seas and the patterns of icebergs they consist of. This might lead to an oversight of important aspects of organizational features or processes. Another famous metaphor amongst organization theorists is that of the garbage can as a model to understand decision making processes (Cohen et al., 1972). It could easily be misunderstood by the novice to the field as implying unpleasant, sinister processes that stink. However, it was used to describe the multitude of factors around a decision making situation (people; time constraints; previous solutions etc.) that all come into play with each other (they all go into the garbage can) to inform the decision.

Metaphors and truth

Metaphors are not 'true' in the sense that they represent an objectively existing reality, but they are part of figuratively understanding social and organizational worlds. They are part of meaning systems that are evoked tacitly whenever a metaphor is used. Metaphors only make sense and can only create new insights, on the basis of the conventionally and habitually known. In the 'machine metaphor' example, we, the authors, rely on the readers to bring some knowledge about what machines are and how they work to the reading of the text. We are drawing on previously established meaning systems. Otherwise the metaphor would not work.

If, for example, a less well-established metaphor is used – let's say, 'organizations are (like) Tai Chi' – the reader might not be able to decode (interpret) the meaning of this metaphor. It might lead to a rejection of the metaphor as non-sensical, it might lead to a perception of the user of the metaphor as weird or incompetent. It is quite difficult to create new metaphors that are sufficiently engrained in conventional and therefore acceptable meaning systems, yet that at the same time challenge the received wisdom and its normative assumptions.

To further complicate the process, a user of a particular metaphor has no means to control how the recipients/audience will decode it. For one recipient, the Tai Chi metaphor might provide new insights into the resolution of conflicts and paradoxes into a harmonious whole organization (the Yin/Yang elements); for the next recipient the metaphor might evoke images of prescribed, rigid sequences of steps, rules and regulations; for yet another recipient it might resonate with pictures of flowery, vague new wave management; for the last recipient it might not evoke anything at all, since there is no previous knowledge about Tai Chi. Metaphors are subject to interpretation and as such they contain an uncontrollable element.

The particularization process

Ortony (1975: 47) in a famous essay "Why Metaphors are Necessary and Not Just Nice," describes this as the particularization process: particularization is the "process of filling in the details between linguistic signposts present in the message."

The linguistic signposts in our example are 'organization' and 'Tai Chi'. How and whether the recipient of the metaphor makes sense of the relationship between the two signs is not controllable by the sender. It is the recipients who establish the meaning through the particularization process. Indeed, a successful metaphor implies the right mix of similarity and difference between two signs. Too much or too little similarity might mean that the point is not understood and that the metaphor remains unsuccessful in the communication process.

Metaphors also express an emotional reality in so far as they can capture the values of a social collective. The image of the organizational team is a metaphor drawing on the notion of team games, often competitive ones, such as football or hockey. These games are a part of a culture, that most members of Western industrial societies can be expected to be familiar with. A manager might use this metaphor in order to communicate to her staff how they ought to conduct themselves – as a team that shares the same objectives and that overcomes internal rivalry. In this example, the metaphor is an attempt to direct behaviour by evoking cultural values, such as being a good team player. The 'team' metaphor provides a communicative device that simultaneously appeals, evaluates and directs.

Of course, team metaphors – as much as machine metaphors – are established metaphors, culturally sanctioned, but hardly fresh or innovative. It could be argued that it is a dead metaphor that has "become so familiar and so habitual that we have ceased to become aware of their metaphorical nature and use them as literal terms" (Tsoukas, 1991: 568). Dead metaphors, however, while not providing new insights, can be used to analyse organizational processes, because they point to normalized, ideological assumptions (see Chapter 5). This means that we take the imperative of having to be a good team player at face value, we don't question it, we start to view ourselves as part of a team and behave as such. The metaphor has become such an engrained, yet invisible, part of how we see and understand the world, that it becomes taken-for-granted. It is normalized and its very tacitness starts to control us. It has become a "metaphor we live by" (Lakoff and Johnson, 1980). The team metaphor has become part of our conceptual system, that "structures what we perceive, how we get around in the world, and how we relate to other people" (Lakoff and Johnson, 1980: 3). The team metaphor has become part of our culture, to an extent that it shapes how we view, experience and enact organizational realities.

A powerful metaphor?

One of the most powerful metaphors in the Western world is the metaphor that time is money. Do you think it is possible to live your life outside this metaphor?

The linguists George Lakoff and Mark Johnson published their highly influential book on *Metaphors We Live By* in 1980. Their main thesis is that metaphors are pervasive in everyday life, not just in language but in thought and action. They argue that metaphors govern our everyday functioning, that they structure what we perceive, how we get around in the world and how we relate to other people. Metaphors form our conceptual system and thus play a central role in defining our everyday realities.

For example, *Time is money* is one of the most powerful metaphors of industrialised societies. Time is viewed as a limited resource and valuable commodity. We measure our time in terms of money as expressions like Time is money; Don't waste my time; Is that worth your while?; and You're living on borrowed time all illustrate. This has affected the world of paid work to an extent that everyday practices are based on this metaphor. Work is typically associated with the time it takes to do, and time gets precisely quantified. We pay people by the hour, week or year; telephone messages are counted in time units; yearly budgets and interest on loans are calculated within the conceptual frame that time equals money. Many companies offer incentives based on money as well as on time bonuses. We conceive and act of time as if it were a valuable commodity, a limited resource. "Thus we understand and experience time as the kind of thing that can be spent, wasted, budgeted, invested wisely or poorly, saved, or squandered" (Lakoff and Johnson, 1980: 8).

The metaphors of strategy

The language of business strategy is couched in the metaphors of the military and warfare. Following Lakoff and Johnson's theorising, this has consequences for the processes and content of strategy formulation. What would happen if the language of business strategy was to be couched in the metaphorical framework of 'dance'?

Table 3.1 The language of business through the metaphors of military and dance

	Military	Dance
Process	Plan; linear	Movement; pattern
People	Planners; doers	Partners; crowd
Structures	Hierarchy	Explorations within rules
Communication	Top-down	Mutual; ambiguous
Objective	Victory; to be the best	Enjoyment; aesthetics; emotional release
Value	Finite; linear	Infinite; circular

(Continued)

- Did you find it difficult or easy to think about 'strategy' in the metaphors taken from the subject domain of 'dance'?
- If the answer is 'yes', what are the reasons for this difficulty?
- Can you find other metaphorical concepts (for example, navigation; mapping) to apply to strategy formulation and execution?

Following the definition of metaphor as a figure of speech linking two previously unrelated signs or subject domains, its main features are:

- it can create innovative and new perspectives;
- it can constrain the generation of new insights;
- it can obscure features of organizations;
- it contains an uncontrollable element;
- it captures emotional realities;
- it expresses and sustains values;
- it is part of our conceptual systems, which we enact in the social world; and
- it normalises how we see the world and establishes what is taken for granted (the ideological value of metaphor).

Metaphors as reframing in organization theory

The debate about different ways of seeing organizations was fundamentally influenced by the work of Gareth Morgan. In 1980 he identified the two most frequently invoked metaphors in organization theory: the machine and the organism. The machine metaphor views organizations as closed systems, in which the emphasis is on formal structures, the efficient accomplishment of pre-specified ends by people cast into specific organizational roles. The organism metaphor, in contrast, works from an open system perspective, viewing organizations in a dynamic and changeable relationship with the environment. Morgan's approach rests on the assumption that we do not really know what organizations are, in the sense of having a single authoritative position from which they can be viewed.

In his *Images of Organization* (1986) Morgan further develops the reframing approach by exploring new images of organizations beyond the machine and organism metaphors. He uses diverse images such as organizations as brains, as psychic prisons, as flux and transformation and as instruments of domination. Morgan favours a pluralist approach to using metaphorical frames, in so far as he views organizational life as complex and ambiguous and one metaphor would never fit all situations. For example, in the same organization, one department might work in a machine-like fashion, another department might be full of strife and conflict, while yet another department works in a collegial spirit as a team. The metaphor approach, then, is not to be understood as a rigid model, but as a sensitizing process which aims "to unravel multiple patterns of significance and their interpretation" (Morgan, 1986: 342). However, images and metaphors are more than just neat interpretive constructs, aiding in analytic processes. Morgan concludes by under-lining metaphor's potential in the active construction of organizational worlds: "They [metaphors] are central to the process of *imagination* through which people enact or 'write' the character of organizational life" (1986: 344).

Table 3.2 Summary of common metaphors used to describe organizations

Metaphor	Features; Applications	Value	Weaknesses
Machine	Closed system; efficient goal-oriented activity; clear order and structure; division of labour; classic management theory; scientific management; ideal type of bureaucracy	Formal rationality	Hides human aspects; resistance to change; paradox of consequences
Organism	Open system; changeable; adaptation; relationship with environment; organizational needs; good fit; Hawthorne Studies; Human Relations approach; contingency thinking	Natural selection	Ascribes agency to the environment; ignores the role of conflict
Brain	Self-organization and creative action; double-loop learning; learning throughout the organization; holographic; decision-making; cybernetics; learning organization	Learning	Overlooks realities of power and control; overlooks role of inertia as based on existing beliefs
Culture	National cultures; corporate culture and subcultures; meaning systems; shared beliefs and values, norms and rules, enacting shared realities; organizational change; corporate culture writers	Quest for meaning	Underplays role of fragmentation, ambiguity and complexity of cultural dynamics; leads to mechanistic culture management
Political system	Limited resources; conflicting interests; distribution of power; wheeling and dealing; negotiations, analysis of power and conflict; sources of power	Distribution of power	Can generate cynicism and mistrust; pursuit of personal interest; can overstate power of individuals
Psychic prison	Influence of the unconscious; fears and desires; repressed sexuality; patriarchal family structures; unhealthy patterns; psychoanalysis; psychology	Unconscious desires and fears	Ignores interests and ideologies of control as well as material base of control
Flux and transformation	Self-referring systems; evolving entities, change unfolds through circular patterns of interaction. Taoist philosophy Marxist analysis	Change	Is difficult to translate into practice due to existing ideologies
Instruments of domination	Exploitation of natural resources; exploitation of employees, discrimination; class; workaholism	Concentration of power	Ignores non-exploitative organizational forms; allocates blame, distracts from developing sense of collective responsibility

Since Morgan's contribution there has been an increasing and continuing interest in using metaphorical approaches for purposes of organizational analysis and development. For example, metaphorical frames included seeing organizations as clouds and songs (Gergen, 1992); theatre (Mangam and Overington, 1987); spider plants (Morgan, 1993). Clearly, these frames seek to disrupt established ways of thinking and imply that other frames are also appropriate (or even more so) for capturing organizational realities.

Currently, the field of organization study is in search of new metaphors. Czarniawska's work (1992, 1997, 1999) is exemplary in this search to establish a new vocabulary to understand institutional transformation and newly emerging organizational realities. She develops a narrative approach to knowledge in and around organizations by turning to the metaphors of anthropology, literary theory and the institutional school of sociology as a conceptual base to understand institutional and organizational transformations. Thus, the search for new concepts continues, and new metaphors might allow us to understand the new by relating it to what we already know.

Some applications

The generative potential of metaphor has attracted much attention, particularly in the field of organizational change and organizational development (for example, Barrett and Cooperrider, 1990; Marshak, 1993, 1996; Oswick and Grant, 1996; Sackman, 1989; Srivastva and Barrett, 1988). Metaphors are used to diagnose organizational problems and then to construct solutions to these problems. Metaphors are used to capture experience and emotions. Barrett and Cooperrider (1990) and Srivastva and Barrett (1988) provide persuasive examples of how metaphors helped in enabling organizational groups to overcome the negative perspectives they held of each other and improve communication and understanding. Changing the metaphorical frame proved indeed liberating and beneficial for the organization.

However, other researchers maintain that the degree to which managers or consultants can trigger a perspective shift amongst employees of the workforce remains a subject of debate. Sinclair (1994) provides examples where management attempted to facilitate organizational transformation by using new images, but failed – indicating that metaphors are not unilaterally changeable at the will of a particular person or group. Dunford and Palmer (1996a, 1996b) evaluate the effectiveness of reframing from the perspective of managers, who have undergone reframing training. While most of their respondents were enabled to use multiple frames, half of them could not implement their new vision due to lack of resources, political interests and lack of power. Their reflections stress that reframing occurs in a context of interest and power.

Product development

A new product development team attempted to design an improved paintbrush. The problem was set as brushing paint onto a surface; attention was focused on how paint clung to the bristles and rubbed off on the surface. However, during a discussion an observation was made that the brush worked like a pump. Thus, attention was shifted onto how the paint flowed through the spaces in between the bristles. With the change of perspective, the key function of the brush came to be viewed differently, leading to a new way of viewing the task. An improved brush was developed.

Adapted from Schön (1993).

Some criticisms of the metaphor approach

While viewing organizations as clouds, songs, icebergs and machines might result in a series of images and rich and sensuous descriptions, one could argue that these images remain quite superficial – that they lack analytic rigour and do not provide a basis for reliable and scientific inquiry. For example, likening organizational processes to processes of navigation might result in rather cliched descriptions of ships passing in the night and simplistic and rigid understanding of organizational roles (the captain, the officers and the crew). This criticism has been voiced by Pinder and Bourgeois (1982) who took issue with Morgan's theorising about metaphor and argued that the use of metaphors and tropes in administrative theory and research should be constrained, because they can be misleading: the language of research must not become ambiguous and must remain literal for the sake of clarity. Tsoukas (1991) agreed with these warnings against vagueness and argued for a similar constraint, although he concedes that metaphors can capture the "flow of experience" (1991: 571) as a necessary stage to the development of a literal language.

Alvesson (1994) attempts to address the criticism that metaphors provide only a broad and imprecise picture of the phenomenon they seek to capture by offering a more refined approach to understanding and using metaphors. He develops the concept of **first-level** and **second-level** metaphors. As a case in point he uses the 'organization as game' metaphor. He analyses several pieces of work that have used this metaphor and shows that the first-level metaphor (organization as game) is further developed into a sub-set of metaphors (organization as domesticated jungle; organization as brokering power relationships), which he calls second-level metaphors. These, so he argues, yield more precise insight and are more useful for organizational analysis. Rather than leaving analysis on the first level (organizations are games), he suggests that any analysis ought to become more sophisticated and look for the metaphors within metaphors to exploit fully metaphor's generative and stimulating potential.

Thus, Alvesson would argue that the organizations as games metaphor could only give the impression of communicating a rather distinct image. However, it can be interpreted in a multitude of ways, and therefore it is neither reliable as a communicative device nor does it provide a clear interpretative framework. In addition, viewing organizations as games creates no new insights, since the metaphor is part of an already established body of knowledge. As such this particular metaphor will hardly ever stimulate innovative and creative thinking. But driving the analysis further by concentrating on metaphors within metaphors might yield more specific and concrete insight. Viewing organizations, for example, as engaged in brokering games of power relationships, focuses the analysis on particular occurrences and renders the images more precise and therefore potentially more useful.

The benefits of second-level metaphors are that:

- they offer a more refined understanding of how metaphors inform conceptualisations of organizations and how to guide research;
- they reduce the problem of metaphorical seducing by being less ambiguous;
- they focus on critique and reflection. Contradiction between first-level and second-level metaphors point to variations in the use of metaphor;
- they share their generative function with first-level metaphors, but they provide new insights; and
- established first-level metaphors can be reinterpreted through second-level metaphors.

Organizations as family

- **Individual task**: Use the organization as family metaphor as the first level. Then, explore it in terms of how this metaphor defines organizational roles, structures, processes and values.
- **Group task**: Compare your findings with that of your group (wherever possible) and discuss reasons for similarities and differences.
- **Plenum discussion**: Are there any dominant ideas about families? What are the societal and historical factors that influence these images?

While the second-level metaphor approach alleviates some of the difficulties associated with metaphorical analysis, it does not address the way that metaphors can be used to legitimise certain actions over others, and can be used to sanction decisions as rational and necessary, when they might also have been influenced by personal or stakeholder interests. For example, within the logic of the open systems metaphor, the environment dictates the changes an organization has to implement in order to survive in the given environmental circumstances. Whatever steps managers and/or owners deem necessary to undertake (for example, downsizing, developing new products, or finding new markets) can be justified and legitimated within the open systems metaphor as necessary and unavoidable. By obscuring the influence of personal or stakeholder interest and institutionalised power relationships, this metaphor legitimises actions and creates what Tinker (1986: 378) describes as "false consciousness that undermines critical social analysis." The open system metaphor is an example of a metaphor that has become such an integral part of how we perceive, understand and run organizations that we are blind to its logic and often unable to challenge it. The power of this metaphor is the extent to which is has become true, common sense and part of our cultural and institutional systems. The more we are unaware of using the metaphor, the more it can create misunderstanding and false consciousness (Reed, 1990).

In summary, it would be misleading to present the metaphor approach as universally accepted. However, a good summary of the debate can be found in Palmer and Dunford (1996a, 1996b) and Grant and Oswick (1996).

Metaphors of the field

In the previous section metaphors were discussed as conceptual frames that are applied to organizations in order to facilitate insight, generate new meaning and provide new perspectives on change. They are imposed by researchers, consultants or managers onto the organization and arrived at conceptually. In the previous task you were asked to impose the family metaphor on an organization. You worked conceptually with the metaphor approach.

However, there is another way to use metaphors for organizational analysis. Within this second approach, 'meaningful metaphors' (Oswick and Grant, 1996: 217) are 'exposed'. They are arrived at empirically. For example, a researcher could study an organization from the inside, observing processes, talking to people, reflecting on her findings. She might discover that organizational members refer repeatedly to each other in terms of family roles; that values of obedience and loyalty seem of prime importance, sometimes more so than expertise and initiative and that the senior manager has got a reputation of being a benevolent, but strict patriarch. She might also come across counter-metaphors, ridiculing the roles – such as in the use of nicknames (for example, the godfather, the spinster auntie). She could then start to theorise the metaphors-in-use as she discovers them and start to engage in a cultural analysis of the organization.

The main benefit of collecting and working with metaphors-in-use, also called metaphors-of-the-field, is to better understand the complexities and paradoxes of organizational life. The strength of this approach is its richness and depth of analysis; its scope to engage with setting-specific uniqueness and the situational and contextual embeddedness of meaning. The most conducive methodology for this approach is perhaps ethnography, that is, the study of an organization in situ from a participant observer perspective. It yields the richest insights into the complexities and dynamics of organizational meaning systems. In particular, the exploration of emotions and values can be linked to an exploration of the metaphors-in-use.

However, the main challenge for the researcher/analyst is to make sense of the plethora of metaphors and tropes she is likely to find. Language users often mix metaphors, use them inconsistently and vary them according to situational contingencies. Sometimes, metaphors that are found in the field are not particularly insightful, innovative or even entertaining. It has been argued (Benjamin, 1968; Gabriel, 2000) that modernity has led to narrative deskilling and few organizational members are skilled in telling 'a good yarn' or using an insightful metaphor. However, while it might be that much of organizational talk and language is likely to be mundane and seemingly insignificant, we would argue that the art of research and interpretation is to look beneath this seeming banality. We are reminded of Boden's comments here about mundane talk being the 'lifeblood of organizations' (1994: 8). The examples provided below might give some indication of the metaphors and tropes that were used in real mundane organizational talk and subsequently used by researchers to illuminate organizational processes.

Same metaphor – different meaning

In her ethnographic study of the role of language in processes of meaning creation, Tietze (1998) collected tropes-in-use to infer about meaning making in organizational context. The following excerpt is taken from an observed meeting and post-meeting banter. The meeting was attended by product managers, who were bitterly protesting about the Centre, which was perceived to cream off an inappropriate amount of the profits. The Head of Production chaired the meeting. His role was to oversee production as well as to liaise with the Centre.

PM1: It is not fair to cream off that amount of the money we make. It's unacceptable.

PM2: And what is it used for? To fund the big offices of some bureaucrats.

PM3: They keep on asking us about what we add to the business ... but we need to know how much overhead they cause. One begins to wonder what value they add! We should just refuse to play their game. We have got ways and means to withhold information...

HoP: You can't just stop the game and put your hand up and shout to the referee: 'Hey, he's been off side' while the others are scoring goals. I mean, shouting to the referee won't help. You've got to get on with the game.

- The Head of Production uses the game metaphor to control the meeting. What are the emotions and values he appeals to in using the metaphor?

The meeting continued to be difficult, but the threatened boycott of withholding information was not mentioned again. After the meeting the Head of Production left and the production managers stayed on to discuss the events. One turned to the observer and commented:

PM2: It's funny, but when we play football it's not really about scoring at all. I mean, I can't actually remember who won last week. It's just brilliant if it's a beautiful game.

- How is *game* conceptualised in this use?
- How is this conceptualisation of the game metaphor different from that used by the Head of Production?

There are indeed a number of ethnographic studies, e.g. Barley (1983); Czarniawska-Joerges and Joerges (1990); Watson (1995a, 2001b) that collect tropes-in-use. These studies often find more than just metaphors-in-use, but make a point that language use is much richer and that ordinary language speakers draw on a multitude of tropes as part of everyday communicative processes. Watson (1995a) frames this as "hunting the tropes" (p. 812). He discovered a plethora of figures of speech in his analysis of an ordinary, spontaneous dialogue between two people in an organizational setting. He demonstrates how these tropes-in-use are part and parcel of organizational meaning making, but also how they are connected to wider, institutionalised discourses – one of empowerment and one of control.

Hunt the tropes

Irony:	says the opposite to what is meant
Simile:	links two subject areas, but does so more explicitly, using *like*
Metonymy:	the parts. The 'head' stands for a whole 'person'. The 'brown envelope' stands for the process of being made redundant.
Euphemism:	represent the whole the metonymy hides the dour fact of making people redundant.
Oxymoron:	combines two seemingly contradictory terms (honest con).
Personification:	treats business as if it were a living entity
Anthypophora:	a rhetorical question

The conversation is between Dick, the Training Manager, and Alan, a junior production manager. Dick sought a decision on whether Alan would prepare a skill module to be offered to employees.

D: Hello Alan. Sorry to interrupt. Just a quickie. You've decided?

A: Aha. Am I going to take on the skill module? (**anthypophora**) Uhm. I think I … Uhm. We.. I… Go on persuade me.

D: I wouldn't do that. It's up to you. You know the way the business (**personification**) needs to go. You know what's in it for you. You know that in the end you've got to persuade yourself. I am not going to twist your arm (**metaphor**). You're ahead of the game on all this. You know the score. You know what's best.

A: I know, I know. If I take it on I've got to own it (**metaphor**). I know the language. I didn't go through the whole teamworking thing for nothing.

D: You got a lot out of that, didn't you.

A: Oh yes. Oh yes I did. Look, I have bought into (**metaphor**) the whole personal development scenario. And if I can show others what empowerment can mean to them … but … No, I'm still not sure. You know the arguments. You tell them it's like making an investment (**simile**). OK, they say. So the pay packet will follow. Well, the pay packet might follow. But people aren't sure, are they? 'Winning culture,' ugh. That's all very well. But people can still go down the road. What do I say to people when they ask, 'will another skill module under my belt stop me getting a brown envelope?' (**metonymy**), the next time Bill's told to take out heads (**metonymy; euphemism**). Can't you see their point? I mean I really do. They talk about it being a con. I don't agree. But I know what they mean. OK it's an honest con (**oxymoron**) But….

D: OK, Alan, forget it. I don't know about all that stuff. It's beyond me. It's E.R. [employment relations] – not my scene. Perhaps you are right. It's best that you say no (**irony**).

A: Oh, sod it. All right. I'll do it.

While a technical analysis is interesting, the point is to demonstrate that a multitude of figures of speech is used as part of an everyday communicative process. The development of argument and counter-argument is part of organizational meaning making as embedded in a context of interests. These interests are individual, but also institutional and political in so far as the background of the dialogue is the turbulent telecommunications industry, its restructuring and the threat of redundancies. Watson shows that ordinary human actors, in pursuing their own as well as organizational interests, use rhetorical means routinely and consistently. This pursuit, however, does not happen in a neutral vacuum, but is shaped by the events and discourses around the organization (see Chapter 5).

Scope for tropes!

Verbal irony – is a figure of speech in which the intended meaning is the opposite of that expressed by the words used. It plays with apparent and intended meanings. It is used to point to incongruity between actions and their results, between appearance and reality, between what is expected and what actually occurs.

Situational irony – refers to the contradictions in a situation. In Watson's (1995a) study, employees were expected to commit themselves to the organizational purpose, while facing possible redundancies. Johnson and Woodilla (1999) point to a case where employees received more and more training to work as a team, but worked less and less well together.

Irony and humour – there are many studies on the use and meaning of humour (see Collinson, 1988; Linstead, 1985; Watson, 2001b), some of which found irony as part of organizational or managerial meaning making: Hatch and Ehrlich (1993) found that the use of irony indicated ambiguity and paradox in managerial work; Hatch (1997) showed that irony was used by managers to construct their emotional experiences in difficult and complex situations.

Metonymy – builds a relationship between two signs or subject domains based on physical, existential and casual contiguity (nearness).
For example, to refer to a person as a **a suit** or **an anorak** is using this figure of speech, because the garment and the wearer of the garment are physically contiguous (near), that their names can be exchanged. Of course, if you use a metonymy you assume that your audience knows about this changing of names and can make the right connection between the two signs. However, using the metonymy **an anorak** in a cultural context outside the United Kingdom might result in a non-communication, because speakers outside the UK have different bodies of cultural knowledge (see Chapter 6).

Tietze's (1998) study entailed the analysis of buildings and geographical locations as metonymies. She found that frequently people used expressions such as "the Old Manor has decided this" or "Braithwell Block is playing primadonna again." The metonymies-in-use were used like a convenient shorthand system, which allowed the users of the metonymy to reify complex organizational processes and thus transferred agency onto material artefacts.

Can you spot the metonymy and other tropes?

- The world of work has witnessed the transition from hands to brains.
- Headquarters have come up with another report.
- We need some new blood in the organization.
- The managed heart.
- The new product needs to become *the Hoover* of our industry.
- Personnel have not arrived at the meeting yet.

Summary

Metaphors are figures of speech that link two previously related subject domains. In doing so, they create new conceptual bridges and entail the possibility of seeing the world anew. Thus they carry a generative function. Organizational researchers, analysts and consultants use this particular function for purposes of reframing organizations. Studies concentrating on metaphors-in-use, on the other hand, yield deeper insights into metaphors embedded in organizational meaning making, and so can give insight into emotional realties and organizational value systems. In addition, ethnographic studies reveal that spoken language is full to the brim with all kinds of rhetorical figures. These form part and parcel of organizational meaning making. We suggest that the field of organizational analysis could benefit from broadening its approaches to include a wider variety of figures of speech, both as frames and as found in-use.

Table 3.3   **Metaphor**

Contribution	Criticism
Its generative function enables us to see the world anew and is therefore liberating	It constrains knowledge by hiding certain features and accentuating others
It can create new knowledge and insight	Therefore, it can be used for purposes of ideological control and manipulation
It encourages different ways of thinking and experiencing the world from multiple perspectives	It cannot be proven right or wrong. It does not add to scientific inquiry
It offers a way to access organizational meaning systems	It becomes established as common-sense and dominates thinking
It offers a way to access emotional realties and value systems	It creates a false consciousness and hinders critical social analysis

Recommended reading

Key texts include Lakoff and Johnson's (1980), *Metaphors We Live By*. It is an accessible read with many examples and has been widely influential. Ortony's (1975) seminal article on *Why Metaphors are Necessary and Not Just Nice* makes the case for the emotional and educational value of metaphor. Ortony (1993) has also edited a series of theoretical essays, *Metaphor and Thought*, which offer theoretical and philosophical slants on the metaphor debate.

Gareth Morgan's (1986) *Images of Organization*, is the classic text for the conceptual use of metaphors. Czarniawksa's work – notably *Narrating the Organization* (1999) and *Writing Management* (2000) is an attempt to develop new concepts to understand contemporary transformations.

Useful essay collections are edited by Grant and Oswick (1996) on *Metaphor and Organization* and by Oswick and Grant (1996) on *Organizational Development and Metaphorical Explorations*. Helpful summary of the debates around the use of metaphor can be found in the articles of Palmer and Dunbar (1996a, 1996b).

For inspiration on how to work with tropes and metaphors of the field, the reader can turn to Czarniawska-Joerges and Joerges' (1990) work on linguistic artifacts; Oswick and Montgomery's (1999) article on metaphors as elicited in an intervention; Tietze's (2000) study on the use of first-order metaphors and their variations in an organizational setting or Watson's (1995a) reflective tale on sense-making, rhetoric and discourses.

CHAPTER FOUR

Understanding Organizations Through Stories and Narratives

The previous chapter provided an overview of metaphor as a way of understanding organizations. In this chapter we look at the way we can use (organizational) stories or narratives to develop our understanding of meaning making in organizations. Like metaphors, we can use stories to explore otherwise tacit organizational meaning systems. They can provide a window into the symbolic realities as experienced and constructed by organizational members.

First, we introduce the role and function of stories as cultural accounts and depositories of meaning: stories are viewed as part of the cultural heritage as well as providing individuals with a means to express and shape their identities. This section is followed by a discussion of the tacit knowledge that stories often entail and how this knowledge is activated in the processes of narrating stories.

In the next section, the debate that informs the field of organization studies is outlined using the concept of *rich* versus *fragmented* stories as the two different cases in point. This is followed by examples taken from our research that are used to illuminate how organizational analysis based on stories can yield insights into cultural processes. These examples include the struggle over meaning as conducted between different organizational groups.

The section on stories and audiences examines the role of the audience in making meaning through storytelling, the suspension of disbelief and the ideological context within which stories are vetted as true or false. The final section provides a brief discussion of how stories can be used as tools for students of organizations to explore cultural systems of meaning. It also entails a discussion and some examples of how managers and consultants use stories for purposes of organizational learning, strategic development and for constructing the public image of an organization. This use of stories implies exercising social control so as to shape a particular image or to create a particular set of values.

Objectives

In this chapter we will:

- discuss the function and performances of stories;
- introduce and discuss stories as depositories of meaning and knowledge;
- introduce and discuss the emotional and cultural value of stories;
- discuss the fiction-fact balance in stories and the role of storywork done by the audience; and
- provide examples of how stories are used by organizations for learning and development.

Stories, storytelling and meaning making

Stories are a core component and constitutive part of culture. They are said to represent, reflect and confirm cultural values; they can provide templates for behaviour and moral judgement. In telling stories, cultural heritage is evoked, and both storyteller and audience position themselves in particular traditions and contexts – although this is not necessarily a conscious or deliberate act. Examples of such cultural spinning are the widely known stories of religious accounts (for example, as captured in the Koran or the Bible) as well as fairy tales. The latter are interesting cases in point, because they are still available and recounted in forms that have changed little over the past hundred years; but they have also been transformed and challenged and are used in a variety of forms including novels, films – including Walt Disney productions – theatre, comics, television programmes and jokes. They continue to reach children as well as adults. In their original form they function as providers of values and mores and in doing so provide guidance on what it means to be good, and as a consequence what it means to behave in certain ways.

Fairy stories and moral codes

Snow White and the Seven Dwarfs is a well-known fairy tale collected and recounted by the Brothers Grimm.

1 Can you summarise its content?
2 What are the moral codes entailed in this tale regarding gendered relationships, class structures, the work ethic?
3 In which forms is this fairy tale disseminated today?
4 Do you know of any critical reading of this particular fairy tale? What would you say is the purpose of these accounts?

These particular accounts continue to play a key role in cultural collectives – albeit there is more variation and fragmentation in how and why these accounts are told or reproduced. A critical account of the Snow White story could be, for example, the feminist re-interpretations that abounded in the 1970s. These accounts challenged the gendered roles and behaviours and constructed a different identity for Snow White.

Stories also play an important part for individuals in establishing and creating their identities. Indeed, human beings have been called "homo narrans" (Fisher, 1984, 1987) and "all forms of human communication" have been seen "fundamentally as stories." (Fisher, 1987: xiii). Within this thinking, storytelling is at the core of human activity, through which identities are constructed, changed or confirmed and through which human beings take cognizance of their social worlds. Social actors engage in storytelling throughout their lifetime and in all settings to make sense of the complexities and dynamics of human relationships, to define and shape the concepts of themselves, to influence unfolding events as much as to make sense of experiences.

Thus, the meaning of the term *story* is manifold: it ranges from accounts of traditional cultural heritage as captured in folklore and fairytales, the foundations of religions as laid down in their sacred books, to early bedtime stories, to gossip exchanged over lunch, to stories as read in newspapers or followed on the television. Stories constitute an ongoing part of how meaning is made, values are shaped and through which socialisation is achieved.

There are similarities in all stories in so far as they function as depositories of meaning and in that they perform symbolic acts. The difference in cultural accounts such as a fairy tale and a story exchanged between friends as part of a shared meal resides not so much in their function as depositories and inventories of meaning, but rather in the extent to which this meaning can be generalised.

Tales from childhood

- Can you remember stories that were told to you within your family or a similarly close-knit community?
- What was the purpose of telling the story?
- Was it recounted frequently?
- Did it begin to develop and change over time?
- Who told the story? Who did the listening?
- Were there different interpretations of the story?

If you have done the above exercise, it is likely that you identified different functions that a story performs. Notwithstanding the different contents of your stories, stories are a key ingredient of social processes such as establishing or confirming group identity; relationship maintenance and collective cohesion are performed. It could also be possible that you just had to think about one sentence or one word even and a whole chain of events, together with streams of images and people, sprang to your mind. However, in telling the story you would need to provide more details and narrative logic for your audience.

One story told to us as part of a project about how values informed management practice was the following:

> When I came home from my last day at national service, my mum was waiting for me. She said, 'come on, sit down, your tea is ready on the kitchen table.' I said,

'just give me five minutes, mum.' I went out into the garden and made a fire. I threw my uniform, my boots, my rucksack and anything that bloody reminded me of those days on it and burnt it. Then I sat down and had my tea … I made a promise to me on that day. Never again, in my life would anyone push me around.

The burning of the standardizing clothing (uni – form) can be interpreted as a highly charged symbolic act, that serves as a ritualistic cleansing of the experience of having been a cog in the machine. While the story itself referred to a unique event, it was also used to explain to the listener of the story, why this particular manager *had become the kind of manager I am now*. Highly (and often provokingly) unbureaucratic and challenging, this particular manager constructed his identity through the telling of this story. He loathed any kind of stand-offishness and showed his dislike in no uncertain terms regardless of the seniority or rank of the other person. He boycotted bureaucratic fiat as often as he could and acquired a reputation as a bit of a maverick – a reputation he cherished and cultivated – through the telling of this and similar stories to others.

Stories and storytelling, then, serve in this example as a way of interpreting experience and thus rendering it meaningful. If the audience does not acknowledge the symbolic importance of the act of burning the uniform for how the values of this manager were shaped, the story would be without significance or purpose. In turn, this meaningful experience can be shared and communicated to other people through the medium of the story. In this sense, stories are particular ways of carrying encoded meaning. It needs to be decoded as part of the communicative process. If this decoding does not occur in the way that the narrator intends – we do not always get the point of a story – one of the main purposes of storytelling, that of satisfying the need for meaning (Baumeister and Newman, 1994) remains frustrated.

Stories and knowledge

Consider the following example:

> My brother-in-law went shopping at Meadowhall on Good Friday. Later, they found that their car keys had been lost or stolen…

This is how a story could begin, and in this simple beginning, several knowledge propositions are entailed. The reader of this fragment is expected to make certain assumptions about the context of this story. It is based on a plethora of tacit (cultural) knowledge or cultural literacies as we refer to them in Chapter 5.

1 The narrator has got a sister.
2 The sister is married.
3 We (the narrator, the audience) talk to each other – since I (the narrator) is in a position to recount the story.
4 The narrator's brother-in-law goes shopping.
5 He was not alone.
6 He or the other person/s can drive a car.
7 It is March or April.
8 They are in a shopping mall.
9 The narrator's brother-in-law does not follow particular religious practices.

Furthermore, there are several wider contextual assumptions that are implicitly alluded to. For example, the changing cultural and legal traditions of when and where to go shopping: Good Friday is an important Christian day, on which particular commercial practices were not supposed to happen until approximately 1995. Also, the audience is likely to be able to visualise the particular environment of a shopping mall: shreds of music and murmurs, wafts of smells from stalls selling baked cookies or French fries, large potted palm trees and water features, the sliding motion of glass lifts and escalators. In doing so, it becomes clear that the shopping trip is less likely to entail the purchase of groceries, rather it is more likely to be a leisure activity, typical of the discourses and practices (see Chapter 5) in developed societies at the beginning of a new millennium. It is even possible to imagine that the audience of the story – consciously or subconsciously – frowns upon the decadence of the 'temples of consumerism' or on the contrary feels a sense of joyous anticipation and mentally begins to plan the next shopping trip. Thus, in this seemingly trivial couple of sentences that mark the beginning of a story, tacit knowledge needs to be activated to create the cultural context within which the story is anchored. Furthermore, subconscious thoughts, hardly ever captured or discussed, inform the reception of the story, too. Thus, particular formal relationships (brother-in-law), as well as cultural practices and their transitions form part of the context of the story.

Indeed, the context of the story is so culture-bound, that in different cultural contexts the knowledge propositions as we have portrayed them here would be changed. For example, in Holland homosexual people can marry, thus knowledge proposition two ("the sister is married") needs to be qualified to "the sister or the brother is married" – though more 'traditional' interpretations of marriage between man and woman are likely to linger on. In Bavaria, a mainly Catholic federal state in Germany, Good Friday and similar high religious days continue to exercise strong normative control over practices. Shops are closed and socialising activities are kept to a minimum. In other cultural contexts outside the UK and USA in particular, the language, practices and artefacts of consumer behaviour are less widespread and would perhaps meet with less understanding. In these instances, questions such as, "how come they go shopping on Good Friday?" might interrupt the flow of the story.

Some key principles of stories

- Tacit knowledge is the invisible glue that holds stories together.
- Stories are meaningful only in particular cultural contexts.
- Stories are part of the narrative mode of knowing.
- They capture the experiential specificities of human actions and include reason, intentions, beliefs, goals and values.

The continuation of the thus begun story is likely to elaborate the specifics of the unfolding event. For example, it might turn into "this-is-typical-of-my-stupid-brother-in-law" story, or it might be used to demonstrate the superior customer care of *Meadowhall* staff, who went to unheard lengths to help the hapless protagonists. Or, it could turn into a story in which the so far faceless other person/s turn out to be the hero/es who intercept the activities of a car key thief. Whatever meaning these unfolding events might hold for the audience, it is important to realize that whatever the plot of the story, each story is embedded in knowledge that quite often remains mute. For the audience, working with stories implies activating the tacit or mute knowledge(s) in order to contextualise the story and thus to render it meaningful. For the researcher, working with stories implies articulating the tacit or mute knowledge(s) in order to reveal underlying meaning systems that are taken for granted.

The knowledge that stories are embedded in is not presented or extrapolated in context-free abstractions, it is not contained in abstract (moral) rules or inferences. Rather, knowledge is embedded in a particular experience, which is "temporally structured and context sensitive" (Baumeister and Newman, 1994: 676–677). Baumeister and Newman refer to this as narrative knowledge: "that much of the thinking of ordinary people does not follow the patterns of inference, abstractions, and generalizations that science itself favors. But people do learn and store a great deal of information about their lives". Therefore, one means of understanding these patterns of thought and interpretation is the study of stories and storytelling.

Stories, narratives and organization

Stories and storytelling have entered the imagery and vocabulary of many spheres of public and private life. We all have a story to tell and everything tells a story. Within the field of organization studies, the intensifying fascination of organizational scholars with organizational folklore, including storytelling, can be located in the early 1980s as part of the emerging interest in organizational and corporate cultures. Stories together with myths, rites and rituals, language, jokes and so on became established items of research agendas (for example, Martin, 1982; Martin et al., 1983; Wilkins, 1984; Wilkins and Thompson, 1991). These researchers started to collect organizational stories as told by organizational members and worked with them analytically. Since then, narrative forms of knowledge have entered the field of organizational studies in many different ways, such as organizational research that is written in a story-like way (research cases), but also as accounts deliberately compiled for purposes of teaching (for example, Sims et al., 1993; Watson, 2000, 2001a).

Meanwhile, researchers continue to theorise cultural processes based on the analysis of either elicited or overheard accounts of organizational members (Boje, 1991, 1994; Boyce, 1995; Brown, 1992; Gabriel, 1993, 1995; Hansen and Kahnweiler, 1993; Mallon and Cohen, 2001; Salzer-Mörling, 1998; Taylor, 1999; Wilkins and Thompson, 1991). From this perspective, stories are viewed as the preferred meaning making currency of organizational members as well as external stakeholders. They are attractive, because they are the form in which knowledge is cast and within which meaning making occurs.

In addition, consultants and managers have latched on to the persuasive and didactic power of stories and a burgeoning industry flourishes that views and uses stories/ storytelling for purposes of social control; the construction of public images; and for organizational learning and strategic development. Thus, the efforts to use stories as analytic or conceptual tools, as well as tools for management, are immense and continue to develop (see Chapter 8).

The challenge to metanarratives

According to the writer Jean-Francois Lyotard, the postmodern condition of knowledge is defined by incredulity towards metanarratives. These grand stories used to provide the universal, conceptual and moral framework by which the world could be explained and which also provided the bedrock of morals and values. These, in turn, provided a stable and unquestionable basis for social and political (and organizational) conduct. While Lyotard's (1979) critique centred on the Enlightenment project (that is, the claim that science legitimates itself as the bearer of emancipation), other examples of metanarratives or grand stories are, for instance, any ideology or orthodoxy such as Marxism, liberal capitalism or religions.

In the field of organization studies, frameworks such as scientific management, human relations, contingency thinking and so on used to act as metanarratives. These have become subject to criticism and debate, to the extent that most of today's scholars and managers would reject a single unified conceptual framework for action. This is not to say that these frameworks have disappeared or are not being used to legitimate practice, rather it is the claim to absolute right that has been dented.

For example, *globalisation* or *capitalism* are functioning as such metanarratives. They provide an inescapable logic and legitimise actions. However, they have become subject to debate and controversy and are by no means accepted as universal grand stories, although their power to convince and to provide an inescapable logic continues to inform public and private debates.

The return of the little narrative

Concomitant with the demise of metanarratives, we can observe a return of the "little narrative" (Lyotard, 1979/1986: 61) of the everyday. These little narratives focus on the stories of (organizational) lives in terms that emphasise the situational and temporal embeddedness of (moral) choices. The onus of responsibility is on each individual/individual organization – rather than on institutions and their bodies. This includes the responsibility to make sense of the complexities of (organizational) circumstance: the big questions – if answerable at all – are to be addressed not within universalist and potentially totalitarian ideologies, but within the contingencies and expediencies of an increasingly complex world.

The love affair with organizational stories is to be seen against this background. Using organizational stories and storytelling to understand organizational processes is both a process of exploring how meaning is made, as well as a process of creating meaning in an otherwise opaque, potentially chaotic, world. By engaging with little narratives a means has been created to write meaningful accounts of organizations, while avoiding the reversal to the potential moral totalitarianism of metanarratives.

The focus on and interest in little stories has led to a proliferation of the term **story** to the extent that every occurrence, every sign, every object, every snippet of organizational talk can be framed as having a story to tell. People in organizations are, then, born storytellers, who "construct the categories-in-use, the frames-in-use, the histories-in-use, and the capitalisms-in-use" (Boje, 1994: 435) in a dynamic, collective process that constructs knowledge and power relationships. This view is challenged by Gabriel (1998a, 2000), who criticises the trend in organization studies to label every conversation, snippet of narrative, every text, every cliché or sign as a story or as having a story to tell. This undifferentiated use of the term "story", so he argues, results in obliterating any distinction between stories and other types of texts. Stories will thus disintegrate into "chic clichés into which meaning disappears" (1998a: 86). Therefore, they will become useless as tools for social research or as windows into the cultural and emotional side of organizational life. Following the concept of story through the folkloric, modern and postmodern tradition, Gabriel distils the key characteristics of stories as entertaining, interpretivist (containing hidden symbolism) and as maintaining inchoate meaning systems.

Gabriel (2000: 22) defines stories as "narratives with simple but resonant plots and characters, involving narrative skill, entailing risk, and aiming to entertain, persuade, win over." However, other writers and researchers use the terms **narrative** and **story** as interchangeable (for example Polkinghorn, 1987; Weick, 1995). Weick's influential framework of meaning making views stories as part of the wider meaning making process. Stories posit "a history for an outcome" (1995:128). The very sequencing that happens in a story provides an efficient causal chain and thus sequence is the source of sense.

We can see then that there is no one accepted definition of a *story* or *narrative*. Most pieces of writing use a wider definition of stories and *include other forms of text* such as *narratives, dialogues and exchanges* within their definition.

A question of definition?

Use the *Oxford English Dictionary* or any dictionary of literary terms and find the definitions for the following terms.

Legend
Myth
Narrative
Saga
Story

- Can you find any examples for each taken from a social/organizational context?
- When doing the task ourselves, we did find it problematic to find good examples in all cases. Do you agree? If so, why should this be the case?

Rich versus fragmented stories

We have found it useful to differentiate between **rich** and **fragmented** stories to reflect on the differences in concepts and application of the term story in the academic debate. On the one hand, Gabriel's definition of story protects its conceptual purity and in doing so provides the organizational researcher with a sharp analytical tool to investigate emotional realities, cultural processes as well as the constitution and challenge of meaning making processes.

An inquiry based on this narrow definition of stories, however, is likely to be faced with the following problem: despite claims that human beings are defined by their desire and ability to narrate (homo narrans), despite claims that organizations are supposedly brimful with wonderful stories, despite the fact that people talk and communicate incessantly and perhaps obsessively, there is a void of meaningful, rounded, noticeable stories. It is highly improbable that the hopeful researcher will come across a plethora of these narrative gems, because few people are effective storytellers, nor do all organizations possess a rich and flourishing folklore. Following Benjamin (1968), Gabriel reasons that the dearth of these kind of stories can be explained by the social and technical conditions of modernity that undermine the act of storytelling. Facing a deluge of information, people are turned into skilled information handlers, but become deskilled as narrators. However, Boje and Dehenney (1993) argue a different case: the more mind-numbing the mountains of information become, the more importance will be attributed to stories, because they provide a means to turn information into meaningful experience.

Table 4.1 Differences between rich and fragmented stories

	Rich story	*Fragmented story*
Property	Cast of characters; beginning and end; for example, dense and easily identifiable 'gem'.	Sometimes several and simultaneous listeners/tellers; for example, research interviews; organizational talk.
Purpose	Entertainment; emotional/symbolic; meaning making	Meaning making
Process	Teller-listener/audience clearly defined	Multi-authored; unfolds in conversation; punctuated
Focus	An action	Continuous flux

In an influential article on the storytelling organization Boje employs a different notion of story. His participant observer study of an office-supply firm showed stories not to be told from beginning to end. Rather, they were dynamic, done in conversation and involved the listeners in various ways: "people told their stories in bits and pieces, with excessive inter-ruptions of story parts, with people talking over each other to share story fragments, and many aborted storytelling attempts" (1991: 112–113). Boje refers to stories as potentially **terse** – they become abbreviated over time into one sentence (you know the story!) or even one expression (the parking lot story). The more terse the story, the more sharing of the social context needs to be assumed. This, in Gabriel's terms, robs the story of its narrative richness, its performative, ingenuity and symbolic richness. On the other hand, the collective, fragmented, dialogical storytelling as suggested by Boje is a more frequent, commonplace occurrence in organizations. As such, its inherent meaning making quali-ties are less spectacular, less entertaining than those evoked in a rich story, but they constitute and present storyline patterns that make sense of wider organizational processes and relationships and of past, unfolding and anticipated experience. The sym-bolic value of the fragmented story is less easily recognisable compared to the rich one. It also relies more on tacit, grounded knowledge.

Stories about change

The following excerpt is adapted from Boje (1991). Managers of the organization talk about resistance to change.

Manager 1: Over and over again in all your notes and blurbs and all on what people saying, I think paranoia ran high in this company in the last ten years, especially under Ralph Jones. I'm sure Paul could share a few examples (laughter). Examples of when he was out pulling invoices out in the warehouse while he was the frigging controller of the company. People were afraid to hire people that were better than they were. I mean, we have an assistant controller that can't run Lotus and it's not a jam but we do. You see I don't understand, I have – never have. In order to have a company that is going to grow, we actually have to hire and nurture people that are better than we are.

Manager 2: And unfortunately the frame of mind, the mindset that has been in the company for so long, because of all of the turnover and the turmoil with upper management, is I could lose my job tomorrow.

Manager 1: But the interesting thing is that nobody has ever come in and taken their job.

- Can you find instances of **terse** storytelling?
- Do you think that this kind of story is devoid of narrative richness?
- What are the advantages of working with these fragmented stories from the point of view of the researcher?

Of course, rich stories and fragmented stories are not mutually exclusive. In many instances, one will find that a rich story is referred to routinely in exchanges that are locally and temporarily fragmented. It could be argued that these different approaches to applying the story concept to organizational analysis are merely a question of definition and that it is possible to work with both concepts. However, this would pose problems in so far as every single titbit of talk, every banality needs to be treated as a story, leading to the loss of interpretative rigour as articulated by Gabriel (2000). However, the practicalities of research and studying prove that the number of original stories and gifted storytellers is few. Boje (2001) in his book on the use of narrative methods for organizational and communication research offers the new concept of the **antenarrative** as a way to engage with narratives. Antenarratives are the incoherent, non-linear and fragmented 'stories' the researcher will come across in the field. Boje offers a variety of approaches to working with such antenarratives. For example, his **causality analysis** does not look for simplistic causes of events, but he uses **causal map methodology** as a way forward to consider and acknowledge the complex ways in which causality attribution is done retrospectively.

Thus, espousing a purist approach might impose serious difficulties in so far as one might not find many stories worth their while. While there is no immediate consensus in the field of organization theory about the parameters of using stories as a analytic tool, we have used different approaches in our own work – comprising the purist approach (Tietze, 1998) as well as the more pragmatic approach of using accounts as part of our data (Mallon and Cohen, 2001). It might be helpful to consider at the outset of a research project what one is looking for and which forms of talk are to be regarded as a story. But our concern to understand and work with language in all its diversity makes us more predisposed to accept definitions and concepts as useful heuristic devices, and therefore to apply them beyond the boundaries of strict definitions.

Exploring collective meaning making through stories and storytelling

Boyce's (1995) study into collective meaning making, for example, views stories as the main symbolic form by which groups and organizational members construct shared meaning. These processes include both everyday conversations of organizational members as well as formal communication by managers. Focusing on *Friendship International*, a religious organization devoted to converting international students to the Christian religion while they study in the United States, Boyce shows how this regionally dispersed collective of individuals, creates a unifying organizational sense through storytelling events, cultivating an experience of unity: "How we are. This is what we do. This is what we stand for" (1995: 113). Boyce elicited stories from the members of *Friendship International* and investigated the processes and content of these accounts. She concludes her study by listing five intentional uses of shared storytelling that warrant utilization by organizational members, managers and consultants.

- Confirming the shared experiences and shared meaning of organizational members.
- Expressing the organizational experience of members or clients.

- Amending and altering the organizational reality.
- Developing, sharpening and reviewing the sense of purpose held by organizational members.
- Preparing a group for planning, implementing plans and decision-making in line with shared purposes.

A good yarn: emotions, evocations, entertainment

In this section we introduce various features of stories by narrating three different **rich** stories that were told to the authors during research projects. We arrived at the characteristics of these stories inductively, in that we interpreted the stories so as to arrive at some insights. In telling these stories, we pursue several intents. The first intent is a didactic one of providing examples of stories for the reader, and demonstrating how in the interpretation process we made sense of the data. We show how the interpretation of stories can be used to explore, for example, cultural change, group identities and counter-cultures. The three examples we provide are taken from fieldnotes. They are all rich stories and are imbued and reflect the emotional undertows of organizational life. Other than edify, we also hope to entertain the reader.

A tale of teaching

This story was narrated to us during a semi-structured interview. The intent was to explore whether the conceptualisation of teaching and its social relationships had changed over time. In particular the impact of shifting models of universities from collegiate academy, to bureaucracy to entrepreneurial model were examined. The interviewee, Claude, had been working as a teacher in further education and more recently in higher education. At this stage of the interview he expressed his increasing disillusionment with the current HE environment, its instrumental purpose and the bureaucratisation of human relationships. By point of contrast he said:

> When I used to work in FE, I used to enjoy 'Return to Study'. Anyone over the age of twenty-three who wanted to return to education could attend. And I used to teach them English ... and there is a chap there, who is about forty, and I was teaching on the top floor and I said: "Has anyone ever noticed how water always starts freezing at the top floor and then works down?" And I spent about an hour and a half talking to these people about autumn. At the end I needed to give some homework and I guess, it just seemed right to give them something to write about autumn. "What do you want us to write?", they asked – "Anything" I said. Following week this chap came in and said:

"Look at this for us." First poem he had ever written, that is. What provoked action like that and here, isn't that sense to me, that feels like something has been achieved. But here, it doesn't feel.

Before reading on, answer the following questions:

1   Who are the characters in the story?
2   What are the emotions expressed in the story?
3   What is the action of the story?
4   What does it symbolise, what does it mean to you?

Our interpretation is as follows. The story presents the poetic experience of a former existence. The season of autumn is evoked and used to frame the classroom experience as a transformational process. It enables the student to re-see the minutiae of everyday drabness through a poetic way of seeing, adding (possibly) beauty and truth to Claude's existence. Learning and teaching are best understood as poetic, spiritual experiences, by which internal change in the way one sees the world can be achieved.

The story resonates with notions of nostalgia as 'a state arriving out of present conditions as much as out of the past itself' (Gabriel, 1993: 121). Nostalgia expresses the yearning for a golden past (Gabriel, 2000), characterised by authenticity and genuine achievements. Within this story, it is the antidote to the present that is troubled by the increasing dominance of bureaucratic fiat and regulated, prescribed social relationships. The gamut of emotions entailed in the story ranges from feelings of self-worth and appreciation of a kindred spirit to dismay, frustration and anger at the alienating aspects of bureaucratised educational systems that are a feature of Claude's present condition. The story criticises the present, by metaphorically evoking a past in which education was meaningful, because it was transformative.

A story of a prank

While we interpret Claude's story to be one of melancholic beauty and reverie for things past, we interpret the following account as also expressing feelings against the excesses of bureaucratic control, but from a humorous perspective. A colleague told the story to us during a chance meeting on a bus. Recently, there had been a series of emails by the department's facility manager, Rosie, reminding staff of the out-of-control photocopying budget and requesting that staff be more careful when using photocopying materials. Implicit in the emails were indications of having to rationalise the photocopy paper supply.

The following exchange occurred:

–   Have you read Rosie's latest email?
–   Yes, em – the one about the photocopying costs?

(Continued)

> – Yes, that one – there is another one about this, sent this morning
> – Oh?
> – Yes, anyway. You know Peter managed to sneak into Eric's office while he had his elevenses and he had left his email switched on. So Peter sends an email as Eric, officially expressing his support for any future plans to ration the photocopy paper per person, and also drawing attention to the irresponsible squandering of paper in the mens' loo – suggesting that this paper supply be rationed to one sheet per go!

This humorous account tells of a prank by this particular group of men. They all had their offices on the same floor and frequently played tricks on each other. We also interpret it as poking fun at the formal organization and its representative, the facility manager. It satirizes the cost cutting efforts as petty and as part of a bureaucratic control discourse (see Chapter 5). As such the story could be seen to be expressing a dissenting voice, a counter-culture satirizing the rationalization plans by mimicry and mockery. The story carries a spectrum of emotions: feelings of belongingness and friendship as based on the solidarity among the group; heroic feelings of (self) righteous rebellion against absurd bureaucratic fiat, as well as amusement and/or disapproval on the side of the audience. Satire can seem cruel and petty towards the recipients, however as a recurring occurrence it can also resonate with dissent that can question power balances and social structures.

To continue with our interpretation of this story, there were follow-on pranks in the form of official looking signs put on the doors of the male toilets: "Be careful. Every sheet you use, every flush you make, means pennies down the drain. THE MANAGEMENT." For some time after the email, the group of men kept on humming the tune and the lyrics of a particular pop song when in (informal) public settings. The lyrics of the Police song, *Every Breath You Take* had been changed to: "Every breath you take, every dump you make, every sheet you use, I'll be watching you." Whether these follow-on pranks are interpreted as merely childish, possibly misogynistic acts, or expressions of genuine resistance, or act as emotional safety valves sustaining bureaucratic structures, is a matter of debate (see Ackroyd and Thomson, 1999, in particular Chapter 5 and Gabriel, 2000, for more detailed discussions on humour and resistance). Whatever, as a story the entertainment tenet has been fulfilled. But it can also be said to express more than the entertainment function, enabling the researcher to explore the dynamics of group identity maintenance through the expression of a different voice, which challenges and mocks the powers that be.

A story of achievement

The following story formed part of a speech made by a senior manager at a celebratory event of a public sector organization. It started off with a brief glance back to the bad old days, and then it focused on the present and ended with a vision for the future, based on customer focus and total quality. The particular manager's role was to imbue the departments of the council with some entrepreneurial spirit by setting up internal market mechanisms, developing stronger profiles for the portfolio of services and nurturing customer focus. He started off his speech as follows:

> There we were, trying to get people going, trying to move forward. It was like running a race with your ankles shackled together. Whatever we wanted to do, it needed to go through a committee. It took four months to decide who would be on it, five months for it to agree on a date for a meeting and six months to book a venue... and then you went there and the room was double-booked! [Some laughter] It's true! Once I had to persuade Steve and his gang to cut their meeting short by thirty minutes – toughest negotiations I ever had!

Before reading on, address the following questions:

1 Why do you think the manager opens his speech with this story?
2 Which emotions does the story evoke in you?
3 What is the difference between the heroes of the previous story (the pranksters) and this one in terms of the purpose, the audiences and the role of the protagonist?

Our interpretation of the story is as follows. The story begins by taking a look at the past and describes the agent as being constrained by using the shackle metaphor (see Chapter 3). The impact of the bureaucratic structures are humorously embellished (four months, five months, six months; the showdown with the villain of the piece, Steve) and made fun of by pointing to the inefficiency of the system (rooms are double-booked). There are insinuations of heroism (facing Steve), albeit played down. This epic story (Bowles, 1989; Gabriel, 2000) is one in which the speaker/hero emphasises his agency and achievements such as overcoming the red tape of irritating officialdom.

The story formed part of a public speech, that is, a rehearsed and prepared communal event, in which values are communicated and meanings are forged (see Chapter 5 on **genre**). In this sense, the story is used as an indirect and unobtrusive method of control (see Chapter 8). One point of the story then could be to prepare the ground for the shaping of an agenda which is anti-bureaucratic – more flexible and customer-focused. Thus, the story can be seen as part of the unobtrusive art of indoctrination by persuasion, offering the audience an opportunity to identify with the hero, inspiring to emulate his behaviour, to share his values. The means of control are indirect, rather than direct, perhaps controlling the employees from the inside – to capture their hearts and minds. Since the story was part of a speech, which was part of a larger event, it can be interpreted as an attempt at managing the corporate culture by instilling appropriate values through giving a humorous account of the 'bad old days'. In this sense the story has become part and parcel of controlling values and meaning systems. However, our interpretation of the previous stories shows that a story can contain an unmanageable element, in which meanings can be challenged. They occur in spaces that are beyond the gaze of management and skilled orators. In this terrain, people both as individuals and in groups engage in spontaneous and subjective activity. They reinterpret, redefine and refashion formal

Table 4.2 Comparing three stories

	Claude's story	The Pranksters' story	Manager's story
Protagonist/role	Teacher – student, victim	Pranksters, Anti-hero, rebel	Manager, hero
Emotion	Nostalgia, alienation	Belligerency	Overcoming of adversity
Purpose	Contrast and escape from oppressive present	Entertainment, resistance	Edify, entertain, control of values
Tropes	Metaphorical	Joke, satire	Metonymic (past-present-future)
Meaning	Symbolic contra-point to present	Existence of self-determined counter-culture	Culture management

stories or events. Neither completely conforming, nor completely rebelling, they are suspended between pleasure and control, emotionality and rationality.

Audiences make meanings

In narrating a story – be it in rich or fragmented formats – a dynamic relationship between teller and audience is created. If stories are depositories of meaning, the meaning is made not only by the narrator, but also and perhaps more importantly, by the audience. Just as with the use of metaphor (see Chapter 3), the narrator has little immediate control over the audience's reaction to the story, be it as an immediate response while the story is being told, or as a later response when the story might very well be corrected, amended, reinterpreted or even rejected. The audience of the manager's story of achievement might laugh politely during his performance, but post-celebration might very well ridicule and reject the attempts at value management (see Höpfl, 1993; Tietze, 1998). The pranksters' story might be interpreted as genuine attempts at resisting the excesses of bureaucracy or alternatively as infantile recalcitrance. The meaning of the story depends on the audience's position. Someone who had to make difficult financial decisions might sympathise with the facility manager and frown on the unprofessional behaviour of the pranksters. Claude's account might be judged as romanticising the past, as celebrating the transformative power of teaching or as a ray of beauty in an otherwise grey world. Thus, the meaning of a story is dynamic, and can change over time or be subject to a group's belief system. Stories then are polysemic, that is, they can have several meanings.

More key principles of stories

- The reception of a story is contingent on the ideological assumptions of its audience.
- The truth of a story is judged in relation to the existing beliefs of a particular social collective.
- Stories are both unique and general. Through processes of interpretation, they transcend their uniqueness to take on a deeper symbolic meaning.

When we listen to a story we suspend our disbelief, that is to say, we allow the storytellers to use their poetic licence to embellish the narrative, to exaggerate some aspects, to sketch out the particularities of the situation. If we witness a physical fight between a group of people, we are likely to attempt to give a descriptive and detailed account to the police (a report). The account we are likely to give to friends is probably less descriptive and detailed, but will be more lively, evaluative and entertaining. We will tell a different story. In our culture we have learned to trust a report, because it appears to be objective and based on facts (see role and function of genre in Chapter 5). After all, we assume that we can always go and check the facts ourselves. How do we trust a story that is based on facts, but openly and deliberately plays with them, distorts some, obliterates others, uses poetic devices as part of the narrative process? Partly, we come to trust a story if it is in line with our own belief and value system. In this case the audience is prepared to suspend its disbelief and become part of the storytelling. Once the audience decides to reinstate its disbelief, storytelling becomes near impossible. Storytellers propose interpretations that audiences "may test, trying them out in their own imagination and seeing whether they work or not. If a particular interpretation 'resonates' with them, they may accept it; alternatively, they may reject or modify it" (Gabriel, 2000: 43).

Whether a story resonates with the audience or not is contingent on whether it is in line with the audience's belief and value systems as well as its experience. However, the truth of a story has to have a symbolic value for it to be acceptable. Thus, the pranksters' story, the manager's story and Claude's story, while being based on factual, unique episodes or events, also carry a deeper symbolic truth. Claude's story refers to one particular teaching session, yet the meaning of it transcends its time and space bound uniqueness into a symbolic meaning. The pranksters' story relates a particular, unique turn played on management, but it resonates with a deeper meaning about the state of affairs of life in bureaucracies in general. The manager's story refers to particular identifiable events, but also contains a symbolic truth about the inefficiencies of bureaucracy. Thus stories refer to the unique and the particular, located in the here and now (or there and then), but their meaning transcends the temporal and spatial boundedness and renders them deeply symbolic. Stories are more likely to be accepted if they are both unique and generalizable.

- Stories are more likely to be accepted as true if the audience recognises their symbolic value.
- Stories are subject to interpretation work by the audience.

- The meaning ascribed to stories is only partly controllable by the narrator.
- Stories are both unique/specific and symbolic/universal.
- Stories are judged in relation to the beliefs and values of social collectives.

Organizational stories can be collected and/or elicited in order to explore cultural processes, to reflect on the emotions of organizational life, to investigate specific and universal meaning making within ideological belief systems.

The examples we have used show how the analysis of stories can help to illuminate and understand the nostalgic construction of the past, the establishment of dissenting voices and processes of cultural change – all of which are essentially emotional processes. Thus the interpretation of stories opens windows into the emotional arena of organizational life.

Understanding organizations inductively through stories entails:

- Viewing social realities as constructed: agents both shape their social worlds through their stories and accounts, as they are shaped through collectively shared stories;
- Working with 'meaning' rather than expecting to discover the truth;
- Admitting and confronting one's personal feelings, assumptions and preconceived ideas; and
- The researcher's willingness and ability to view the world as polysemic and therefore as potentially ambiguous.

Understanding organizations through stories is an enjoyable way to engage in the exploring of meaning systems. While there are some technical decisions to be made about research design (for a useful discussion of technical and philosophical aspects see Gabriel, 1998b, 2000), researchers using stories as research instruments must not seek to 'set the record straight' or to 'write the ultimate story about the organization'. Rather the research process will entail the engagement with and confrontation of the researcher's own emotions, preconceived assumptions and value systems.

Stories as part of the management and consultancy process

There is a second strand of application of the story concept, which is particularly practised by consultants and managers. It is the deductive use of stories for purposes of organizational development. Just as with metaphors (see Chapter 3), the concept of stories can be used inductively as resources from the field. This is the way we have used stories in the chapter so far. However, stories can also be used conceptually, as devices that are applied/imposed onto the organization to achieve certain objectives or to construct a public image (corporate stories for example). Latter approaches play an increasingly important part in managing organizations (see Chapter 8).

The point of a good story is easily remembered. Famous stories that have become part of the collective wisdom of organization studies are, for example, *The H–P way* or *Taylor's ox story* or indeed *Banana time*. A good story is more easily remembered for longer than a factual report. Therein lies their extraordinary power as didactic devices. "Successful businessmen do not, by and large, express the reason for their accomplishments in terms of abstract, general principles, but instead they tend simply to keep all the relevant information in their memory in narrative terms. The story, rather than the generalization, was the medium for presenting and communicating information" (Baumeister and Newman, 1994: 676). Of course, this kind of storytelling is enacted by particular people within particular situations for particular purposes, exploiting the edifying potential of stories. Often, the stories encode particular corporate values or codes of conduct, or are part of the construction of a 'corporate story', which promotes the public face of the organization (see Chapters 5 and 8). Also, these stories enhance and strengthen the 'corporate ego' (Salzer-Mörling, 1998), an image of the company as an autonomous and strategically alert actor (in Chapter 5 on Discourse and Chapter 8 on Leadership we provide examples of corporate stories).

Do you know the story?

Can you fill in the details of these tersely presented stories? They require you to draw on quite specific tacit knowledge. If you have it, the task is easily completed. If you don't, you might draw on the collective knowledge of your group/as codified in books/as embodied in your lecturer.

1 **Taylor's ox**
2 **The H-P way**
3 **Banana time**

To make your task a little bit easier: for examples one and two, consult the textbook by Huczynski, A. and Buchanan, D. (2001), *Organizational Behaviour. An Introductory Text*, Prentice Hall; for example three consult Roy, D. (1960), "Banana time: job satisfaction and informal interactions," *Human Organization*, 18(2): 156–168.

The writers of the corporate culture school, in particular Peters and Waterman (1982), Peters and Austin (1986) or Deal and Kennedy (1988), are skilful rhetoricians. Their books provide useful examples to study how to make a point by using a plethora of stories and other means of persuasion. These and other accounts narrate many stories of high achievement, which fulfil a practical point – they provide a trajectory of how to behave, but also a moral one – about what is good management. The readability of these books hinges largely on the authors' skilled use of stories to make their point. Combining both the entertaining and edifying functions of storytelling, the narratives are geared to inspire and convince. Indeed, the skill of a consultant is the ability to tell a convincing story (Akin and Schultheiss, 1990; Clark and Salaman, 1996), interpreting the past and offering a vision of the future that provides – to use an oxymoron – a safe challenge (see Chapter 8).

Increasingly, there is also interest in stories as containers of knowledge and in storytelling as knowledge disseminating processes. Early work by researchers (for example, Wilkins, 1978; Wilkins and Martin, 1979) saw one of the function of stories as transmitting knowledge among organizational participants. The importance of stories as cognitive repositories becomes even more urgent in the information age with its insistence on making the point quickly, succinctly and memorably. The sharing of organizational knowledge is considered to be a key competitive advantage. **Knowledge management** is a current label to categorise attempts to systematise and share collective knowledge. Stories within this emerging field are both the means to transform information into knowledge, as well as the transmitters of the thus created knowledge (Choo, 1998; Davenport and Prusak, 1998).

In particular, large global organizations face the challenge of accumulating their combined knowledge in ways that are flexible and process-oriented, rather than centrally driven. To this purpose some companies have formalised knowledge management systems, creating knowledge management roles, databanks, including the establishment of electronic means to share knowledge through stories throughout the company. For example, IBM has established web pages on storytelling to facilitate the sharing of knowledge, that is, to facilitate organizational learning.

Company storytelling on the world wide web

Search for IBM's – or a similar company's – storytelling web pages: http://www.research.ibm.com/knowsoc/project_whystories.html

Take some time to browse through the pages.

- Identify which stories are used.
- How are they used and why are they used?

Other companies that are quite adept at using corporate stories are *The Body Shop* and *Ikea*. Their websites provide ample material to access and analyse how public images are constructed through the use of stories (see also Chapter 9).

From this perspective, stories can be used by organizations for purposes of organizational learning, the sharing of knowledge and for purposes of social control. Storytelling can also be used for purposes of strategic development. Shaw et al. (1998: 41) provide an interesting example of how 3M uses strategic storytelling for purposes of business planning. They begin their account as follows:

At 3M we tell stories. Everyone knows that, in our earliest days, a share of 3M stock was worth a shot of whiskey in a local St. Paul bar. We tell stories about how we failed with our first abrasive products and stories about how we invented masking tape and Wetodry sandpaper. More recently, we've been telling the story about one of our scientists who, while singing in a choir, wished he had book-marks that wouldn't fall out of the hymnal – and later created Post-it notes.

Shaw et al. show how stories are used in 3M. For example, the sales representatives are trained to "paint stories through word pictures so that customers will see how using a 3M product can help them succeed" (1998: 42) and stories are told at employee award ceremonies to explain what happened and to demonstrate the significance of events and certain behaviours. In this way stories become central to the construction of identity as a 3M employee. Shaw et al. also tell a story themselves, to show how storytelling was taken one step further in 3M to become incorporated into 3M's approach to strategic planning. They use the example of Robert Brullo, a divisional head and hero of the success story, demonstrating the virtues of originality and tenacity, individuality in the face of adversity, resulting in a successful adaptation of the strategic process.

Compare and contrast

Read the complete case study about 3M as printed in the *Harvard Business Review* (Shaw et al. 1998, May–June).

- Compare and contrast the **bullet point** approach to strategic planning with the **narrative approach**.
- Clearly, the case study shows the **narrative approach** to be superior. By what means do you think this is achieved?

If stories are used as part of the management process, similar issues that face the academic approach to storywork need to be heeded. Thus, managers and consultants should be aware of the polysemic and ambiguous character of the organizational world and that in using stories one deals in meaning rather than truth. In particular, using stories as part of the management process entails an acknowledgement:

- That all stories need to be interpreted by an audience, and that this process is ulti-mately beyond management's control.
- That stories are part of a collective process of meaning making and do not belong to any one person or group, even a particularly powerful one.
- That claims of omnipotence or omniscience need to be relinquished.

Summary

Against the said background of declining metanarratives there is a vigorous interest by organizational scholars, researchers, managers and consultants in the little narratives of stories and storytelling. There are different definitions of what stories are, and what storytelling entails, which we compared and contrasted using *rich* and *fragmented* stories. We introduced three (rich) stories to explore some functions and features of storytelling as polysemic, part of meaning making, expressing emotional realities and values. These raised issues of the use of stories as forms of social control. The meaning of stories and their trustworthiness were shown to be contingent on the simultaneous evocation of the unique and the universal, which persuaded the audience to suspend its disbelief and engage with the emotional and symbolic undertones of the story.

We also briefly outlined applications of stories and storytelling to organizational settings. These included the application of stories as inductive means to understand and theorise organizational meaning making processes better. We also discussed the deductive application of stories, where the story is used mainly by consultants and managers to facilitate organizational learning and strategic development as well as for purposes of social control. The questions "whose stories are being heard," "whose are being suppressed," and "whose count" imply that stories and storytelling are subject to processes of power and manipulation. These ideas are discussed in more detail in Chapter 5 on Discourse and Chapter 8 on Leadership.

Recommended reading

The literature on organizational stories and how they can be used is burgeoning. Gabriel's work (1993, 1995, 1998a, 1998b) provides important contributions to the establishment of stories as a serious means of organizational analysis. His book on *Storytelling in Organizations. Facts, Fictions and Fantasies* (2000) provides a comprehensive, readable account of the topic area. Boje's book on *Narrative Methods for Organizational and Communication Research* (2001) provides a useful discussion on narratives and stories and approaches how to work with such messy and fragmented narratives. It makes for a rewarding but challenging read.

Boje's (1995) and Boyce's (1995) articles are useful examples of a different definition and approach to organizational storytelling. They make useful reading to supplement one's understanding of how this concept can be used to investigate meaning making processes. Boyce (1996) has also written a review highlighting the contributions of several key studies: "Organizational Story and Storytelling: A Critical Review," in the *Journal of Organizational Change Management*.

The work of Czarniawska (1997), *Narrating the Organization. Dramas of Institutional Identity* and (2000), *Writing Management. Organization Theory as a Literary Genre* offers theoretical approaches that draw on literary theory – including narratives and stories – and can be seen as attempts to develop conceptually the field of organization theory. These two sources are challenging reads, but for those students wishing to engage with how subject areas are conceptually developed, they make for worthwhile reading.

CHAPTER FIVE

Understanding Organizations Through Discourse

This chapter explores the ways in which we read and understand cultural texts, using the concepts of **genre** and **discourse**. In the chapter we use genre to refer to the **form** of a particular text, and discourse to refer to its **content**. We acknowledge that it is difficult to draw distinctions between form and content – such distinctions might be thought of as artificial, and there is, in any case, considerable overlap between these concepts. However, for the purposes of this introduction, we have separated them out. We feel that such separation makes these rather slippery concepts a bit more accessible, and therefore more useable.

In our discussion thus far we have suggested that meaning making must not be seen as a purely individualistic or idiosyncratic process, nor can a particular text be understood as a unique occurrence, in isolation from other texts and contexts. Rather, we have described meaning making as a fundamentally social and cultural process. In particular we have emphasized the idea of texts as situated within particular cultural contexts, and the importance of cultural knowledge in all social interaction. The question then arises: how can we understand the cultural knowledge that individuals bring to bear on a particular text and that informs the way in which that text is understood? In this chapter we use the concepts of genre and discourse to help us make sense of cultural texts, providing useful insights into how signs work together to form patterns that underpin our understandings.

In the first section we introduce the idea of **cultural frames** as a metaphor for illuminating the relationship between texts and their cultural contexts. In the next two sections we discuss the concepts of genre and discourse, respectively, and explain how both work as framing devices. While genre has received very limited attention in the organizational literature, there is a rapidly growing interest in discourse and organization. Key issues and debates within this literature are discussed in the final section of the chapter.

Objectives

In this chapter we will:

- introduce the idea of cultural frames and cultural literacy and examine two important framing devices, genre and discourse;
- discuss the relevance (but neglect) of genre in organizational theory;
- examine the concept of discourse and highlight key debates raised by commentators in this field; and
- discuss the ways in which discourse has been used in organizational research.

Frames

As we have already noted, we do not make sense of texts in isolation. As we suggested in our discussion of metaphor (see Chapter 3), for a text to be recognizable it needs to draw upon established and shared meanings. The point here is that we understand cultural texts, be they language, objects or behaviour, in terms of what we already know about them: their contents, contexts, and what we know about other texts **like that**. That is, we approach cultural texts with certain expectations. When we find ourselves in new situations, we draw on knowledge of other similar situations to get by. The idea that our encounters are mediated through the cultural knowledge that we bring to any situation was central to our discussion of storytelling. That is, our competency in one setting enables us to make sense of and operate within other settings. As Schirato and Yell explain, "in a given context, members of a culture can predict, to an extent, the kind of meanings which are made" (2000: 53). They describe this tacit knowledge, knowledge that in many cases we are not even aware of, as **cultural literacy**.

Cultural literacy

Schirato and Yell define cultural literacy as "a knowledge of meaning systems combined with an ability to negotiate those systems within different cultural contexts" (2000: 190). They argue that as individuals, we have different cultural literacies which we draw upon continuously as we encounter new texts and situations.

Within organizations, members' cultural literacy, their knowledge of the implicit and explicit 'rules' (including values, attitudes, norms etc.) enables them to operate comfortably within those settings. In contrast, newcomers arriving in the organization with knowledge of other organizations and with different cultural literacies can feel lost and insecure. A respondent in Cohen's (1997) study of women's career transition described her experience of starting a new job: "I just didn't know what was expected because nothing was explained outright. I continually felt like I was about to be dragged in front of some disciplinary panel for breaking some rule, but I had no idea which one."

Consider an organization you know well.

- Are there some people who you would describe as culturally literate? How can you tell?
- Are there members who you feel are not so literate? How can you account for this?
- Can you think of a setting in which you have felt culturally literate, and one in which you have felt illiterate?

Crucially, cultural literacy is not something that an individual achieves in isolation from others. Indeed, the whole idea of cultural knowledge is that it transcends the individual – it assumes that people operate in social worlds (even though these collectives can of course be very diverse). Becoming culturally literature, therefore, is a process of learning and participating in shared systems of meaning.

Some commentators refer to these systems of shared meanings, as **frames**. We find this a salient metaphor for understanding the diverse **packages** of knowledge that we bring to our reading of a particular communicative event or text. When we encounter a new situation we use our existing frames to make sense of it. In this way the new situation is not experienced as a barrage of totally unfamiliar stimuli, but is understood in terms of things that we already know. Thus, frames provide us with structures for making sense.

Using cultural frames

When we watch a film, read a book, or hear a speech, our interpretation of the text is framed by what we already know about texts like that (their contexts, authors etc.). In the case of film, for example, we bring to the text our knowledge of film generally and of the topic in particular, and sometimes of the director or the main actors.

We recently saw Ang Lee's film *Crouching Tiger, Hidden Dragon* (Dir: Ang Lee, 2000). In many ways this was a very unusual and original film that combined elements from a variety of film types, including Kung Fu films, love stories and feminist cinema. Our interpretations, therefore, were framed by prior knowledge of these styles. In addition, we had already seen Ang Lee's earlier film, *The Ice Storm* (Dir: Ang Lee, 1997), so we had certain expectations of his new work. These different knowledges thus worked as 'cultural frames', providing us with ways of accessing and making sense of that new and very different text.

Sometimes, of course, our existing frames are not a perfect fit. In such cases, the process of becoming culturally literate is about developing new frames of knowledge.

Breaking frames

In our research we have frequently come across cases where new computer systems have been introduced in organizations and, lacking adequate training, individuals have reported feeling deskilled and incompetent. Because the language of computers often uses familiar words and redefines them in wholly new ways (desktop, window, home page, memory – see also Chapter 9) and also makes up whole new words and phrases (pixel, disc compression, virtual memory, RAM etc.), respondents have explained how they were unable to use existing frames to understand the new system. Indeed, trying to apply prior knowledge often resulted in even greater confusion – and frustration.

The metaphor of the frame helps us to understand the process of meaning making as embedded within social and cultural contexts. Discussing the meaning of Sabina's bowler hat (noted in Chapter 2) Kundera, the author of *The Unbearable Lightness of Being* explained that: "each time the object would give rise to a new meaning, though all former meanings would resonate (like an echo in a parade of echoes) together with the new one." (1984: 88). That is, new meanings do not just erase those that came before. Rather, each new meaning is like another strand in a complicated, tangled and slowly evolving web. Here we have another example of the process of **ventriloquation** discussed in Chapter 2.

The frame trope becomes even more useful – and more precise – if we try to break it down and consider different kinds of frame, and their implications for meaning making. Genre and discourse are two important kinds of frame. While discourse has received a great deal of attention in the field of organization studies, the notion of genre has been basically ignored. We feel that both can be really valuable analytical concepts, and can work to enhance further our understanding of organizations.

Genre

Genres are forms of communication practice. They include forms such as:

- speeches
- sermons
- interviews
- informal conversations
- presentations
- sales transactions
- poems
- novels (with sub-genres including romance, thriller, fantasy, horror, slice-of-life, etc.)
- flirtations
- arguments
- negotiations
- appraisal interviews

- meetings
- instructions
- jokes
- email messages

The concept of genre does not refer to the text itself. Rather, it refers to its form – or the type of encounter it is. As social semiologists Hodge and Kress explain, genres are "typical forms of text which link kinds of producer, consumer, topic, medium, manner and occasion" (1988: 7). That is, within each of the genres listed above are certain sets of rules and social relationships. We hardly ever discuss these explicitly. But our facility with these different genres shows that we know they are there. If we take workplace meetings as an example, we can see that they are organized around sets of rules – implicit or explicit – which define the ways in which people interact: who can speak, when, how and to whom they can speak and on what topics. They define those who have the power, and those who are subordinate. While some of these rules may be general, others will be specific to an organization or department. That is, while in many cases meetings are conducted by a chairperson following a set agenda, rules about relative formality or informality, the extent to which people digress from the agenda, degrees of openness and the likelihood of consensus or conflict will vary among local contexts. Indeed, an important dimension of cultural literacy is an appreciation of these subtle variations in the ways in which different genres are enacted. Although many of these rules are unstated, it is all too obvious when someone violates them. Sometimes individuals violate genre rules intentionally as an act of subversion or resistance – or even just to get attention. However, this can also happen unintentionally. Indeed, all three of us can remember uncomfortable and embarrassing instances when we have unwittingly broken these genre rules.

Knowing the rules of the game

Having just recently been socialised in a business school environment and the dress codes that come with business/management conferences, a young lecturer tried to get it right for a conference on organizational aesthetics. Dressed in a navy blue, classically cut trouser suit, a smart brooch on her lapel, polished fingernails etc. she arrived at the conference somewhat late. On entering the conference room she found to her dismay that everyone was dressed extremely casually, artistically or downright sloppily. Also, her slick presentation – prepared on PowerPoint (as would have been expected by her MBA students) came over as excessively formal and business-like. It did not go down well compared to the improvised, performance-art styles used by the other presenters. She felt uncomfortable and left early.

- Choose three of the genres listed at the start of this section.
- For each, identify the key social relationships, and any implicit or explicit rules that govern how these activities work.
- Try to think of an example of intentional or unintentional rule breaking.
- For all three, what would be the consequences of these violations?

Each genre thus codes "particular relationships among sets of social participants" (Hodge and Kress, 1988: 7). However, this is not to suggest that the distinctions between genres are watertight, nor should these patterns of relationships be seen as static or deterministic. First, some genres are clearer and more distinct than others. For example, the rules governing social interaction in the university lecture theatre are highly institutionalized, and rarely contested or seen as ambiguous. Indeed, if someone was to violate that genre (if the lecturer came to the session in pyjamas, or a student suddenly stood up and started singing), it would be all too obvious. However, those concerning email at work are in a state of flux – in terms of sender, receiver, style, content and context. Indeed, as email becomes more established, it is fascinating to observe how such rules are becoming codified and formalized (see Chapter 9). Many organizations are now seeking to regulate practice through the development of email policies.

Second, genres often overlap. This can happen implicitly, as meetings, conversations and presentations can all include elements of argument, or appraisal interviews can include negotiation. It can also happen explicitly, as in the case of political speeches when a conversational genre can be effectively used to create an emotional link between the speaker and the audience.

Mixing genres

In his book on the language of New Labour, Fairclough describes how in his speech after Princess Diana's death Tony Blair effectively combined conversational and political speech genres:

> I feel like everyone else in the country today – utterly devastated. Our thoughts and prayers are with Princess Diana's family – in particular her two sons, two boys – our hearts go out to them. We are today a nation, in Britain, in a state of shock, in mourning, in grief that is so deeply painful for us. (2000: 7)

The results were an address that was both emotionally charged and also statesmanlike.

While in the example above we see Tony Blair's genre mixing as appropriate and actually very effective, at times such overlap can cause doubt and uncertainty. This was the case in David Mamet's play, *Oleanna* (1992), about a university student's allegations of sexual harassment by her professor – and his denial of the accusation. What the professor apparently saw as legitimate tutorial behaviour was interpreted by the student as an attempt at seduction. The drama unfolds around the tension between the characters' different understandings of these genres.

Finally, although genres can be seen as shaping the way we communicate, they do not determine our interaction. Rather, they are socially constructed and as such are continuously reproduced, challenged or transformed through social practice. In other words, although the way in which a group has historically conducted their meetings might provide a frame for current practice, this frame can of course be subverted and ultimately changed.

Genres provide us with knowledge about particular types of social practice and the rules and relationships embedded within them. Because we understand how genres work, we are able to perform as culturally competent and literate social actors. Curiously, within the growing literature on language and organization, genre is rarely considered in an explicit way. However, for students, researchers and managers wanting to understand organizations better, we see genre as a very valuable analytical tool, illuminating the rules and social relationships situated within a particular social practice, and linking a text to its wider social context.

Identifying genres

Below are four texts. For each one, consider the following questions:

- What is the genre and how do you know?
- What are the rules of this genre? How established are they?
- Who are the people typically involved in this genre and what is their relationship?
- How well defined is this genre? Can you think of any instances where confusion or ambiguity might arise?

1. At 04:08 PM 1/30/01 +0000, you wrote:
   dear laurie
   >>I've just noticed that we are both due to teach the PhD students next week Would it work for me to do the morning session rather than the afternoon? (I have a meeting of the Faculty Board to attend Tuesday pm, but if I can't attend the world will not come crashing down!)
   >>
   Let me know. thanks
   >>best wishes john

2. I set out today the next steps of our journey to renew our country. Prosperity is spreading to all parts of Britain....

   I'm the Prime Minister and that's supposed to be the great reader of public opinion. After the events of two weeks ago, it's no wonder the government has taken a knock. It happened on my watch and I take responsibility. And, yes, there are things we've done wrong…

3. Apologies for absence
   Dr R. Robson
   Dr P.B. Shah
   Ms N. Ebbs
   Dr J. Lingard

   15.1 Minutes from previous meeting

(Continued)

> 15.1.1 The minutes from the 15th Staff Meeting were accepted as an accurate record.
> 15.2 Welcome to new colleagues and matters for report by Director
> 15.2.1 PBS welcomed Dr G. Barnett, Mr C. Emory and Dr Y. Roland to the Department.
> 4. Right. The first thing I'd like to ask is what originally attracted you to this post
> – Well, as you'll have seen on my CV, I finished my PhD in 1999, and have been working as a Research Assistant on the ESRC project on networking since then. As you know, that project comes to an end next month, and I'm keen to find a position in which I can continue to develop my research, and also to get involved in teaching. In this department, I feel I could do both.
> – Can you tell me a bit more about your current research interests, then?
> – Yes, as you'll have seen on my list of publications…

Discourses

Discourses, like genres, can be understood as framing devices, systems of shared meaning which we use in making sense of cultural texts. However, whereas we are using genre to refer to specific types of text, discourse is more concerned with their subject matter. As Fairclough explains,

> Discourses correspond roughly to dimensions of texts which have traditionally been discussed in terms of 'content'… 'topic', 'subject matter' and so forth. There is a good reason for using discourse rather than these traditional terms: a discourse is a particular way of constructing a subject-matter, and the concept differs from its predecessors in emphasizing that contents or subject-matters – areas of knowledge – only enter texts in the mediated form of particular constructions of them. (1992: 128)

Consider this example taken from Pat Barker's novel, *Another World* (1998). The scene involves a conversation between Geordie, a veteran of the Great War, and his grandson. Geordie is dying, and has been in and out of hospital. The two men are discussing and trying to understand Geordie's recent habit of wandering the streets at night.

> 'It's the pills', Geordie says. 'I've never been one for pills'.
> It's not the pills, and they both know it, but somehow the hospital prescribes the kind of conversation they can have with each other. (1998: 76)

In this quote, "the hospital" defined the ways in which Geordie and his grandson could talk about the old man's nocturnal activities. Geordie's wandering was attributed to the medication he was taking – his doctors flatly rejecting the possibility that it could be linked to his wartime experiences or the memories which continued to haunt the old man until the day he died. Similarly, writers on discourse and organization have suggested that discourses define the ways in which we think, talk and act in and around work contexts. In Barker's words, such discourses "prescribe the kind of conversation" we can have with each other. In creating certain ways of looking at the world, discourses also impact on action.

Changing discourses, changing behaviour. Passengers, patients and students – or customers?

Writers on organization and culture have argued that in the current context, the consumer is at centre stage, "god-like" and "triumphant" (Gabriel and Lang, 1995: 1). At the heart of the consumer culture, the discourse of the market reigns supreme. Thus we have seen the renaming of passengers, patients and students as **customers**. Indeed, within our own universities we three have all participated in vigorous debates in which colleagues express their (sometimes diverse) views on what a customer focus means in the context of higher education: about the relabelling of students as customers, its implications for the learning/teaching process, our own roles as experts and for the practice of academic pursuit. As one of our MBA students recently pointed out:

> We are customers now, not students. And that means that we have certain rights and expectations which you need to meet. You need to do things differently now. Taking account of my time out of work, this course has cost me x pounds altogether. I expect value for money.

How might this customer discourse impact on:

- Relationships between teachers and learners?
- Practices including course preparation, dissemination, assessment and feedback?
- Notions of academic expertise?
- Academic research (particularly in terms of WHAT gets studied)?

The concept of discourse has been defined in a myriad of ways, ranging from everyday, commonsense understandings to highly specific, academic definitions reflecting particular theoretical positions. Indeed, the term can be seen to have roots in linguistics, cognitive psychology, sociology, poststructuralism and literary theory (Potter, 1997). Within organizational theory the concept of discourse has been taken on much more recently, and its application in this field reveals traces of these earlier disciplinary origins. The eclectic use of discourse within organization theory has had both benefits and limitations. On one hand, its transdisciplinary background provides tremendous richness and analytic potential. However, the lack of consensus can also result in a certain fear about using the term at all – for fear of using it incorrectly.

Michel Foucault

French historian and philosopher, Michel Foucault, has been a very influential figure in the development of ideas about discourse. Foucault's work was highly abstract, concerned with the ways in which knowledge is constructed through discursive practice. Broadly speaking, it can be divided into two phases. In the first phase, often described as his 'archeological work' (Foucault, 1972), Foucault was concerned with the ways in which different types of discourse establish rules for constituting areas of knowledge. Fairclough points to two important insights developed in this phase: first, the idea that discourse constructs social life – constituting the subjects and objects of knowledge as well as social relationships; second, the notion that discourses are inter-related. That is, discourses do not stand alone as separate entities, but rather are defined through their relationships with other discourses (this echoes the semiology principle of meaning as relational).

The second phase of Foucault's work is described as 'genealogical' (Fairclough, 1992) and is primarily associated with *Discipline and Punish* (1979). In this phase Foucault was interested in relationships between power, knowledge and language. Power, in this view, is central to all social practices and processes. He argues that power is not imposed by particular groups or collectives; rather, it is generated "from below," in institutions such as prisons, schools and psychiatric hospitals. In this sense, the exercise of power involves becoming knowledgeable – and language is central to this process. An analysis of power necessarily involves an examination of language. Linked with the idea that power struggles are enacted through discourse is Foucault's view of social change as essentially discursive – that is, that changing discursive practice is central to social change.

Foucault's analysis has made a significant contribution to developments in organization theory, and has been applied to contexts and issues as diverse as HRM (Townley, 1994); strategy (Knights and Morgan, 1991), organizational change (Cohen and Musson, 2000; Pritchard and Wilmott, 1997), organizational identity (Phillips and Hardy, 1997), emotions at work (Mangham and Overington, 1993) and emancipation (Parker, 2000). However, his work has also been widely criticized. In particular commentators have taken issue with what they see as Foucault's deterministic analysis of discourse and neglect of individual agency, his rejection of social structures, and for his excessive abstraction and lack of empirical grounding (Fairclough, 1992; Layder, 1994; Reed, 1998, 2000).

Paradoxically, Foucault is credited both with popularizing the concept of discourse (Fairclough, 1992), and also with its mystification (Watson, 2000).

In this book we are using Tony Watson's definition, which is loosely based on the work of Foucault (1972, 1979, 1981, 1984). Watson's approach is particularly relevant to our concerns about meaning making. He describes discourse as:

A connected set of statements, concepts, terms and expressions which constitutes a way of talking or writing about a particular issue, thus framing the way people understand and respond with respect to that issue... [discourses] function as menus of discursive resources which various social actors draw on in different ways at different times to achieve their particular purposes – whether these be specific interest-based purposes or broader ones like that of making sense of what is happening in the organization or of what it is to 'be a manager'. (1995: 814)

So there are, for example, legal, medical, socialist, bureaucractic, entrepreneurial, Christian, Jewish and Islamic discourses which systematically give expression to the beliefs and values of particular social institutions. It is important to note that discourses can be highly codified and regulated, as in the case with legal, medical and some religious discourses. However, other discourses such as feminism, atheism, anti-globalisation or university student discourses are less so.

Competing discourses at *ZTC Ryland*

Watson's article is based on participatory research in a telecommunications company. Analysing managerial talk, he identifies two key discourses: one of "empowerment, skills and growth" and one of "control, jobs and costs" (1995: 815). Watson discusses the ways in which these conflicting discourses impact on managers' ideas about what their jobs are for and how they are best carried out, in terms of long-term business strategies as well as day-to-day practices and social relations. Central to these competing discourses are issues about power – and whose view holds sway.

The analysis of these discourses illustrates the political dimension of language.

That language, however, is deployed in a context where power is exerted, where there are winners and losers. The owning interests behind ZTC are continuing to make profits from the company, as I write, and simultaneously, there are people in the process of losing their jobs at the Ryland plant. The two things are not unconnected. (1995: p. 11)

Significantly, in his definition Watson makes what we see as an important link between thought and action, emphasizing the idea that discourses frame the ways in which we understand and respond to things. This is consistent with Fairclough's point cited earlier that subject-matters are mediated. In this view, areas of knowledge are never neutral. On the contrary, they are always constructed, or framed in particular ways. So, the subject of penal reform might be constructed one way within a legal discourse, and quite differently within a social work discourse. Similarly, Watson's "empowerment" and "control" discourses will have different implications for human resource management and account-ability procedures. Knowledge, in this view, is not objective or arbitrary. Rather, it is shaped in a particular way, reflecting "prevailing values, norms, beliefs and relations of power" (Jackson and Carter, 2000: 66). The important point here is that it is not the case that the two dominant discourses at ZTC happily co-exist: rather, they vie for power and control. At stake is what is seen to be the accepted view of reality – and who is seen as the legitimate representative of this view. Thus, the relationship between power and knowledge is essential to the notion of discourse that we are presenting here.

Using the concept of discourse

The ideas that knowledge is mediated through discourses, and power relations are constructed within discourses, are further developed through Jackson and Carter's analysis. They explain that discourses define **who** can speak, about **what** issues, in **which contexts** and **styles (how)**, and for **what reasons** (2000: 66) (as we noted earlier, these criteria are also central to genre).

The discourse of teamwork

As we noted in Chapter 3 on Metaphor, in recent years, a teamwork discourse has emerged as a powerful resource within sectors as diverse as healthcare, manufacturing and financial services. This discourse is typically characterized through terms like empowerment, collectivism, participation and collaboration – and is constructed in opposition to "out-dated" Taylorist notions of linear production processes and individual effort (Baldry et al., 1998: 168).

Given its current salience, in the section that follows we will use this discourse to illustrate how Jackson and Carter's analysis can be applied in practice.

Considering their points in order, Jackson and Carter argue first that, "a discourse defines **who** [our emphasis] is allowed to speak authoritatively on a particular subject" (2000: 66). Within the teamwork discourse, Baldry et al. maintain that it is not the workers' view of "team" which holds sway, but that of the managers: "Teamworking can … be seen from a managerial perspective to perform, at least rhetorically, the function of sharing (and thus increasing) the workload in a period of cuts and lean staffing" (1998: 175). In contrast to this managerial agenda, a teleworker in their study explained that:

> Although they sit in teams it's not really a team because everybody is responsible for their own casework. You don't feel that everyone is pulling their weight and you're all mucking in. It's not like that. It's misleading to call it teamwork. (1998: 175)

Within the teamwork discourse, however, these voices go unheard. In other words, people who are outside of the legitimate group of speakers will find it difficult to make their views known. In this way, embedded within discourses are questions about power and status – about those who are eligible to speak (and are thus in a position to pursue their own interests), and who are not.

Turning to **what**, the subject matter of discourses, Kress explains that discourses "define, describe and delimit what it is possible to say and not possible to say (and by extension what it is possible and not possible to do)" (1985: 6–7). Within the discourse of teamwork, certain people are constructed as good "team players" and others are not. Likewise, the discourse implies those attitudes, norms, values and behaviours which are acceptable, and those which are unacceptable or deviant. For those who are not skilful in demonstrating their engagement with the discourse (that is, presenting themselves as team players), or who choose to resist or subvert it, the stakes can be high. As Tietze (1998) demonstrated in her work on higher education, renegades face the prospect, at the very least, of marginalization.

Sennett (1998) offers a contrasting view of the teamwork discourse. A far cry from the joys of collaboration and partnership, he suggests that: "Teamwork, though, takes us into that domain of demeaning superficiality which besets the modern workplace. Indeed, teamwork exists in the realm of tragedy to enact human relations as a farce" (1998: 106). However, this voice is rarely heard. Rather, it is routinely drowned out by the overwhelming chorus of approval of the benefits of teamworking arrangements.

Turning to the questions of **where** and **how**, Jackson and Carter maintain that discourses define "where knowledge is located" (2000: 67) and how it is disseminated. One might assume that within the teamwork discourse social interaction would play an important role. However, rather paradoxically in their study Baldry and his colleagues found quite the reverse. Although the team members at the Finance Bank all sat at one long table, their work was non-stop, intensive and individualised. There were no formal breaks and no opportunities for team talk. Indeed, the only time they were officially allowed to converse was during their weekly team briefing session. Because talk was precluded at other times of the working day, presumably it was during these briefing sessions that teamwork issues were explicitly considered and debated. Here the idea that discourses define where and how things get talked about interacts with the notion of genre introduced above. Although Baltry et al. do not delve into this area, the team meetings they refer to will no doubt unfold according to a certain format and structure. Being a good team player will mean conforming to these (probably unwritten) rules and norms, and getting on with one's work – alone – at all other times.

Finally, Jackson and Carter maintain that at the heart of the questions of who, what, where and how are questions about **why** we speak about a particular topic. Within the teamwork discourse, while increasing management efficiency and effectiveness may be seen as an appropriate motivation behind the development of work teams, creating a more enlightened, more articulate workforce may not. Another question which arises is why a particular discourse becomes resonant at a particular time. Perhaps the current salience of the teamwork discourse could be a result of changing organizational practices where networks and network knowledges seem to be overtaking individual knowledges (Sewell, 1998). Or maybe it could be attributed to widescale organizational restructuring, the predominance of short-term, temporary arrangements and the need to make more with less (Sennett, 1998). Relatedly, its emphasis on affiliation and collectivism (even though research indicates that this is manifestly not borne out in practice) provides feelings of security and harmony in an uncertain and divided world.

Mediated knowledge

Jackson and Carter's analysis elucidates our point that knowledge must not be thought of as natural or objective. Instead, it is mediated through different discourses, reflecting the interests and values of particular groups and institutions. However, such is the pervasiveness of these discourses that they appear to be 'true'.

(Continued)

Preferred readings and reading against the grain: the diversity of discourses

In their excellent critique of the corporate strategy discourse, Knights and Morgan note that, "so powerful are these truth effects that it is exceedingly difficult for us to disengage ourselves from such a view. Can there be any other way of looking at organizations other than one which derives from the discourse of corporate strategy?" (1991: 260). Indeed, it could be argued that the teamwork discourse is an offshoot of this strategic perspective.

However, this is not to reify the concept of discourse, or to suggest that discourses are wholly determining and can only be interpreted in one way. Knights and Morgan go on to say that in spite of its power:

> If we take a more long-term view, we can see that there are alternatives to the strategic discourse. For example, it is clear that there are groups both within management and in the wider population of the organization who will reject the discourse of strategy per se. Certain managers may cling to some sort of entrepreneurial ideology in which conformity to the top-down demands of a strategic plan are anathema. Others may reject the credentialist ideology in favour of the emphasis on experience or instinct. Still other managers may cling to a notion of the traditional way of doing things which does not need to be sanctified by 'strategy.' Within the lower ranks of an organization, we are likely to encounter mass indifference or even cynicism about the way in which the discourse of strategy is used by management. (1991: 260)

The purpose and process of science: views from above and from below

The two extracts below discuss the purpose and process of scientific research. The first is from the 1993 Government White paper on science and technology, "Realising our Potential" (Cm 2250). The second is an extract from an interview with a public sector research scientist.

> The understanding and application of science are fundamental to the fortunes of modern nations …The history of the United Kingdom has shown the intimate connection between free trade, the application of science to tradeable products, and national prosperity. The industrial revolution which played so large a part in creating the modern world was made possible by our great engineers of the 18th and 19th centuries. In a world where ever fiercer competition prevails, history's lessons are highly pertinent…Thus science needs Government and public funds. The decision for Government, when it funds science, as it must, is to judge where to place the balance between the freedom for researchers to follow their own instincts and curiosity, and the guidance of large sums of public money towards achieving… the generation of national prosperity and the improvement of the quality of life. (1993: 1–2)

At the moment I am trying to fight off the Government's White Paper because I am not a great believer in that White Paper. I always have had a very very great fear that it would have the effect that it is having. You are forever being pushed to find short-term economic gains out of what you are doing and I personally believe that we are heading for the dark ages in science if we are not careful because of this. It's about having to forever justify yourself, trying to convince people that the work you are doing is valuable for some national purpose when it may or may not be ... I argued very strongly when the White Paper was being put together that we should see science as a cultural activity, like the Arts, but one which occasionally has a real tangible benefit, but one that you can't predict. You can not predict that somebody sitting in a room in the 20's would come up with the Heisenberg uncertainty principle and that would result in us having computers and God knows what. Now nobody would have given Heisenberg money. You could just imagine the grant committee now, 'Oh yes, Mr Heisenberg, you don't know where it will be, what it will be or when it will be'. Sod that. Most of the time scientists don't know where it's going. People don't know the value of their research and it doesn't become apparent for a long time. It is the cutting edge, fundamental science that's the sequel for 50 years ahead, and what we're doing now is we're stifling that. We are a short-term game.

- Can you use the concept of discourse to explain the different views expressed here?
- Try to apply Jackson and Carter's who, what, where, how and why analysis to the way in which science is constructed within the discourses you identify.
- Can you think of any other examples of different discourses constructing knowledge in different ways?

In the section on genre we suggested that although our literacy in different genres frames the ways in which we make sense of social practice, we must not see genre as **determining** our understanding of or participation in different social situations. Similar issues have been raised with regard to discourse. As noted earlier, Foucault's work has fueled heated debate as to the status of discourse in the construction of the social world (Chia, 2000; Grant et al., 1998; Reed, 2000).

A hot debate

Some critics take issue with what they see as Foucault's tendency to dissolve all social life into discourse. In a stinging criticism, Reed argues:

Discourse attains ontological and methodological primacy within Foucault's universe because it determines the strategies and rules by which we can speak about and act on a domain of objects ... [It] is very difficult, if not impossible,

(Continued)

> to shake off 'Foucaultland'. We escape Weber's iron cage of bureaucratic rationalization and Marx's immutable laws of capitalist development only to be trapped, indeed trap ourselves, within a Foucauldian disciplinary society where we become incarcerated within a total organizational world in which we play no conscious part or active role in making. (1998: 197–198)
>
> However, others maintain that this is not the case, that an emphasis on discourse as constituting social reality does not necessarily lead to a view that discourse is all there is, and furthermore that criticisms such as that cited above are based on an incomplete reading of Foucault (Chia, 2000).

Although this debate is compelling, it is not our purpose in this chapter to provide a definitive reading of Foucault. What is important, though, is to clarify our position on the status of discourse. Here we find Mumby and Clair's analysis useful. In their view:

> **Organizations exist only in so far as their members create them through discourse. This is not to claim that organizations are 'nothing but' discourse, but rather that discourse is the principal means by which organization members create a coherent social reality that frames their sense of who they are. (1997: 181)**

Here again we have this notion of discourse as a framing device. However, while discourses do play an important role in creating patterns of understanding which we carry with us and apply to our social interactions, we are not wholly constrained or determined by particular discourses. Rather, as in the case with genre, individuals can – and do – subvert these frames, challenge conventional understandings and introduce new meanings and social practices. Referring back to the Ang Lee film *Crouching Tiger, Hidden Dragon* we said that our understanding of this film was framed, in part, by our knowledge of kung fu films – in other words, by a kung fu discourse. This discourse typically involves brawny, young Southeast Asian men fighting in the streets – often over questions of honour, usually about power and sometimes about women. Bruce Lee is, of course, the quintessential kung fu hero. What Ang Lee does in *Crouching Tiger, Hidden Dragon* is to subvert this dominant discourse, confounding it with other discourses about love, work and freedom, and by presenting us with a different, feminist alternative.

Here the concepts of **preferred readings** and **reading against the grain** are useful. Although at any given time certain discursive frames might appear dominant, this is not to suggest that they eradicate all other interpretations. Rather, as Knights and Morgan argued in the long passage cited above, individuals can and do resist. They can draw on different, oppositional bodies of knowledge, skilfully reading against the grain, reconstructing dominant discourses and negotiating understandings in light of their own circumstances.

Discourses of enterprise

In their research into the discourse of enterprise, Cohen and Musson (2000) found a dominant interpretation of this discourse, expressed by government policy makers and business leaders, and codified, in part, through changes in employment policy and training initiatives. Within this "preferred reading" were implicit rules about who was included and who was excluded, about what types of organizations and workplace practices were allowable etc. However, their empirical work into (a) self-employed women and (b) general medical practitioners revealed that individuals did not necessarily adhere to these dominant prescriptions.

Discussing entrepreneurship in general and whether they considered themselves entrepreneurs, women's responses varied widely. There were some who strongly identified with the term: "think of an entrepreneur as someone who makes the most of what's available and who manages to build a successful business"... "On reflection I would say that yes, I am an entrepreneur". Others saw it as repellent: "Someone who stood on other people's toes... a money grubber product of the 1980s."

Interestingly, one woman explained how our assessment of terms like that change over time. When in the early 1980s someone referred to her as an entrepreneur she said she was "horrified. I thought it was the worst thing anyone could say." However, at the time of interview (in 1996) she said she was now "wearing the label with pride. It's brilliant stuff! I am an entrepreneur and think it's great!"

These case studies demonstrated how people read against the grain, constructing the discourse of enterprise in relation to their particular contexts and experiences.

Using the discourse concept in organizational analysis

As suggested above, discourses must not be seen as unitary, but as diverse and changeable. In our own research we have taken this idea of discourses as **polysemic** as our starting point, and applied the concept of discourse in two main ways. First, we have found it very useful to track the articulation of a particular discourse, both through the accounts of different organizational members and those of a single individual through time. Our study of the discourse of enterprise, noted above, is an example of this approach, illustrating that dominant and subordinate readings can and do exist. Significantly, though, our data revealed that the relationship between dominant and subordinate interpretations is not static, but a site of constant tension and negotiation.

Second, researchers can examine relationships between discourses. As noted earlier (most specifically in the discussion of Watson's (1995a) work at ZTC Ryland), discourses do not work in isolation. Rather, as Grant et al. suggest: "'organization' is comprised of a multiplicity of discourses...Potentially, this permits a multitude of 'organizational realities' which, although relatively autonomous discourses, may overlap and permeate each other" (1998: 7). Thus, organizational analysts can examine discourses, not only in relation to the people who use them, but also in terms of other discourses. Fundamental to this approach is a semiological view of language as relational. Discourses, in this sense, derive their meaning from their intersection with other discourses. This was aptly illustrated in Cohen et al.'s (1999a and 1996b) studies of research science institutions in which a discourse of management was constructed in opposition to a discourse of good science. And similarly, in Musson's (1994) work a clinical discourse was understood in opposition to the discourse of small business management.

However, **relational** does not always mean **oppositional**. Instead, a discourse can also derive its meaning through its **colonisation** of other discourses. This is clearly illustrated in the case of the discourse of enterprise which, as Du Gay points out, can partly be understood in relation to what came before it, "a permissive and anti-enterprise culture fostered by social democratic institutions since 1949" (1991: 45). In the process of appropriating other discourses, such as that of excellence and quality, the discourse of enterprise gained acceptability, and began to make sense to people situated diversely within society. Interestingly we could argue that in 2001 the discourse of enterprise has now been superceded (or colonized) by discourses of teamwork, partnership and collaboration. Discourses thus struggle for acceptance and dominance, sometimes colliding, often overlapping and frequently competing – existing in a dynamic hierarchy which can change over space and time. A consideration of these relationships can be a useful tool in illuminating the tensions and challenges of organizational life, and the ways in which these are understood and enacted by organizational members.

Read the following extract from a *Body Shop* leaflet

- Identify the key discourses articulated through this text.
- How would you describe their relationship with one another (competing, complimentary, dominant/subordinate)?
- Can you think of any different interpretations of these discourses which organizational members might make?
- What does an analysis of these discourses tell us about the organization?

From *'The Chairman's Wife's* statement':

As I look back on 20 years of a multi-local business within the gigantic cosmetics industry, I spend a lot of time smiling. How delinquent we were! It was absurd having five sizes of everything. It was absurd having the products packaged in cheap bottles. It was absurd calling it *The Body Shop* next door to a funeral parlour in Brighton. How absurd it all was! But, as dear old Albert Einstein said, "If at first the idea is not absurd, then there is no hope for it"... Today we are less delinquent, but still challenging...
So, it will be business as unusual. Let's celebrate that together with lots more attitude, by resisting the ordinary.

On the adjoining page, superimposed on Anita Roddick's face are the following statements:

- 20 years of listening to Mum say, "Get a real job"
- 12 years of trying to fit into a pin-striped suit made for a dinosaur

- 3 decades of campaigning for social change
- 53 years of environmental degradation
- A quarter of a century spent arguing with the old man
- Learning to do business the American way, the Japanese way, the hard way… all ways
- 17 times around the world in one year
- 20 years of trying to tell jokes in board meetings
- Forever trying to get the media to print what I say
- A lifetime looking for signposts in a world without them

Consider the key discourses at work in an organization you know well. What does this analysis tell us about the tensions and challenges facing this organization?

Summary

This chapter has used the notion of framing devices to explore the cultural knowledge that individuals use to make sense of cultural texts, informing the ways in which such texts are understood and acted upon. We introduced the concepts of genre and discourse as two important framing devices. Defining genre as forms of communication, we suggested that genres code certain cultural rules and social relationships that inform the ways in which we make sense of social practice. However, our view of genre was not deterministic. Rather, we emphasized the dynamism of the concept, highlighting in particular overlap between genres, as well as social actors' capacities for challenging and subverting established genres.

The concept of discourse, in contrast, was used to describe ways of speaking about particular contents or subject-matters. We suggested that discourses give expression to the beliefs and values of an institution or topic, and inform the way in which that topic is talked about, by whom, in what contexts and for what reasons. However, like genre, we do not see discourse as wholly determining. While not underestimating the power of discourse or the dominance of certain interpretations, we argued that individuals can – and do – read against the grain, reconstructing discourses according to their particular life experiences and circumstances. Finally, we offered some ideas about how the concept of discourse can be used in organizational analysis.

In summary, we see both genres and discourses as framing devices, linking cultural texts to wider social contexts. Genres are types of communication practice and imply particular sets of rules and social relationships. However, the distinctions between genres are not watertight; rather there is considerable overlap between them. In contrast, we see discourses as ways of talking about a particular issue, reflecting certain institutional values and beliefs: they define what is talked about, by whom, it what ways and contexts, and for what purposes. Researchers use the concept of discourse in two key ways: tracking the way in which a single discourse is used by different organizational members, and exploring the relationship between discourses. Significantly, neither genres nor discourses are static or wholly deterministic – both are reproduced and transformed through social practice.

Recommended reading

As noted earlier, within the organizational literature little has been written about genre. However, Fairclough's discussion of the concept in *Discourse and Social Change* (1992) provides a valuable introduction. Other useful analyses of genre can be found in Schirato and Yell's *Communication and Culture* (2000) and Agar's *Language Shock* (1994).

In contrast, there is a vast literature on discourse, encompassing a wide range of academic disciplines and theoretical perspectives. Here we shall note those contributions that we have found most useful in our own research, and which are most consistent with the approach taken in this chapter. On a general level, we have found the work of Norman Fairclough illuminating. *Discourse and Social Change* provides a critical review and analysis of the field. His more popular *New Labour, New Language?* (2000) is an interesting example of how these theoretical ideas can be applied to the contemporary political scene. As noted, Michel Foucault has been an extremely influential figure in the development of discourse theory. Some of his most noted works include *The Archeology of Knowledge* (1972), *Discipline and Punish* (1979), *History of Sexuality* (1981) and his essay "The Order of Discourse" (1984). For an excellent analysis of Foucault's work from a management perspective, see Knights (1992).

Within organization theory, Jackson and Carter's (2000) discussion of discourse in their analysis of knowledge provides a succinct and accessible introduction. Also, the extensive work of Grant, Keenoy and Oswick has been very influential. Their edited collection *Discourse and Organization* (1998) is a fascinating collection of empirical and theoretical pieces, as are their on-going debates in *Organization* (Keenoy et al., 1997, 2000). Knights and Morgan's (1991) paper on the discourse of strategy has made an important contribution to the debate. Finally, Watson's discussion of discourse and application of the concept to organizational and management contexts (1995a; 2000) provides fascinating empirical insights and further enhances our understanding of how people make sense of their organizational worlds, and the links between these meaning making processes and action.

CHAPTER SIX

Language, Culture, Meaning

This chapter takes as its point of departure the notion that cultures are meaning systems and can therefore be investigated within a semiological framework. We propose that social realities are formed through the simultaneous existence and interaction of several cultural systems. In the chapter we discuss the concepts of linguistic determinism and linguistic relativity, followed by a discussion of the themes and issues of intercultural encounters. These include the role of English as a communicative tool; the role and function of non-verbal communication and a definition and contemplation of 'ethnocentrism' as the main barrier to intercultural communication.

Objectives

In this chapter we will:

- define culture in semiological terms;
- explore the relationship between language and culture;
- discuss and assess the role and consequences of English as the main communicative tool in international encounters;
- investigate the nature and role of non-verbal communication; and
- define and discuss ethnocentrism as the main barrier to effective communication.

Cultures as webs of meaning

There is a multitude of different definitions and understanding of what culture is. For example, the field of organization theory has welcomed the concept of organizational culture as one of its grand ideas and developed a multitude of perspectives and alternative angles (for an overview see Brown, 1998; Eisenberg and Riley, 2001). Our understanding of cultures is rooted in the semiological approach of cultures as meaning systems. The anthropologist Clifford Geertz (1973) in a classic selection of essays on culture provides the following explanation:

Culture = web of meanings

The concept of culture I espouse … is essentially a semiotic one. … Believing with Max Weber, that man is an animal suspended in webs of significance he himself has spun, I take culture to be those webs, and the analysis of it to be therefore not an experimental science in search of law but an interpretive one in search of meaning. (1973: 5)

Geerzt describes the essence of culture as being **webs of meaning**.

In many regards this book is written to develop practical help on how to disentangle these webs as well as to raise awareness that as human beings we are both spinning the threads of the webs as well as being suspended in them (see Chapter 1).

The same tradition is developed by industrial sociologist Tony Watson. Watson (1995a) defines culture as, "The system of meaning which is shared by members of a human grouping and which defines what is good and bad, right or wrong, and what are the appropriate ways of members of that group to think and behave" (1995a: 12). Culture is a 'signifying system', through which social order is communicated, explored and reproduced. Watson (2001b) investigates the culture of a particular occupational group – managers – at an organization in the UK and showed management to be perpetually in search of an identity and the meaning of that identity.

Schneider and Barsoux's (1997) book on *Managing Across Cultures* is an example of a partly semiotically driven approach to the understanding of different national cultures. For example, the word **management** carries different meanings contingent on the cultural context. The easy use of this 'word' across different cultural contexts is not as unproblematic as it seems, since the differences in meaning become obfuscated by the use of the same signifier (see Chapter 2). In the United States, for example, managers carry a particular status: "Members of this class [management] carry a high status and many American boys and girls aspire to the role. In the United States, the manager is a cultural hero" (Hofstede, 1993: 81). The set of values, the prestige and roles associated with the signs **management** and **manager** are not consistent with the meanings in other cultures. In Germany, managers are expected to be experts and to have mastered their subject area practically as well as theoretically. In France, intellect and rational analysis define the concept and practice of management.

Compare and contrast

"Management is getting things done through people."
"Management is developing people through work."

- What are the implicit assumptions entailed in these two definitions.
- Can you attribute them to different cultural frameworks?

Language and culture

We view meaning, culture and language as intrinsically bound together. Agar (1994) adopts the term **languaculture** to express the inseparability of language, culture and meaning. The connecting ties between language, culture and meaning were investigated earlier on in the twentieth century. An important contribution to understanding the dynamics between language and culture was made by the anthropologists and linguists Benjamin Lee Whorf and Edward Sapir. Their works and writings comprise a raft of essays, poems, books, articles, but what they have become famous for is called the **Sapir-Whorf hypothesis** or **linguistic determinism** (Whorf, 1956). Linguistic determinism proposes that the language one grows up in determines how one will see the world, how one thinks about it, and what kind of consciousness one has about it. This resonates with the deterministic view of Foucault's ideas about discourse discussed in Chapter 5.

Whorf and Sapir worked with Hopi Indians both in New York City and on reservations. In particular Whorf wrote extensively about the language of the Hopi Indians and argued that the Hopi language was a "timeless" language, that is, that there is no concept of "time" in this language. A useful summary of his main ideas can be found in Agar (1994). A Hopi Indian does not see time as a thing or substance that one can measure, count or divide into units. Thus, sayings such as "time is money," "don't waste my time," "see you next week," would make no sense; neither would practices based around efforts to save time or writing books about time management be considered sensible, necessary or feasible. Whorf argued that a speaker of American English and a speaker of Hopi English live in different worlds. As Agar puts it (1994: 64), according to Whorf, "the American chugs along in his world of clocks and calendars, the Hopi in a world of events that happen."

Different language – different world

The real world is to a large extent unconsciously built up on the language habits of the group. No two languages are ever sufficiently similar to be considered as representing the same social reality. The worlds in which different societies live are distinct worlds, not merely the same world with different labels attached. (Sapir, 1949:161)

Of course, linguistic determinism raises questions about whether one can really escape one's own language and its conceptual construction of the world. From this perspective, language is like a prison one is confined in. Within the weaving metaphor used at the beginning of this chapter, one is rather passively suspended in webs of meaning that have ossified into rigid structures.

A weaker version of linguistic determinism is known as **linguistic relativity**. From this perspective, language is seen to "lay down habitual patterns of seeing and thinking and talking when you learn its grammar and vocabulary. But it does not have to be a prison" (Agar, 1994:18). Linguistic relativity could also be linked to an architectural metaphor: that of a room. Language is like a comfortable room that we know well. Therefore, we can manoeuvre in it, find our jumpers and socks quickly and feel very much in control. Leaving this comfort zone always implies a modicum of initial disorientation, confusion and even discomfort, but it may also lead to rich discovery.

Linguistic determinism and linguistic relativity

Linguistic determinism   =   Language as prison
Linguistic relativity   =   Language as comfortable room

Anthropology and ethnography provide an endless variety of examples to support the relevance of linguistic relativity to understanding the social realities in different cultural contexts.

A multitude of words ...

Hindi: has several words for "uncle" and "aunt" (father's/mother's oldest brother, father's/mother's youngest brother and so on)

Navajo: language expresses the notion of a moving and ever changing universe. The Navajo would not say "One dresses," but "one moves into clothes" or they would not say "one is young," but "one moves about newly."

Sami: (of Kiruna/Sweden) has five hundred words to explain snow and several thousands for reindeer. For example, one word describes "where reindeer have been digging and eating in one place and then left, so it's no use to go there."

German: is known to have more words to express feelings of "angst" than other nation.

All examples are adapted from Samorvar and Porter (2001).

These words shape a particular understanding of the world: who is who in it, how individuals relate to social others, how this relationship is ordered and how it is to be performed appropriately. The different words that exist in the Hindi language for a particular social relationship allows a Hindi to grasp nuances that remain literally and metaphorically unperceivable and ungraspable to someone from outside this culture.

The concept of linguistic relativity can be used to understand why misunderstandings between people from different cultures occur. Even if they use the same language (in international encounters mainly English), they might still remain in the comfort zone of their own meaning system. For example, the concept of **brainstorming** is often quoted and used as a way to be creative and generate new ideas. Frequently, this approach works. However, in our experience with international groups of students we found that brainstorming means different things to different people. For example, German students took it to mean an opportunity to demonstrate their knowledge and intelligence. British students often took it as an opportunity to let their wit shine. Malaysian students did not participate a lot and it turned out later in the reflective period of the seminar that they understood the word brainstorming, but felt uncomfortable with its associated practices and were doubtful about its usefulness as a means to elicit ideas.

A multicultural world

Travel, international business, and electronic communication make it possible and likely that people from different backgrounds or cultural spheres will interact with each other. These cultural spheres are by no means only national and regional. They include backgrounds such as professional, industrial, social class, ethnicity, gender, age and so on. These make up the cultural literacies that we talked about in Chapter 5. Together they form a complex and rich fabric within which people communicate and make meaning of a plethora of signs, symbols and behaviours. Modern societies and organizations are composed of people who differ hugely in terms of their demographic profile or social background. Concomitant with more integrated societies, markets and the globalisation of business, individuals are more likely to interact with similar and different others. Thus, global changes in politics, economics and in the movement of people around the world are experienced in the interstices of everyday practice. In business contexts this implies that companies need to become more culturally adept. For example, how, when and where to make initial contacts with potential business partners, greeting behaviour, gift giving, the pace and style of negotiation, and the establishment of social trust are part of an organization's cultural agenda, as are culturally influenced functional approaches (such as marketing, HRM etc).

Much has been written about this – but very little of the literature goes below the surface and investigates the underlying assumptions of the behaviour and practices that make up cultural literacies. However, we argue that in intercultural encounters previously separate 'meaning systems' come into contact with each other. In these intercultural encounters the ability and sensibility to interpret the meaning entailed in the other's behaviour, symbols and artefacts becomes crucial in establishing and retaining worthwhile relationships.

Meaning, then, changes according to cultural contexts. The **national context** provides primary contexts for such meaning systems. For example, the business practice of exchanging business cards carries both functional and symbolic values. However, in some cultures the symbolic value of the business card is much more pronounced than in others. The textbox below tells a story to illustrate.

On business cards and insults

Meishi etiquette: A *meishi* is a business card, an important component of any business encounter in Japan. *Meishi* must be exchanged before conversation can begin and business can be conducted. The exchange of cards follows distinct rules: the junior of the two people offers the card first, held in both hands with the writing turned face up, so that it can be read by the receiver. The card is offered, accompanied with polite words. Then, the recipient offers her *meishi*. Cards are then scrutinised since the richness and texture of paper, the elaboration of the design, encode subtle clues about the role and position of each person. The *meishi* is an extension of its owner.

The story: Mr Tanaka, flamboyant politician, magazine columnist and social flaneur was elected governor of Nagano, a Japanese prefecture. His eponymous ways made him few friends in the bureaucratic corridors of the prefectural offices. Mr Fujii, the bureau chief did not take to Mr Tanaka's drinking, womanising and his preference for reforms. However, personal criticism was unthinkable. Instead, Mr Fujii refused Mr Tanaka's *meishi* in the first instance. On Mr Tanaka's insistence, Mr Fujii accepted the *meishi* – and then folded it.

Faxes and emails of denunciation came within hours, many calling for Mr Fujii's resignation. The story made its way into all national newspapers. Mr Fujii had to apologize and tender his resignation. Mr Tanaka did not accept it, since it was time for all public servants of the prefecture to pull together. Rumour has it that Mr Tanaka granted Mr Fujii some grudging respect, his very rudeness showing that he is nobody's *baka* (fool).

Based on an article published in *The Independent* on 1 November 2000. It was adapted from *The Asian Times* by Richard Lloyd Parry.

An appropriate interpretation of the *meishi* story's meaning (see Chapter 4) needs to be seen against a cultural context, in which the business card carries an important social value, that goes much deeper than the value or meaning that is attributed to the exchange of business cards in most Western cultures. The latter are more likely to be viewed from a functional perspective. Merely observing the exchange of the business cards, that is, the behaviour, would not necessarily explain how the insult was achieved. This can only be understood if one looks beneath the surface of behaviour into the meaning system on which behaviour is based. Cultures, as Guirdham (1998: 59) argues, are more conducively differentiated on the basis of **deep culture**, which means "underlying values, worldviews and ways of social organization."

In the story the meaning of the artefact "business cards" carries a nuance that is not as pronounced in other cultures. Tied up with the artefact is a protocol of behaviour, hierarchical positions and social etiquette. The story also shows that an individual can make a difference – that webs of meaning are spun by human agents and thus meaning can be changed.

Table 6.1   Politeness from German and British perspectives*

	A German perspective	A British perspective
Value	Conversation is based on respect.	Conversation implies friendliness.
Conversational topics	Controversial topics (e.g. politics) can be discussed, because you respect the intellect and opinion of your partner. Chit-chat is considered shallow.	Controversial topics are avoided to maintain friendly atmosphere. Serious discussion is considered rude.
Routines	High formalisation: formal greetings (shaking hands), use of titles, formal addresses (Herr, Frau); formal form of 'you' (Sie).	Low formalisation: use of first name; small talk, banter.
Style	Can be very direct; direct debate (konstruktive Kritik).	Can be suggestive, implicit.
Humour	Expressed in private realm. In public it may potentially insult conversational partner.	Used more widely; plays down social differences; lubricates relationships.

*Based on author experience

As individuals, we are likely to interact most of the time with other individuals from the same national culture. Interactions with family and friends, work colleagues, subordinates, managers, professional advisors, doctors, teachers, sales assistants and fellow exercise enthusiasts are part of our everyday experience. Yet they, too, comprise intercultural encounters. Most of these encounters have become an unnoticed part of our routine behaviour – others require more circumspect and active interaction. When going shopping we routinely interact with sales assistants, this genre or context dictates following the cultural scripts (or discourses as we discuss in Chapter 5) we have acquired. In our interactions with other professional groups such as doctors or teachers we still use highly recognisable and repeatable patterns – however, in many cases the scripts or discourses of these genres are subject to change and we can no longer routinely prescribe how to interact with each other. For example, patients are now frequently called **clients** and **customers**, who are entitled to a good service to be provided by service deliverers. This renaming is more than just surface re-labelling, but implies a change in what it means to be a patient, what it means to be a doctor or consultant, and how these two are to interact, what their expectations are, how they are to talk to each other and who is more powerful in this relationship (see Chapter 5).

What's 'normal'?

This excerpt is taken from a contemporary novel by Nick Hornby (2001: 122). The main protagonist is faced with her husband's increasingly strange behaviour (for example, giving away all their children's toys; inviting strangers for Sunday lunch). She reflects:

> You're turning our kids into weirdoes. Please don't say it's everyone else who's weird please don't say that please, please. Because it isn't true, is it? It can't be true, unless the word 'weird' means nothing at all. (But then, is it weird not to want to watch "Who Wants to be a Millionaire?" when everyone else does? Is it weird to find Big Macs inedible, when millions of people eat almost nothing else?) Aha: no it isn't because I can draw a circle within a circle – a circle around my particular postal district, as it happens – and place myself in a majority, not a minority. The only circle I can draw encompassing people who want to give their Sunday lunch and their kids' toys away, however, would be a circle around my house. That's my definition of weird. It is also fast becoming my definition of lonely, too.

- What is the class background of the protagonist?
- Why did you arrive at your assessment?
- How is her identity constructed in this text?
- How is normality constructed?

Many everyday encounters, then, whether international or not, make us engage with 'different' cultural worlds. In intercultural encounters meanings linked to one cultural system come into contact with meanings from a different cultural sphere. While many intercultural encounters are successful, there is also failure due to misunderstandings and miscommunication. These occur due to the different interpretative systems that are activated in the communication process. For example, lecturers and students belong usually to the same organization, a particular university or college. However, providing feedback to students on their progress is often fraught with difficulties, because the lecturers often use a professional discourse that students find difficult to follow. Comments such as, "this piece of work is descriptive rather than analytic" might be highly meaningful for the lecturer, but it might not be quite as meaningful to the student.

A week in the life of ...

Recall the previous seven days and your activities, including encounters with other people.

- How many different encounters can you list?
- Which ones would you describe as **intercultural** and why?

While nationality is an important part of an individual's cultural make-up, other markers such as ethnicity – the heritage, history and origin outside or preceding the present nation state – social class, age, gender, occupation, religion and disability provide sources of cultural identities, too. Also, political affiliations, leisure activities, organizational, industrial and regional or local identities contribute to the complexity of how many people experience their realities.

Commonalties or differences?

How many cultural commonalties and/or differences do you think the following pairs of people share?

- An American academic and an Hungarian academic.
- A shop floor worker and a manager – both working for the same company.
- One student of business and management and one student of comparative dance of the same university.
- An octogenarian, former soldier in WW1 and an octogenarian, former officer in WW1.
- A 30 year old German woman from Frankfurt and a 30 year old German woman from Halle.

The above exercise is intended to draw your attention to the existence and interaction of several cultural systems, of which the national culture may be an important one. However, it is also possible that, for example middle class people across the world share a set of values and meanings independent from national contexts, but which bind them together, contributing to that specific cultural literacy (see Chapter 5).

In the business and management literature the emphasis is put very much on the importance of national cultures. The contributions of the Dutch management researcher Geert Hofstede (1984, 1991), for example, have become famous beyond academic circles. The cultural dimensions he discovered through his research provide different axis (dimensions) to categorise national cultures.

Cultural dimensions

- **Individualism – collectivism:** the extent to which individual behaviour is influenced and defined by others. The extent to which the group is viewed to be more important than the individual, or vice versa.
- **Power distance:** the degree of separation of people based on social status (egalitarian versus hierarchical).
- **Uncertainty avoidance:** the degree to which people prefer to avoid ambiguity and how they resolve uncertainty.

(Continued)

- **Masculinity – femininity:** the social implications of having been born male or female and the privileging of one orientation over the other.
- **Confucian dynamism:** this dimension was discovered in later research (Hofstede and Bond, 1988): the degree of short-term or long-term orientation.

Hofstede (1999) has shown that these dimensions are remarkably stable and continue to be central to the conduct and practice of management and business affairs. We find Hofstede's and other authors' contributions (for example, Trompenaars,1993) helpful in so far that they can help to explain particular communication patterns. Chen and Chung (1994) provide examples of how the values of Confucianism continue to influence organizational communication processes such as socialisation activities, socio-emotional communication in the workplace and non-confrontational conflict resolution.

Confucianism

Kongfuzi or Kong Fu Ze (550–478 B.C.) was a Chinese scholar. Later, Jesuits latinized his name to Confucius. In his writings he proposed a government based on morality and merit rather than heredity. He set up an ethical-moral system intended to govern all relationships within the family as well as within the community and the state. Confucianism stresses virtue, selflessness, duty, hard work and respect for hierarchy. Its value orientation is collectivist, guiding social relationships to live in harmony, with the universe and with fellow humans, through proper behaviour.

These values mandate a style of communication that stresses group harmony, avoidance of loss of face, modesty and the avoidance of direct, potentially hurtful statements. Verbal strategies include compliments and greeting rituals, which are developed to maintain good relations. A Confucian understanding of communication views all parties as seeking to develop and maintain social relationships through the evocation of shared beliefs. Concepts of communication as based on "winning an argument" and "frank discussion" are Western concepts, and alien to this culture.

An interesting and personal account of life in a Chinese family in communist China, based on Confucian values, can be found in Adeline Yen Mah's (1997) auto-biographical life story *Falling Leaves* (London: Penguin Books).

However, we would advise caution in using only nationally based cultural frameworks, since they detract from the inherent dynamism and complexities of cultures (Collier and Thomas, 1988; Tayeb, 1996). They also do not include sufficient emphasis on human agency, that is, the active weaving of webs of meaning by the individual, nor on the roles of interest, power and ideology in the design and maintenance of (business) structures (Wilkinson, 1996).

Intercultural encounters

Intercultural encounters happen when two people or two groups from culturally diverse contexts meet and (attempt to) communicate. They imply leaving one's comfortable room, one's comfort zone. According to the logic of semiology, leaving a comfort zone implies at least momentarily the experience of its opposite – discomfort, which is a side effect when representatives of different meaning systems meet.

The following sections investigate three issues of intercultural encounters: English as the lingua franca of particularly international encounters, the role of non-verbal communication as part of cultural encounters and thirdly, the role of cultural blindness, or to use the technical term, **ethnocentrism**.

A diverse world – one language?

Communicating in English appears to be an ideal solution to the vagaries of uncharted cultural territories. Theoretically, using the same language creates an even playing field in which everyone knows the rules and everyone is an equal player.

In terms of national and regional encounters, in particular in business and professional contexts, the lingua franca is English (Agar, 1994; Guy and Matlock, 1993; Hanson, 1995). Today, the spread of English is propelled through the computer industry and the use of electronic communication and the Internet (see Chapter 9). One could argue that the use of the same language in intercultural encounters should render communication less problematic and should lead to communicative convergence. However, evidence from research and experience shows that this is not the case at all. Why should it be that every person who uses the English language for purposes of communication is actually drawing on the same cultural codes, meaning systems and behavioural rules? Gudykunst (1998) argues that most of the time when we interpret strangers' messages, we use our own frame of reference – our own cultural literacy. This is to say, we use the cultural assumptions we are familiar with to make sense of signs that might very well be based on different assumptions. Therefore, ineffective communication often occurs – we do not leave our comfortable rooms.

Divided by the same language

During the Korean War, a British brigadier reported the position of his troops (the Gloucesters) – they were outnumbered 8 to 1 by the Chinese Communist infantry – to his American superior in the United Nations joint command. The British brigadier did so with typical British understatement: "Things are a bit sticky, Sir." This was understood by the American officer to mean: "We're having a bit of rough and tumble but we're holding the line." Consequently, no reinforcement or order to withdraw was given.

With no extra support, the Gloucesters made their stand: for four days they held off 30,000 Chinese troops, killing 10,000 of them with bren gun fire. On withdrawal, over 500 were captured and spent years in Chinese prison camps, 59 were killed or missing, 39 escaped and two were awarded Victoria crosses for bravery.

(Continued)

Sir Anthony, then a young adjutant of the Gloucesters, was captured. Now aged 77, he commented: "the two nations spoke military [language] in a slightly different way. It's certainly a good example of the old saying about Britain and the US as *two nations divided by a common language."*

(adapted from John Ezard's "Needless Battle Caused by Uncommon Language," *The Guardian*, 14 April 2001)

We do not necessarily dispute the advantages and the advance of English as the international lingua franca. However, there are also signs of (cultural) resistance that are aimed at protecting both the languages and identities of national and regional cultures. The French, for example, virulently oppose the hegemony of the English language. France has a list of 3500 foreign words; many of those are English words that cannot be used in schools, bureaucracies or companies (Samovar and Porter, 2001). This linguistic resistance is not only about the use of particular words, rather words are tied up with meanings and with a way of life (see Chapter 2), which are at the heart of cultural identity.

It is not only words that carry different meaning depending on the cultural context. Of course, this also holds true for symbols and artefacts, as the example below demonstrates.

The meaning of flowers?

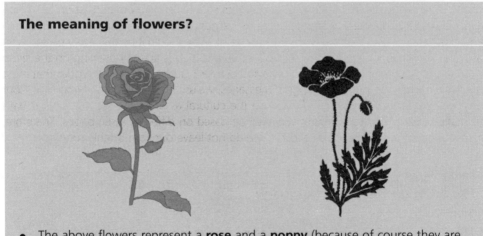

- The above flowers represent a **rose** and a **poppy** (because of course they are not actual flowers at all, but representations). What is their symbolic meaning for you?
- Both carry a strong symbolic value in some cultures. The rose is likely to be more universally recognised, standing for romantic love. Its meaning and the meaning of practices associated with giving roses as gifts can be decoded in many different cultures. The rose has become, so to speak, a **pan-cultural symbol**.
- The poppy is a more country-specific symbol, standing for remembering in the UK. It is worn during the month of November to commemorate (Remembrance Day) as a sign of tribute to those soldiers who gave their life during times of war.

> • When we discussed this in a multicultural student group only the UK students decoded the meaning of the poppy in the way we have defined above. A Dutch student ventured the interpretation that, "it is a bright spring flower the British wear in grey November, to cheer themselves up." In the following discussion some students interpreted the meaning of remembering the war in this particular way as glorifying and sentimentalising it. This led to a heated discussion, since some UK students took offence at that interpretation.

The previous two examples show that signs, words and artefacts are tied up with symbolic meaning and that meaning varies within different cultural contexts. The consequences of the first example are of course more significant, changing, brutally and irreversibly, the lives of many people. Both examples show that English as a shared communicative tool does not prevent different interpretations and different values pervading, directing and challenging the discussion.

A further important aspect of English as the lingua franca of business is the issue of power. The use of a particular linguistic resource (English) can reinforce power realtionships. Assuming that English is the shared discursive resource in business encounters might well disadvantage some people. The choice of language can create winners and losers, as language dominance is often synonymous with power and influence (Davison, 1994; Donnelon, 1996; Schneider and Barsoux, 1997).

In terms of practical applications, in international and polyglot teams, one of the first items to agree on is the working language. For example, compromises can be used to defuse the often emotionally charged choice of the working language. The composition of the team, the fluency and language ability of the team members need to be taken into account in these encounters. A global training and development manager comments:

> We make several rules for participants: speak slowly; ask for clarification at any point and if anyone gets too frustrated in trying to make the point in English, the participant can revert to his or her native language and someone will translate ... there is often an amazing transformation in body language, tone of voice, facial expression and confidence when someone switches to his/her native language. (quoted in Schneider and Barsoux, 1997: 196)

Stohl (2001) quotes examples of organizations such as the EU and UN, where quite competent speakers of German, French and English use their language ability only very selectively and frequently insist on employing simultaneous interpreters. By insisting on this course of action, non-native English speakers attempt to subvert the practices of an English-only culture, and thus assert their own cultural identities and standing. Thus, the use of language in social and business contexts, is tied to issues of power and control, and the choice of language is thus not exclusively pragmatic, but demonstrates "who and what is respected, validates certain types of knowledge claims, and creates expertise and privilege" (Stohl, 2001: 354).

Barriers to intercultural communication: ethnocentrism

Communication between people can never be perfect, because differences in making sense of the world will always exist, even between long-standing friends. In the case of communication with people from different cultural backgrounds, stereotyping and prejudice can be universal barriers to mutual understanding. Stereotypes come to the fore in inter-group communication. They are a set of beliefs or preconceived ideas, which the members of a group share about the characteristics of other groups. Using stereotypes allows us to categorise people in order to avoid information overload. Stereotypes simplify social life. Prejudice, however, is a derogatory attitude towards all or most of the members of one group (for example, racism, sexism). All these mechanisms act together when intercultural communication goes wrong.

We go further, and suggest that beneath prejudice, excessive stereotyping and rigid conceptions and ideas, lies the belief that one's own world is better and superior to some-one else's. That meaning springs from and resides exclusively in one's own culture and that everyone else's can only be understood as being in an inferior relationship to one's own meaning world. This is known as **ethnocentrism** and underpinning it is the relational argument to meaning making (discussed in Chapter 2). The classic definition of ethnocentrism was formulated by Sumner: "the technical name for the view of things in which one's own group is the centre of everything, and all others are scaled and rated with reference to it" (1940: 13).

The following example is taken from a newspaper. It is the reply letter to the editor following another reader's letter, which praised the experience of that person in Singapore.

Letter to the editor

I disagree with X.Y. about Singapore being a Utopia. I lived there for four years and found, although the living standards etc may be higher, one is forced to trade this off against living in a country where a person's individual beliefs are permanently squashed. The nation is brought up, through its education system, to think as one mass and not to dispute its leaders. I was frustrated with the way the West (parti-cularly the UK) is negatively portrayed in Singapore's media. Although I felt a lot safer living there, I became increasingly bored and frustrated with myopic attitudes of a majority of the people and its leadership. Yes, they may all speak at least a basic form of English (better known as Singlish) but when it comes to thinking independ-ently, they fall short. This country [the UK] may have a number of problems but freedom of thought and expression is surely a fundamental right.

Letter to the editor to daily regional newspaper (*The Metro*, 21 March 2001)

- Do you agree with us that the author of this letter does not seem to have left her "comfortable room" in the four years that she lived in Singapore?
- Can you identify the textual markers of ethnocentrism in this text (for example, use of pronouns, role of English etc.)
- What are the cultural assumptions about the relationship between the individual and the group?
- Do you think that a pan-cultural understanding of freedom of thought and expression exists, or ought to exist, or that there is, or ought to be, agreement on what fundamental rights are?

The ability to communicate between cultures, whether national or otherwise requires a particular mindset, to engage reflectively with one's assumptions about what is normal and what is not, what is right and wrong and why. We propose that this ability implies a willingness to leave one's room or country, not only physically, but also intellectually and emotionally.

Non-verbal meanings   Some researchers claim that non-verbal communication carries 93 per cent of the social meaning of a message (Singelis, 1994: 11) – and that NVC constitutes a considerable barrier to intercultural communication. There is research evidence that suggests that some aspects of non-verbal communication have pan-cultural meanings. The emotions anger, fear, happiness, sadness, purpose, and disgust are recognisable in all cultures (Eleman, 1975; Sogon and Mascutaine, 1989). While emotions can be universally recognised, how they are to be displayed is culture-specific. NVC can convey attitudes such as liking or affection (as displayed in proximity and touching), conveying engagement and attention, confidence/competence, and status and respect.

However, cultures differ in the rules that govern the display of emotions – that is to say, in their assessment of when to display emotions, which ones to display and how to display them. For example, an American mother might say to her child, "look at me when I talk to you." In America, direct eye contact is a sign of respect and attention. In Laos, a mother might say, "Don't look at me when I talk to you." In Laos, downcast eyes are a sign of respect and attention. Thus, different non-verbal behaviour carries the same meaning. The decoding of these non-verbal signs can only occur within their specific cultural meaning systems.

NVC changes meaning by modifying the verbal communication. For example, loudness and tone of voice are used for emphasising meaning, but they can also be used to contradict the verbal message. Clearly, if this is not understood, there is room for compounding misunderstandings. NVC also regulates social interaction. Turn taking (who is to speak next in a conversation) follows quite rigid cultural rules, including eye contact and body language. However, the rules vary within different cultures.

Mind your ...

- **Proxemics** – the use/meaning of spaces or territories in the communication process. Hall (1956) introduced the notion of the "space bubble" in which we all live. Cultures differ in their use of personal and social space.
- **Kinesics** – the use of gestures, movements, facial expressions including eye contact in the communication process.
- **Chronemics** – how time is used and attributed with values.
- **Paralanguage** – the non-verbal elements of the voice such as laughter, sobs, intensity and segregates such as "uh," "um."
- **Silence** – more valued in some cultures than in others. In Western culture, silence is experienced as uncomfortable.
- **Haptics** – the use of touch to communicate.
- **Olfactics** – the use of smell as part of the communication processes.
- **Oculesis** – the use of eyes in the communication process.
- **Clothing and physical appearance** – the importance of clothes to convey social meanings.

It is possible to categorise non-verbal behaviour into the groups listed above. Many of these behaviours occur simultaneously, adding, amending, moderating and changing the meaning of the spoken communication. Mainly, language speakers are unaware that they are using these behaviours as part and parcel of the communicative process. They have become so ingrained in the communicative behaviour that they are considered natural. They are, so to speak, the glue that holds the furniture of our comfortable room together; they are the fabric of our normality.

Learning a culture

Eva Hoffman, of Polish-Jewish origins, immigrated to Canada at the age of 13. In her book *Lost in Translation. A Life in a New Language* she describes the experience: this particular episode (1989: 109–110) gives insight into the very processes of enculturalization.

> Mrs Lieberman is among several Polish ladies who have been in Canada long enough to consider themselves well versed in native ways, and who seem to find me deficient in some quite fundamental respects. Since in Poland I was considered a pretty young girl, this requires a basic revision of my self-image. But there's no doubt about it; after the passage across the Atlantic, I've emerged as less attractive, less graceful, less desirable. In fact, I can see in these women's eyes that I'm a somewhat pitiful specimen – pale, with thick eyebrows, and without any bounce in my hair, dressed in clothes that have nothing to do with the current fashion. And so they energetically set out to rectify these flaws. One of them spends a day with me, plucking my eyebrows and trying various shades of lipstick on my face. "If you were my daughter, you'd soon look like a princess," she says, thus implying an added deficiency in my mother. Another counsellor takes me into her house for an evening, to initiate me into the mysteries of using shampoos and hair lotions, and putting my hair up in curlers; yet another outfits me with a crinoline and tells me that actually, I have a perfectly good figure – I just need to bring it out in the right way. And several of them look at my breasts meaningfully, suggesting to my mother in an undertone that really, it's time I started wearing a bra. My mother obeys.
>
> I obey, too, passively, mulishly, but I feel less agile and self-confident with every transformation. I hold my head rigidly, so that my precarious bouffant doesn't fall down, and I smile often, the way I see other girls do, though I'm careful not to open my lips too wide or bite them, so my lipstick won't get smudged. I don't know how to move easily in the high-heeled shoes somebody gave me. Inside its elaborate packaging, my body is stiff, sulky, wary. When I'm with my peers, who come by crinolines, lipstick, cars and self-confidence naturally, my gestures show that I'm here provisionally, by their grace, that I don't rightfully belong. My shoulders stoop, I nod frantically to indicate my agreement with others, I smile sweetly at people to show I mean well, and

my chest recedes inward so that I don't take up too much space – mannerisms of a marginal, off-centred person who wants both to be taken in and to fend off the threatening others.

Eva's body is made subject to the regimes of a different culture in order to become a culturally acceptable body. Note, that those social actors in the cultural know are more powerful than Eva and her mother (see Chapter 5). Much of the power relationships reside in the non-verbal enactment of disciplining Eva's body.

Can you find instances of:

- proxemics
- kinesics
- paralanguage
- silence
- haptics
- olfactics
- oculesis
- clothing and physical appearance

Summary

In this chapter we have explored cultures as meaning systems that are constituted in and through language and other symbolic sign systems. We investigated how and why it is sometimes difficult to communicate across different cultural systems and argued that the deep reason is to be found in the existence of diverse meaning systems. They comprise of more than just national cultures – rather, several systems are interacting with each other and thus they bestow a changing, unstable quality to intercultural encounters.

In suggesting the use of semiology as a conceptual tool to understand such encounters, we do not wish to over-rationalise the equivocal complexity that characterizes many of those encounters; nor do we wish to provide another alluring tool of the "how to" (as in, "how to become a successful intercultural negotiator in ten easy steps") school of business and management. The dynamic mix of different worldviews, values, behaviours, individual preferences and idiosyncrasies, as well as organizational and situational expediencies, cannot be explained within one theoretical framework. Rather, we suggest that when leaving one's comfort zone, some understanding of how meaning is made, makes for a good travelling companion.

Lifelong project

Learn a foreign language. You will have achieved considerable linguistic and cultural competence, once you succeed in being able to joke and be witty in this language.

Recommended reading

Michael Agar's (1994) book *Language Shock. Understanding the Culture of Conversation* is a key source for understanding the relationship between language and culture. It is a highly approachable book that makes fascinating reading.

Larry Samovar and Richard Porter have edited/written two important texts on inter-cultural communication. Their *Intercultural Communication. A Reader* (2000) is a collec-tion of different essays, spanning a multitude of aspects, ideas and concepts. In their book *Communication Between Cultures* (2001) the authors demonstrate communication con-cepts by exploring differences in perception, worldviews, values and verbal and non-verbal messages. Both books are written for a (North) American audience, but are useful for anyone interested in intercultural communication.

Gudykunst's (1998) book on *Bridging Differences* is a reflective account on intergroup communication.

Geerzt (1973), *The Interpretation of Cultures*, laid important foundations for the study of cultures. It is not easy reading for the newcomer to the field, but since it is made up of self-contained chapters, readers can pursue the themes in their own time.

A comprehensive overview of organizational culture is given by Brown (1998) in his book, *Organizational Culture*. An example on how to research and understand culture is given by Tony Watson's (2001a) ethnography on managers' lives. The seminal text on national cultures is Hofstede's (2001) book on *Culture's Consequences*.

The reader is most warmly invited to read Eva Hoffman's (1989) account of losing her self and finding a different self while adapting and surviving in an alien culture.

CHAPTER SEVEN

Gender and Language

In the introduction to this book we talked about the webs of meaning in which we are suspended, and which at the same time we are constantly spinning. Gender is one of the strands in these complex and intricate webs. Although, like a thread in a spider's web, it might appear thin and insignificant (and at times we might hardly notice it), it is an integral part of the robust cultural system in which we are embedded. In this chapter we examine this **gender strand** as a **meaning system** and consider the role language plays in reinforcing existing patterns, unravelling strands which are frayed and worn, and contributing to new designs. Gender, of course, refers to both women and men. However, in this chapter we are looking at gender primarily from the perspective of women.

There is now a rich and diverse literature on gender relations in organizations. This has developed from concerns about how men and women are distributed in organizations and labour markets, to analyses of power and ideological control, critiques of such grand theories, and considerations of how gender is constituted in particular local contexts. Researchers interested in gender have studied a wide range of issues, from traditional organizational behaviour topics like motivation and leadership, to human resource management, career, organizational culture, technology and knowledge management.

While few would dispute that language is a central feature of many of these issues and processes, it is rarely dealt with head on within organization behaviour texts. There is a flourishing literature on gender and language, much of which is highly pertinent to organizational contexts. However, this resides largely within the fields of linguistics and communication studies, and apart from some notable exceptions (which we will be discussing in this chapter), its significance for students of management and organization is largely unacknowledged and untapped. In this chapter we discuss what is known about gender and organization and about gender and language, and consider what can be gained through their synthesis.

Objectives

In this chapter we will:

- consider gender as a social construct;
- present perspectives on gender and language – and how these are played out in organizations; and
- present perspectives on gender and organizations – and where language fits in.

Consider these questions in light of an organization you know well

- Where are the women and men positioned overall within the organization? How are they distributed in management roles?
- How would you characterise the key values of this organization? Would the labels **masculine** and **feminine** help you to categorise these? Why or why not?
- What kind of behaviour is most valued in this organization? A good way to think about this might be in terms of promotion. What kind of behaviour/ performance/ style gets promoted? Could you categorise these as masculine or feminine?
- What is the typical pattern of the working day/week? Consider this in relation to the lives of men and women outside of the organization.
- Whose voice would you say gets heard most often? Whose is heard least often? How can you account for this? Is there a difference in the profiles of men and women in the organization?
- Have you noticed any differences in the ways in which women and men communicate? If so, how would say these differences are evaluated by people within the organization? How is this demonstrated?

Understanding gender

The issue of gender has been approached from a variety of theoretical perspectives. Although diverse in many ways, these perspectives agree on the significance of gender in social relations and on the unequal distribution of power within such relations. Underpinning these points is the idea of gender, not as an immutable **fact**, but as a **social construct**. As Crawford explains, "gender is what culture makes out of the 'raw material' of (already constructed) biological sex" (1995: 13). In her view (which we share), gender can be seen as a meaning system, an ideology within which interactions are organised and power relations are prescribed. In this sense, gender is a strand in the cultural web that we talked about earlier: "gender is not an attribute of individuals but a way of making sense of transactions. Gender does not exist in persons, but in transactions it is conceptualised as a verb, not a noun" (Crawford, 1995: 12). Thus, feminists talk about

doing gender and, as we will discuss below, organization theorists refer to the **gendering of organizations**.

Crawford suggests that we can understand the way in which gender is played out at three levels: **societal**, **interpersonal** and **individual**. By societal, Crawford is referring to where women and men are located within our social structures – within institutions such as government, education, law, the media and academia – and to the (unequal) power relations associated with these positions. The interpersonal level concerns the **gender cues** which signal appropriate behaviours in social interaction. In work settings researchers have found that the same behaviour exhibited by women and men is often evaluated very differently (Wilson, 1995). Finally, Crawford discusses the gender system at the level of individuals. She maintains that the discourse of gender is divided into two oppositional poles: the masculine and the feminine, each with its particular sets of characteristics, attitudes and behaviours. The individual level refers to the internalisation of these codes. This process, she maintains, is central to the construction of one's sense of self, and these ascriptions are not neutral. Rather, embedded within our notions of masculinity and femininity are ideas about relative value, status, dominance and subordination.

We agree with Crawford that other social classifications, such as ethnicity, class and able-bodiedness can likewise be understood systematically. Here again, central to the ways in which such groupings are constructed are issues of power and control, and whose view of normal is seen to hold sway.

Power as a legitimating framework

Here we are using the concept of power, not in terms of particular roles or positions, clear-cut hierarchical domination or physical strength. Rather, we are using it as a framework for understanding whose view of the world is seen to be legitimate, normal or natural.

In all cases, language has a key role to play in the creation and representation of these categories. Consistent with our own perspective, Crawford sees language as a socially constructed phenomenon, "a set of strategies for negotiating the social landscape" (1995: 17). In her book she critiques approaches to language and gender that assume fundamental differences between the sexes, and explores the relationship between these two dynamic social systems.

Interestingly, Crawford does not talk about organization. We note this not only because organization is our primary interest in this book, but also because we feel it would add a very useful dimension to her analysis. Whilst we find her work insightful in its emphasis on gender as a **system**, as it stands, the gap between her interpersonal and institutional levels appears excessively wide. We see rather more happening between these levels. In particular, an analysis of gender must take into account the ways in which concepts of gender are mediated through, reproduced and reconstructed by, the kinds of organizations in which we participate: from formal to informal groupings, from places of work to spiritual organizations, sports, arts and community associations.

If we take the field of healthcare as an example, people working in organizations such as hospitals, general practice surgeries and health trusts do not all understand or enact gender in the same way, and significantly they do not all reflect dominant understandings as expressed by government policy and policymakers. Rather, the ways in which notions of masculinity and femininity are constructed within such organizations could be seen as resulting from a whole web of factors, including government policy, as well as sectoral issues and local interests and intraorganizational factors. Such understandings constructed at the level of the organization then inform activity and meaning-making at interpersonal and individual levels. The addition of the organizational dimension enhances Crawford's analysis, making it a more refined tool with which to examine the gendering of social life.

Considering the relationship between gender and language at the level of the organization, the following questions arise:

- How do women and men at work talk, and how are they talked about?
- How are ideas about masculinity and femininity constituted within organizational talk?

Though they seem straightforward, these questions raise a whole gamut of theoretical, methodological and empirical issues. In what follows we will answer them through overviews of two historically separate, but closely linked fields of academic knowledge: gender and organization, and language and gender.

Are women born or made?

What do you think Simone de Beauvoir meant when she said that, "One is not borne a woman, one becomes one" (1972)?

- Do you think the same can be said for men?

Gender and organization

Gender is thus an important strand in our cultural web, reinforced, unravelled and re-spun through our action and interaction, at institutional, organizational, interpersonal and individual levels. Given our interest in organization, questions arise as to how we can understand these complex and intricate processes in organizational settings. In Chapter 2 we argued that the analysis of sign systems, such as the built environment, décor and decoration, organizational rituals and corporate dress and language, provides the researcher with key insights into organizations and the process of organising. They can likewise illuminate the ways in which gender is played out within organizational contexts and structures. Indeed, bureaucracy is often seen as essentially masculine: rational, hierarchical and emotionless (Savage and Witz, 1992). In the text box which follows we focus on one such system – corporate dress – which during the summer of 2001 became headline news in New Zealand, a site of struggle between notions of femininity and masculinity, visibility and invisibility, power and powerlessness, and most crucially, struggles over corporate legitimacy.

Change your earrings and maybe we can work together

In New Zealand, the summer of 2001 saw a raging battle over the problem of corporate dress. In a two week period, the following headlines (and many more) appeared in *The New Zealand Herald*:

"The Day Fashion Became Political"
"The Grey, Pin-striped Empire Strikes Back"
"Saga of Top Public Servant Skirts around the World"
"Earrings against Sexism"

At issue was the wardrobe of Christine Rankin, former Chief Executive of the Department of Work and Income. During 1999–2000 the flamboyant Civil Servant Rankin was involved in a political wrangle which on 24 May 2000 resulted in her dismissal. In her appeal for reinstatement, which took place in July 2001, Rankin claimed that her sacking was a result of sexism. In particular, she argued that colleagues had objected to her short skirts, big earrings and low cut shirts. Mark Prebble, Head of the Department of the Prime Minister, spear-headed the attack, arguing that "her earrings were a sexual come-on," her short skirts "an absolute distraction" and that he was disturbed by a "glimpse of her moving breast" (*The New Zealand Herald*, 5 July 2001: 1 (Story ID 198442).

Rankin's appeal for reinstatement ignited the country. In the appeal case her critics, including the Prime Minister, stood by the original decision (and the traditional corporate grey), while supporters rallied around their icon, 'ransacking their wardrobes and rattling through their jewelry boxes' (Beston, *The New Zealand Herald*, 3 July 2001) as they prepared for the first ever Christine Rankin Day. Some say that Rankin has become a cult figure. But whatever their views, New Zealanders agree that she "has made long earrings and hemlines dinner topics" (Gamble, *The New Zealand Herald*, 4 August 2001: 1 Story ID 203838).

- Do you think it was appropriate for Christine Rankin to wear what was seen as sexually provocative clothing?
- What is your view of Prebble's argument that such clothing constituted harassment?
- Do you think there should be prescribed dress codes at work? If so, what would they be? Would they apply to both men and women? What would these dress codes 'mean' to different constituencies in and around the organization? Would you extend these to other types of organizations such as universities, or social settings like bars and clubs?
- What do you think Rankin's look might have meant to her critics? And to her supporters? How might these groups have defended their positions?

Research into gender and organization is extremely difficult to pin down. It ranges from the literature labelled **women-in-management**, inspired by the US women's liberation movement and associated civil rights legislation in the 1960s and 70s, to European-led postmodernist and poststructuralist perspectives. We have found Alvesson and Billing's (1997) discussion to be an extremely useful introduction to the field. Their analysis comprises four broad categories: gender as a variable, as a feminist standpoint, from a poststructuralist perspective and finally from a loosely defined perspective which they call critical-interpretivism. With regard to our own research, whilst at times we adopt elements of all four, it is within critical-interpretivism that our work probably sits most comfortably. In the section that follows we briefly summarize Alvesson and Billing's four perspectives, noting the importance (or not) of language within them.

The gender-as-variable perspective

The **gender-as-variable** perspective sees gender, not as socially constructed, but as a fundamental and unproblematic **essentialist** category, indistinguishable from sex. Variable researchers are typically interested in comparing men and women in terms of inequality and discrimination, investigating the different ways that men and women are affected by their different structural circumstances and finding ways of redressing imbalances. Such perspectives are based on the idea that this is achievable, with appropriate policies and management practices. These studies tend to use large-scale surveys, and aim to produce objective, quantifiable results. Early equal opportunities initiatives were based on results from gender-as-variable research.

In organization theory, the gender-as-variable perspective is most closely associated with the women in management literature (Davidson and Cooper, 1992; Kanter, 1977), and has been the dominant gender perspective. However, a problem with these approaches is that they tend to look at male and female as essential, **measurable** categories that can be reliably controlled, tested and compared (Alvesson and Billing, 1997). In this sense, they fail to recognize more subtle, multi-dimensional webs of meaning, experience and activity. Most relevant to this book is the assumption embedded within variable approaches that language simply reflects reality. Where questionnaires are the chosen data collection method and where variability and deviation are rigorously controlled for and measured, language is seen as little more than a vehicle for the transmission of social facts. Clearly this is at odds with our interest in exploring and understanding the ways in which meaning systems (including gender) are constituted and reproduced linguistically and interpreted variously by situated individuals and groups.

The feminist standpoint approach

Alvesson and Billing's second perspective, the feminist standpoint, views gender as a key organizing principle in a patriarchal society. With emancipation and social transformation as their aim, some researchers working from this perspective offer critical analyses of organizations, highlighting the ways in which organizations work to undermine women and reinforce male power (Cockburn, 1991). Seeking to develop radically new ways of organising, others have focused on the processes and practices at work in explicitly feminist organizations (Morgen, 1994).

From the point of view of language and meaning making, feminist standpoint approaches in organizational research have yielded interesting findings into the consequences for women of being cast as "the other" in work settings. Of particular note are the **gender management strategies** (Sheppard, 1989) that women employ to cope with their disempowered status. Deviating from the male norm, in order to survive women need to find ways of coping with their marginality (that is, ways of handling the fact that they are female). This can pose the contradictory problem of at once concealing the feminine aspects of oneself (clothes, body, linguistic style etc) while remaining feminine enough to be unobtrusive. As Green and Cassell note, for women "learning how to manage the world of the organization necessarily means learning how to re-define and manage their 'femaleness' through attempting to 'blend in'" (Green and Cassell, 1996: 172).

Blending in or being seen: managing being a woman at work

Try to think of some gender management strategies you have seen women employing at work (women readers might consider any strategies they use themselves).

- Why do you think these strategies might be important for women?
- What might be their effect?
- Do men also have to do this? If so, how?
- Why do you think theorists assume that this is not an issue for men? Are there any instances where it might be?

To us the idea of powerful (male) and powerless (female) talk has a certain resonance. On the one hand, we appreciate standpoint analyses for their stark reminder of oppression as a lived reality for many women in the workforce. And we have all three witnessed (and in many cases have ourselves adopted) the strategies that women often employ to cope with their precarious organizational status. However, at the same time, we reject the wholesale representation of women (us) as passive victims, powerless in the face of dominant men, assumed within these perspectives.

Post-structural feminism

The third of Alvesson and Billing's perspectives is poststructural feminism. Here any suggestion that male and female are robust or fixed categories begins to falter. Instead, the focus is on the crucial role played by language in structuring our realities. Within these perspectives the world is depicted as a fragmented place. Alvesson and Billing rightly ask:

> What is the common significance of 'woman' when applied to a 70 year old, retired Brazilian schoolteacher as well as a 14-year old girl from the New Delhi Slum, a Norweigan female Prime Minister, a black single mother of several children in South Africa, a young MBA career woman on Wall Street and a lesbian upper-class middle-aged artist in Victorian England? (1997: 37)

The answer is that there probably is none – that even the biological sex of these women might be understood differently. Gender is again a variable, but now ambiguous and shifting – never neutral, but instead arbitrary and, most importantly, **rhetorically**

constructed. There is no whole truth about to be found about gender, just as there are no whole truths generally. Here gender is not used as a static noun, but as a verb: an active, continuing and dynamic process. Within organizations, therefore, gender is not seen as a variable that can be managed through initiatives and policies. Instead, writers from these perspectives speak of the **gendering of organizations**. Their research aims to illuminate the processes through which gender is constituted in organizational settings. In this poststructuralist view language is central, not just reflecting but fundamentally constituting social realities in particular local contexts.

Critical interpretive perspectives

Finally Alvesson and Billing introduce an emerging perspective which they call critical interpretive, to which we are drawn. Sympathetic to some of the insights of poststructuralism and on the key role played by language in particular, it nevertheless allows for some level of scientific rationality. While realistic about the degree of change which research can instigate, advocates of critical interpretivism nevertheless seek to be useful to occupational communities outside of academia. Although cautious in dealing with universal categories like patriarchy and gender, they do try to engage in questions about power and powerlessness, justice and inequality. They seek to reflect both dominant **and** subordinate voices to illustrate the dynamism as well as the durability of gender relations.

As regards language, while critical-interpretivism does not argue that language is all there is (see Chapter 5), it does highlight the importance of language in re-presenting femininity, masculinity and their changing relationship:

> A word like masculinity has for example no simple and absolute meaning. There
> is no one-way relation between the notion and some cultural or social reality
> 'out there'. This does not mean that the term is unable to describe a social
> phenomenon or stimulate thoughts about social reality, extrinsic to language,
> but it is important to recall the hidden and suppressed meanings that give the
> notion a relative and arbitrary meaning. Masculinity presupposes femininity
> which again presupposes masculinity. The meaning is unstable and
> context-dependent. (Alvesson and Billing, 1997: 49)

Gendered noise: examining patterns of domination and subordination

Using the metaphor **gendered noise**, Harlow et al.'s (1995) look at how **silence** and **din** work to create relations of domination and subordination within organizations. The concepts of silence and din are treated both metaphorically and literally, and Harlow et al. apply the concepts to the very structure of our society: the din of the public (male dominated) sphere and the silence of the private (female dominated) world of domestic responsibilities. This pattern is translated to organizational contexts, where the din of male leadership, management, rules, power and decision-making structures (p. 97) is contrasted to the silence of women who are frequently not heard, and who find progress difficult within these male-dominated spaces. The analysis is developed to incorporate the gendering of organizational structures, and the construction and expression of these structures through every-day interaction. It is important to note that while their focus is **gendered** noise, Harlow et al. insist that their analysis can equally be applied to other silenced groups.

Significantly, at the same time that language serves to perpetuate existing patterns of din and silence, Harlow et al. maintain that it is also a vehicle for subver-sion – and change. Thus conventional associations of din with power, and silence with powerlessness are challenged (this resonates with the notion of 'reading against the grain' that we discussed in Chapter 5). It is interesting that they do not restrict their analysis to organizational contexts. Rather, they use these contexts to examine the dins and silences within organizational theory itself, where **din** encom-passes dominant perspectives and theorists, and the silence of those which are seen as irrelevant, unimportant, or which are simply absent.

- Can you find patterns of silence and din in your organization?
- If so, are they gendered? If not, how might you account for them?
- Are there instances in which the dominant patterns of dominance and sub-ordination are challenged or reversed?
- Can you think of any other metaphors that might illuminate how power is played out in your organization?

To sum up, in this section we have briefly outlined four perspectives on gender and organization, as shown in Table 7.1. We see this categorisation as a useful vehicle for making sense of a diverse and complex field. However, like most frameworks for understanding, it is not quite so straightforward in practice. Rather, there is consider-able overlap between the perspectives themselves. Research studies do not always fit neatly into one or other of these categories and many authors resist such attempts at pigeonholing. Thus, the value of such analysis lies not in its blanket applicability, but in its richness as a theoretical resource – providing a range of lenses through which we can examine gender, language and organization.

Making sense of the Christine Rankin story

Think back to the story about New Zealand civil servant Christine Rankin which we presented at the start of this section.

- How would the theoretical perspectives introduced in this chapter shed light on what happened?
- Which perspective do you have most sympathy with?

Table 7.1   Four perspectives on gender and organization

Perspective	Basic principles	View of language
Gender as variable	Gender as fundamental category, indistinguishable from sex. Research compares the different ways men and women are affected by their different structural circumstances and aims to find ways of redressing imbalances.	Language seen as an unproblematic vehicle for transmitting social facts.
Feminist standpoint	Gender as a key organising principle in patriarchal societies. Essential inequality between men and women within such systems. Research aims for emancipation and social transformation.	Language seen as reflecting women's powerlessness and marginality.
Poststructural feminism	No whole truth about masculinity or femininity. Instead, gender seen as socially and rhetorically constructed. Research aims to provide insights into the processes by which organizations become gendered.	Language central in structuring our realities. Gender constituted, reproduced and transformed through language.
Critical interpretivism	Considers gender as socially constructed, but within particular sets of power relations. Research aims to be useful outside of academic communities, and to represent both dominant and subordinate voices.	Language plays an important role in representing notions of femininity, masculinity and their changing relationship within certain social, cultural, political etc. contexts.

Gender and linguistic theory

Within linguistics, questions about the ways in which women and men talk – and are talked about – have been of keen interest to researchers since the 1970s. Early studies into gender and language examined the structural elements of men's and women's talk, highlighting the deficiencies of women's speech patterns.

Nags and requests: words and their meanings

Consider the following list of words: argue, lecture, speech-make, nag, gossip, announce, chat, negotiate, haggle, giggle, pontificate

- Try to categorise these words in terms of these binary opposites: good/bad, important/unimportant, public/private, male/female
- Do any patterns emerge? What are they? Are there any words that don't fit into these patterns?
- How can you account for the patterns, and for the exceptions?

However, subsequent researchers took as their starting point the idea that women and men live in distinct cultural worlds, shifting their focus from **deficiency** to **difference**. More recently, scholars have turned their attention to the idea of **gendering** as opposed to **gendered** language. That is, they seek to understand the ways in which gender is constructed and enacted through talk, and of the gendering of language through social interaction (Coates, 1998). These have been labelled the deficit perspective, the difference perspective and interactionist or constructionist perspectives. In the three sections that follow we briefly describe these, and discuss how they are played out in organizations.

Deficit approaches to language and gender

We "know that in all known societies it is the way men speak that is held in high esteem, while women's ways of talking are compared unfavourably with men's" (Coates, 1998: 2).

Early research into language and gender sought to reveal the inherent deficiencies and limitations of women's language, and by contrast the linguistic dominance of men. Based on an essentialist (as opposed to a constructionist) view of gender (resonant of the gender as variable perspective already discussed), this US-led research focused on structural features – and highlighted the essential powerlessness of the female forms. This female style, or **genderlect** was characterised by tentativeness, exemplified through devices such as softer expletives, persistent question intonation (rising rather than falling intonation at the ends of statements), use of superpolite forms ("I wonder if you would mind removing your chair from my foot?") and frequent tag questions ("That's right, isn't it?") (Lakoff, 1973, 1975; Spender, 1980).

Subsequent deficit theorists moved away from static structural features to real talk (in Saussure's terms, from **langue** to **parole** – see Chapter 2). Examining patterns of interaction and turn taking, West and Zimmerman (1983; Zimmerman and West, 1975) found that women fared badly, they were frequently not heard, were interrupted more often and were only rarely the centre of attention. Similarly, Fishman (1983) described the unequal division of conversational labour, with women typically doing the conversational shitwork, supporting the needs of men and basically keeping the interaction going.

A more radical take on deficit theory was developed by Australian linguist Dale Spender in her best selling book *Man Made Language* (1980). Echoing feminist standpoint perspectives introduced above, Spender argues that within male meaning systems, women are not only seen as limited or restricted, but in effect are rendered mute. As men control meaning, they are able to impose their view of the world upon everyone else. Underlying this notion is a sense of linguistic determinism, a sense that language creates reality (see Chapter 6). According to Spender, meaning is literally made by men, constructing a male view of the world that is at odds with women's experiences – a web within which women are trapped. In organizations, standpoint theorists argue that women, unable to extricate themselves, or to create their own versions of what is right and what is so, develop strategies through which they manage their "femaleness."

Talking about women and men

While deficit approaches typically focus on the ways in which women and men talk, they can also be applied to the ways in which women and men are talked **about**. Do the following activities on your own or with a partner.

- We sometimes use animal metaphors to describe people. Which animals do we typically associate with women? And which with men? What do these metaphors connote to you?
- Can you add any more pairs of words to this list?

  Landlord   Landlady
  Host   Hostess
  Master   Mistress
- Compare the male and female labels for these occupations. How would you explain any similarities or differences?

Although they have a certain resonance, there are some problems with deficit approaches. Some critics say that in focusing on specific linguistic features, they do not take account of the way that language is used in actual interaction, or of social contexts. Others argue that they are based on a view of male and female as objective facts – rather than socially constructed concepts. We agree with both of these criticisms. For example, we have all participated in and observed meetings where tag questions did not signify weakness, but were used to reassert the speaker's point, and to generate support for her idea. We have also witnessed men using superpolite forms to circumvent the authority of a female chairperson. Regarding the second point, we take issue with a perspective in which men are depicted as all-powerful, and women as victims. Not only is it insulting for both men and women – but it also just does not ring true. Alongside other critics, we object to the notion of male as norm, with the female cast as other, deviating from the male standard and in need of remedial support.

Bully Broads: after two decades of assertiveness training, have women executives become too tough?

From the early 1970s popular psychology books claimed that women's lack of assertiveness was holding them back: at work, home and in life generally. Gender socialization was the culprit – in particular notions of femininity, which were seen to foster passivity and submission at the expense of self-esteem, confidence and proactivity. The good news, though, was that women could do something about their limitations. As deficit theorist Robin Lakoff argued: "we could shuck off deferential style just as we did hoops and girdles" (1975: 25). Through assertiveness training, women could learn to be more like men.

The assertiveness movement took America by storm, and the UK was soon to follow. Women executives hoping to improve their job prospects devoured self-help guides and flocked to assertiveness seminars. These programmes were highly mechanised and prescriptive. Certain styles of talk were good and others were not. "Requests should be in the form of straightforward questions, never indirect references or hints. Refusals should be given without excuses, justifications or apologies. Speakers should focus on their own feelings" (Crawford, 1995: 54). Embedded within these prescriptions were ideas about what constituted healthy, productive behaviour (typically seen as masculine characteristics), and in contrast, those dysfunctional, maladaptive, feminine behaviours in need of 'treatment.' By talking more like men, it was thought that women would be able to break through the organizational 'glass ceilings' which were preventing them from realising their potential.

Now though it seems that these 'remedies' are backfiring on corporate women. On 10 August 2001 the lead story in the business section of *The New York Times* tells how women executives have become too tough: "Their no-nonsense ways intimidate subordinates, colleagues and quite often their bosses, who are almost invariably men." Having rectified their 'too feminine' styles, corporate women are now enrolling in courses designed to 'soften them up.' As Jean A. Hollands, founder of the *Bully Broads* training organization explains,

> for women to succeed now, they must become ladies first ... Ditch all that
> hardball stuff from the 80s – being assertive, standing firm – and learn to hold
> your tongue, stammer and couch what you say. Don't choke back tears if you
> start to cry at a meeting (Banerjee, 2001: C1).

The two cultures perspective

In the mid-1980s, approaches to gender and language emerged which were based on the principle of difference rather than deficit. Supporters of these ideas took issue with deficit theorists' assumption of male standards and the portrayal of women as victims. They sought to move away from two-dimensional comparisons between men and women, comparisons which invariably cast women in a worse light. Their starting point was that communication between men and women is difficult because the two sexes operate in essentially different cultural spaces, much like people from different ethnic groups (Gumperz, 1982).

Men are from Mars, Women are from Venus

- What is the title of this popular book saying about men and women?
- To what extent do you agree with this?
- How would this approach account for gender inequality?
- What are the implications of this perspective for women's and men's language use?

Given these **two worlds**, researchers wanted to look at women's language, not as a deficient or debased form of the "standard" (the norm of male language), but as different from men's language and worthy of examination in its own right (Coates, 1998).

Difference not dominance

In their paper "A Cultural Approach to Male-Female Miscommunication" (1982) Daniel Maltz and Ruth Borker launched a new way of thinking about gender and language. Taking what they describe as an anthropological perspective, they maintain that problems in cross-sex communication should not be seen as miscommunication, but as the result of cultural differences between the sexes. Consistent with other linguists, they highlight what they see as key features of both men's and women's language. These include women's:

- tendency to ask questions;
- use of utterances which work to "nurture" interaction;
- adoption of "silent protest" strategies when interrupted; and
- use of collective pronouns ("we" instead of "I").

In contrast, Maltz and Borker suggest that men:

- are more likely to interrupt;
- are prone to challenge their partners;
- are more likely than women to ignore others' comments;
- tend to use controlling language; and
- make more direct declarations.

To explain these differences, Maltz and Borker emphasise the

cultural differences between men and women in their conceptions of friendly conversation, their rules for engaging in it and, probably most importantly, their rules of interpreting it. We argue that American men and women come from different sociolinguistic subcultures, having learned to do different things with words in a conversation so that when they attempt to carry on conversations with one another, even if both parties are attempting to treat one another as equals, cultural miscommunication results. (1982: 420)

Through its popularisation by authors such as John Gray, in *Men are from Mars, Women are from Venus* (1992) and Deborah Tannen in *You Just Don't Understand: Women and Men in Conversation* (1990), Crawford suggests that this perspective heralded a second bandwagon: "the two cultures model has become a metaphor for all the interactional problems of North American women and men" (1995: 88). Whereas previously women were seen as having problems in social interaction due to their linguistic deficiencies (rectified through assertiveness training), two cultures commentators took the view that if women and men were occupying different cultural worlds, how could they possibly communicate? Again, these interactional problems could be remedied through self-help programmes. As Crawford notes, at the time of writing her book over 25,000 people had attended John Gray's relationship seminars where they were offered a myriad of lists, pre-scribing specific rules on what men and women should and should not say in order to live more harmoniously. Above all, they were encouraged not to question inequalities between men and women, but to accept – and even cherish – their differences. "Through understanding the hidden differences of the opposite [sic] sex we can … give and receive … love. Love is magical, and it can last, if we remember our differences" (Gray, 1992: 14, cited in Crawford, 1995: 90).

Two cultures perspectives at work in management of diversity initiatives

In organizational settings, we have recently seen the two cultures perspectives at work in diversity policies and programmes. The idea behind many of these man-agement initiatives is that the workforce consists of a diverse population, and that harnessing (rather than suppressing or ignoring) these differences will bring signi-ficant organizational benefits, creating "a productive environment in which every-body feels valued, where their talents are being fully utilized and in which organizational goals are met" (Kandola and Fullerton, 1998: 8). It is important to note that the concept of diversity does not only relate to gender differences, but also to factors such as age, background, ethnicity, able-bodiedness, personality and work style. While diversity initiatives do not explicitly focus on language, the language in which they are described and promoted is worth noting. As enthusiastic proponents of diversity initiatives Prasad and Mills explain: "diversity is celebrated with the help of evocative metaphors such as the melting pot, the patchwork quilt, the multicoloured or cultural mosaic, and the rainbow" (1997: 4).

(Continued)

- What do these metaphors connote?
- Are there any other possible interpretations? Who might espouse these alternative understandings?
- Have you experience of diversity initiatives? How were they received by organizational members, and what sort of differences have they made?

Significantly, in Gray's book (as in two cultures approaches more generally), the status quo emerges unscathed. That is, such perspectives do not question existing social inequalities that underlie men's and women's patterns of interaction. Indeed, the neglect of issues of power, and failure to account for the political nature of gender relations is one of the key criticisms of these perspectives. On the one hand, commentators applaud two cultures perspectives for their shift away from the portrayal of women as limited and victimised, and for their legitimation and celebration of women's language. However, underlying the differences model is a certain political complacency. As Crawford explains, "Concepts such as sexism, sex discrimination, patriarchy, and gender inequality are barely mentioned, and conversational strategies that have the effect of silencing women are euphemized as stylistic 'assymetries'" (1995: 106).

Deborah Tannen: public acclaim, academic criticism

Deborah Tannen's *You Just Don't Understand: Women and Men in Conversation* (1990) was hailed by the US popular press as "the Rosetta Stone that at last deciphers the miscommunication between the sexes" (Crawford, 1995: 91). During the 1990s she became increasingly interested in organizational talk (1994, 1995, 1996). Focusing specifically on the sphere of management, in an article appearing in the *Harvard Business Review* (1995) she argues that men's and women's fundamentally different linguistic styles have serious implications for their success at work.

Tannen maintains that patterns of interaction learned in childhood, in particular girls' emphasis on relationship-building and boys' on competition, carry over to the workplace, where women typically downplay their achievements and search for collegial support, while men typically vie for prominence, and steal women's thunder (1995: 141).

Consistent with a difference perspective, Tannen suggests that although men's and women's linguistic styles are equally valid – "either directness or indirectness can be a successful means of communication as long as the linguistic style is understood by the participants" (1995: 147). However, they are not equally valued: "within the world of work, however, there is more at stake than whether the communication is understood. People in powerful positions are likely to reward styles similar to their own" (1995: 147). Given that in the US these people are usually men, it is their style which is seen as most legitimate, and which ultimately holds sway.

Like other two cultures theorists, though, Tannen does not talk about structural inequality or argue for social transformation. Rather, she prescribes greater levels of awareness and sensitivity amongst managers:

A manager aware of those dynamics might devise any number of ways of ensuring that everyone's ideas are heard and credited. Although no single solution will fit all contexts, managers who understand the dynamics of linguistic style can develop more adaptive, and flexible approaches ... Talk is the lifeblood of managerial work, and understanding that different people have different ways of saying what they mean will make it possible to take advantage of the talents of people with a broad range of linguistic styles (1995: 148).

Although widely acclaimed by the public, in the academic world her work has been subject to severe criticism:

I find this book not only flawed in its arguments but intellectually and politically dishonest ... the current salience (and marketability) of gender-related topics is exploited. (Cameron, 1992: 467)

Reading Deborah Tannen's *You Just Don't Understand* – the lamentation of the title alone places it squarely into the profuse relationship literature a la Ann Landers [US agony aunt] along with books of the caliber of Norwood's *Women Who Love Too Much* and selling as well – one might believe feminism had never happened in this country ... This is a dishonest book precisely because of its non-engaged and apolitical stance. It veils and conceals the political analysis to which women have given their energy during the last 30 years ... it equalizes where differences have to be acknowledged; it hardly ever talks about inequity – and never with real concern ... The author also shields her readers from linguistic knowledge. (Troemel-Ploetz, 1998: 446)

In particular, Tannen has been taken to task for her apolitical stance and her unabashed public appeal.

- To what extent does Tannen's analysis resonate for you?
- Why do you think her work has attracted such acclaim from the public and such vehement criticism from academic peers?

In our view, it's not the case that a focus on difference necessarily eclipses the idea of dominance. In fact, the two could work together very powerfully. However, in practice they are typically seen as theoretical opposites. In their celebration of difference, then, two cultures perspectives often neglect the deeply rooted inequalities which are reflected in and constructed through these differences. When this happens, existing gender-power relations remain intact.

Interactionist approaches

Both dominance and difference approaches are based on binary thinking: power or powerlessness, male or female – and high levels of abstraction. In response to each, our refrain is that while aspects of these theories do resonate as explanatory frameworks for understanding the relationship between gender and language, they do not hold up. In particular, they fail to illuminate the diverse ways in which gender is played out in everyday social practice (Cameron, 1985; Coates, 1998; Crawford, 1995). As Eckert and McConnell-Ginet powerfully argue:

> The overwhelming tendency in language and gender research on power has been to emphasize either speakers and their social relations (eg. women's disadvantage in ordinary conversations with men) or the meanings and norms encoded in the linguistic systems and practices historically available to them (eg. such sexist patterns as conflating generic human with masculine forms like *he* or *man*). But linguistic forms have no power except as given in people's mouths and ears; to talk about meaning without talking about the people who mean and the community practices through which they give meaning to their words is at best limited. (1992: 492)

We agree. On the one hand we find dominance and difference perspectives thought-provoking and challenging. However, removed from real social interaction, they provide only partial explanations – explanations at the level of Saussure's **langue** (see Chapter 2). Because they work at the level of generalization, they all too often provide answers in the form of "women's language means this" or "men have that conversational style." In our view, such explanations need to be re-connected with **parole**, with actual social practice and language-in-use. They need to grapple with more everyday questions about what words, speech or intonation patterns, or turn-taking routines mean in particular discursive situations and how this links with wider social practice.

Furthermore, consistent with our earlier discussion of poststructuralist and critical interpretive perspectives on gender and organization, **women** and **men** can not be seen as unified or homogeneous categories. As Coates explains, there is no single way of doing femininity, of being a woman or of talking like a woman.

> In the contemporary developed world, many different versions of femininity are available to us. Different discourses give us access to different femininities. More mainline discourses position us in more conventional ways, while more radical or subversive discourses offer us alternative ways of being, alternative ways of doing femininity. (1998: 319)

Different ways of being a woman

In an article called "Competing Discourses of Femininity" linguist Jennifer Coates argues that the meaning of woman has changed through time, and at any given time will vary – between, for example, meanings associated with more Madonna-like images of femininity and meanings associated with more whore-like images. "There is no such thing as a 'woman'; the meaning of 'woman' will depend on which discourse the word occurs in, which spectacles we put on" (1998: 311).

- Try to think of some examples of **Madonna-like** and **whore-like** images of women.
- What are their contexts?
- Can you think of any other representations of women, particularly in work settings?

- How can you account for these differences?
- Do you think the meaning of **man** is also changeable?

A key point here is the idea of meaning making – and in this case the construction of gender – as a fundamentally **social** process. In Chapter 5 on discourse we introduced the notion of **communities of practice** to refer to groups of people who come together around certain activities, and who, through engagement with one another, develop characteristic ways of speaking and acting, based on certain shared values, beliefs and power relations. Eckert and McConnell-Ginet (1992) use this concept to explain the social dimension of gender relations.

Between communities of practice, gender is constructed in diverse ways. This can result from differential membership. For example, men are more likely to belong to football clubs and boards of directors, while women are more apt to participate in secretarial pools, and parent-teacher associations. It is also related to different forms of participation, as in the army where men are more apt to engage in active combat. Of course, as individuals we all participate in a range of such communities of practice – experiencing the tension, frustration and sometimes the freedom that multiple membership brings.

The meaning of queer

Eckert and McConnell-Ginet (1992) highlight the case of a lesbian lawyer who might at once participate in an occupational community, in which gender and gender relations are constructed in a particular way, and in a gay community in which such meanings are subverted and transformed.

- How might the legal community noted above understand the word **queer**?
- What about the gay community?
- What does this suggest about the term itself?
- How might the concept of communities of practice help us to understand these differences?
- Can you think of any other similar examples?

In an organizational context, the work of Collinson (1988) and Hearn (1985) illustrate the powerful role played by language in the construction of gender identities – not language in an abstract, general sense, but as used by particular occupational communities in specific organizational settings. Their work highlights the importance of jokes, humour and smut in creating workplace masculinities. This work is further developed by Gherardi in a study into blue collar work. She argues that:

> In traditional working-class culture, with its sharp gender segregation of occupational opportunities, workplace sexuality is part of a language game in which both women and men participate collectively ... Power, domination,

pleasure and resistance are intertwined in complex practices and elaborated into ambiguous cultural codes. (1995: 56)

Here power and powerlessness are not structural **facts**, embodied in men and women. Instead, they are discursive constructs. Through these language games, gender relations and power relations are negotiated, reproduced and sometimes changed.

Constructing gender at work

Choose a blue collar and a white collar work setting. Think about the ways in which artefacts (décor: pictures, calenders, bulletin boards, photos, dress codes etc. and humour) work to create particular versions of **femininity** and **masculinity**.

● How would you account for the relationship between these constructions of masculinity and femininity in terms of power/powerlessness?
● Are they the same in the different work settings you considered? How can you explain any similarities or differences?

Summary

In this chapter, we have considered the notion of gender as an on-going social process, constructed at the level of society, organization, interpersonal interaction and the individual. We have examined the historically separate but closely associated literatures on gender and language, and gender and organization, exploring points of overlap and convergence. We have acknowledged the contributions of those perspectives which see gender as one of a number of variables, subject to control and manipulation by management, which impact on organizational life, and those standpoint approaches which conceptualise gender in terms of control and subordination, power and deficiency. However, we have argued in particular for the usefulness of constructionist approaches that see gender as situated within specific communities of practice and wider structures of opportunity and constraint, reproduced, challenged and changed through interaction. Threading through our analysis are two central questions identified earlier:

● How do women and men at work talk, and how are they talked about?
● How are ideas about masculinity and femininity constituted within organizational talk?

We return to these questions to conclude our discussion.

With regard to the first question, in our view an analysis of specific linguistic features, including tag questions, interruption, use of expletives, adjectives, and lexical features, such as specialised vocabulary and nomenclature etc., can illuminate important aspects of gender and power relations within organizations. As such, they can provide useful hints into how men and women experience work, into sites of contestation, conciliation and transformation. However, taken as static facts, without a consideration of local contexts or of discursive practices within those contexts, such analyses can lead to reductionist, stereotypical understandings to which few of us would want to subscribe. Static analyses of linguistic form and content fail to account for the diversity or dynamism of organizational life, or to the complex ways in which individuals negotiate meaning in work settings. Thus, we have argued that it is not the **interruption** or the **tag question** per se which signifies male or female dominance, subservience or anything else. Rather, as we have explained elsewhere, our unit of analysis is this tag question – or this interruption – **in the context of the text in which it is situated**, discursive practice (including the processes by which meaning is produced, distributed and consumed) and wider social practice (Fairclough, 1992), and the interplay between these dimensions.

Thus, we come to the second question: what are the processes through which gender is constructed? As researchers we need to attend to how (and why) organizational actors constitute masculinity and femininity, discursively and through other sign systems, and the implications of these meanings for understanding and action. How is it, for example, that in Cohen's (1997) study into career transition a women solicitor came to view her firm as an inappropriate place for a solicitor who was also a mother, a place where the female secretary had a clearly defined role and status, but where the status of the female solicitor (especially when she was also a wife and mother) was marginal and precarious? To take this example further, how can we account for this respondent's comment that women sole practitioners were seen as "people who got out of unsuitable organizations and were brave and radical" while their male counterparts were seen as "being there because they can't get on in firms." Such questions are embedded within more fundamental questions about how the gender system is reproduced, maintained, resisted and changed. In our view, language is a good place to start to find answers. As Crawford says, "Attention to language practices can be a crucial way of unmasking the politics of everyday life" (1995: 180).

Recommended reading

Examining the relationship between language, gender and organization there are two distinct and very rich literatures to consider. As regards gender and language, Cameron's *Feminism and Linguistic Theory* (1985) is a classic text, while Crawford's more recent *Talking Difference: On Gender and Language* (1995), provides a very readable and thorough overview from a social constructionist perspective. Jennifer Coates' *Language and Gender: A Reader* (1998) is an edited collection, containing some key papers in the field, as well as rehearsing significant (sometimes quite heated) debates. Coates prefaces each section with a very clear and useful introduction. Deborah Tannen's work, as mentioned in the chapter, is notable for its huge public acclaim and for the debate it generated amongst feminist linguists. The book at the heart of the debate was *You Just Don't Understand: Men and Women in Conversation* (1990), while *Talking 9 to 5* (1994) focuses more exclusively on work settings. On a different tack, for a fascinating analysis of the commodification of talk, see Deborah Cameron's (2000) *Good to Talk*?

Turning to the literature on gender and organization, as noted in the introduction to this chapter, this is likewise a huge and diverse field. The texts which we have found most illuminating in relation to our interest in language include Alvesson and Billing's (1997) *Understanding Gender and Organizations* and Sylvia Gherardi's (1995) *Gender,*

Symbolism and Organizational Cultures. Also of note is Fiona Wilson's (1995) challenging and highly readable textbook, *Organizational Behaviour and Gender* and Susan Halford and Pauline Leonard's *Gender, Power and Organizations* (2001). Finally, edited collections *Gender, Culture and Organizational Change* (Itzin and Newman, 1995) and *Gender and Bureaucracy* (Savage and Witz, 1992) offer a diversity of empirical and theoretical papers and methodological approaches to the study of gender and organization.

CHAPTER EIGHT

Leadership and Language

The previous chapters have looked at how semiology can inform our understanding of how language works, and how language and meaning making are inextricably linked. We have seen how the processes of encoding and decoding work to generate particular meanings through a variety of symbolic codes, and combinations of codes, including metaphors, storytelling, discourse, culture and gendering through language. Now we want to situate this view in a key organizational function – that of leadership. We want to use the accounts we have generated so far to try to understand what we believe is a central process of leadership – the generation of new meanings and the reworking of old ones into new kinds of "common sense" (Bate, 1994: 257). We are interested, therefore, in looking at leadership as social influence and the linguistic processes that this involves. So, using the language of previous chapters, we want to look at the cultural literacies or **frames** that leaders draw on to tap into the meanings shared by their audience or followers.

Objectives

In this chapter we will:

- introduce the concept of leadership;
- explore the relevance of meaning making for leaders and followers;
- demonstrate how leaders codify some meanings and not others;
- explain the mechanics through which certain meanings are/can be achieved;
- investigate how leadership is performed through small talk; and
- explain and discuss hegemonic processes as part of the leader–follower relationship.

The leadership literature is vast, and much of it is confusing and contradictory

To illustrate, Grint (1997) observes that between 1986 and 1996 at least 17,800 management journal articles concerned with leadership were published. Grint wryly concludes that the time taken to read this staggering amount of writing means that "you can either be a leader or read all about them – but you cannot do both" (1997: 116). We will not rehearse all the arguments contained in this vast literature here, except to situate our own approach, because the central theories can be found in many OB texts (for example, Huczynski and Buchanan, 2001; Mullins, 1999). Rather, we will explore the idea that "leadership is a language game" (Pondy, 1978).

It is pertinent to say here that we are not proposing a new theory of leadership capable of eclipsing all others. Rather, we want to pick up on what others have said before about "deep leadership" (Grint, 1997: 115–145) being "a language game" (Pondy, 1978: 87), of "rhetorical crafting" (Conger, 1991: 32), involving the "necessary art of persuasion" (Conger, 1998: 84). We also want to show through the analysis of examples of leaders' texts how that is achieved. But first we need to situate our approach in the leadership literature.

What is leadership?

There is very little agreement on precisely what leadership is, how or whether it can be learnt by people, or even whether or not it is important (Yukl, 1989). Competing theories abound. We can find great "men" theories, trait theories, exchange theories, behavioural theories, person-situation theories, and perceptual and cognitive theories. There is little consensus about what makes an effective leader in the literature. We have found this lack of consensus echoed in our many debates with students about which leadership theories (if any) reflect or resonate with their own experience. But leadership continues to pervade our ideas about how organizations function, and most writers agree that it involves processes or acts of achieving change through others. It is not simply about the occupation of formal leadership roles in organizations (Hosking, 1997; Knights and Wilmott, 1992). The leadership function, whether formal or informal, is about acting as a bridge for followers between old and new, past and future, linking strategic direction with individual goals (Lilley and Platt, 1997). Clearly then, leadership involves followers as well as leaders, although this dynamic aspect was not recognised until long after the first leadership theories had been established. The question is how is this process of influence or persuasion achieved.

Leaders and followers

1 Think of a time when you think you were influenced or persuaded by someone to do something. What were the factors that persuaded you? How can you explain why you were persuaded?

2 Think of a time when someone tried to influence or persuade you to do something, but you didn't. Why weren't you persuaded? How can you explain why you weren't?

3 Why was the first person more persuasive than the second? How do you account for this?

Conventional and most contemporary theories of leadership focus on what Pondy (1978) has called leadership's surface structures, or what Oswick et al. (1997) refer to as **behavioural action** or **doing**. They tend not to discuss discursive activity or meaning making in any depth. Any standard organizational behaviour text will include a review of these theories, some of which focus on the personality, social, physical or intellectual traits that differentiate 'natural' leaders from non-leaders. These theories are firmly established on common sense assumptions about human character or personality. They tend to focus on universal traits such as intelligence, self-confidence, energy-activity and task-relevant knowledge, and these recur in the literature with some consistency (Grint, 1997). Similarly, a standard organizational behaviour text will include some discussion of leadership styles – usually confined to descriptions of democratic, autocratic or laissez-faire leader **behaviours.** A standard text will also include some discussion of the contingency theories that try to take a more complex approach to the situational aspects of leadership, rather than promoting the idea that there is one best way to lead. In addition, a standard text is also likely to cover more recent ideas such as visionary, charismatic or transformational approaches to leadership.

Despite this plethora of theories, many commentators believe that "the dynamics of leadership is still very much a puzzle" (Kets de Vries, 1991: 752). We believe that this is (in part at least) because theories focus little or not at all on the discursive aspect of leadership, or its deep structure as Pondy (1978) calls it. This deep structure, or discursive aspect, is the key to understanding how leaders make meaning for others. Even though some theories **imply** that language is important in leadership activity – how else can one be visionary, for example? – few writers explore how language functions in this process. So, although the theories that you are likely to come across in standard texts are premised on the idea that leadership is about achieving change through others, they generally fail to acknowledge the central role of language in that process.

Why is this, when even management gurus such as Tom Peters forcefully argue that "A leader has only his or her language … as a 'tool'. To say that language is everything for the leader is not overstatement. It is fact" (cited in Caroselli, 2000: 12). Although we are clearly using this quote from Tom Peters to persuade the reader (a necessary function of this kind of text), we are not certain that Peters would agree with our fundamental premise that leadership functions can only be operationalized through discursive activity. But, in the spirit of this book we go further to say, that language creates the world as well as discovering it, and we offer the view that effective leaders create and discover the world for their followers. Whether in formal or informal positions in organizations, those who act as leaders are the meaning makers in organizations, framing the future and making it meaningful for others.

We start then from the premise that leaders, like the rest of us "talk things into being" (Oswick et al., 1997) – that what counts as leadership is constructed through accounts that are provided of a leader's actions by others and themselves. Most leadership theories start from the essentialist premise that leaders, whether born or taught, embody qualities within themselves that can predominate in a given situation (Grint, 1997). The inevitable effect of this approach is to presume that leadership resides only in the domain of the leader, and not the follower, or the interaction between the two. From this perspective followers don't matter – what matters is choosing the right person with the right leadership qualities for a given situation. We take issue with this. **We see leadership not as an individual activity but as a social or collective phenomenon.** To begin to understand it, we need to focus on the way meanings are constructed and the role of language in this process. What is it that makes some accounts persuasive, and capable of capturing the imagination and commitment of followers?

From our perspective the central questions about leadership are:

1 Why do some leaders appear able to produce more persuasive accounts that followers accept?
2 What is it about these accounts that appear to make them more persuasive than others?

Approaches to leadership and language

Some writers have looked at the questions we raise above and come up with ideas and concepts to explain what it is that leaders do (or more often say) to make them persuasive to their followers. Bate (1994), for example, from his extensive work with the then British Rail, conceptualises five dimensions of leadership: **the aesthetic**, **the political**, **the ethical**, **the action** and **the formative**. Bate claims that the first two of these dimensions contain the "biggest difference" to conventional leadership perspectives and present the "greatest challenge" for leaders (1994: 245). These focus almost exclusively on the leader's ability to move people emotionally through creating new symbolic meanings, and communicating these meanings effectively.

Leaders as image makers and word merchants

Bate (1994) describes the first two dimensions of leadership respectively as **image-makers** and **word merchants** (1994: 257). Clearly, the effectiveness of a leader as an image-maker or a word merchant must depend to a large part on their language ability, on their ability to develop new and exciting ideas and have these accepted by their followers. This is not simply about developing logical, persistent or objectively rational arguments. Rather it is about creating and codifying new meanings that connect or resonate with people's emotional, psychological and intellectual experience. These then become embodied in collective speech acts, which everybody accepts and understands, and which become established as a new kind of common sense.

But we don't want to paint a simplistic picture here of leaders being able to unproblematically influence and persuade naive followers simply by using words which pull the heart strings, or touch the relevant psychological or intellectual chords. The language must resonate closely with people's experiences and expectations, and make connections between events and ideas that echo the listeners' beliefs about truth. Otherwise, emotive, stimulating and creative language is unlikely to move people to action, or be unconditionally accepted as representing reality. Indeed, as Fairclough points out, in his treatise on the language of New Labour, it is dangerous to contrive to "manipulate language to control public perception" in case it is seen as "mere words, empty rhetoric" (2000: ix). The language must combine with other factors for a leader to move followers to action.

Conger (1998) develops these ideas when he talks about effective persuasion involving four essential steps. First, effective persuaders establish credibility, usually via their expertise and their relationships with others. Second, they frame their goals in a way that identifies common ground with those they intend to persuade; the cultural literacy that we talked about in Chapter 5. Third, they reinforce their positions with vivid and emotive language, including compelling evidence. Finally, through these three steps they fulfil the fourth criteria of connecting emotionally with their audience. Conger's approach reflects Pondy's belief that a central ability of effective leaders is to make activity meaningful for others, and to put that into words, so that the meaning of what the group is doing becomes accepted as a social fact (Pondy, 1978). Visions and missions may be said to be the stuff of organizational success, but not if they hold little meaning for people who work in the organization. This often entails profound ideas being restated in familiar language that is significant for large numbers of people.

Profound ideas made simple

We can no longer wait for the storm to pass. We must learn to work in the rain. (Peter Silas)

We put all our eggs in our workplace basket and wonder why they get scrambled. (Robert Rosner)

- What ideas are these two leaders trying to communicate?
- Why do you think they chose these particular words?
- Why does this language seem to communicate these ideas effectively?

From this perspective, the translation of complex ideas into simple, meaningful and significant texts that resonate with people's cultural literacy becomes a key leadership skill. In the next section, we use Conger's (1991) dual classification of contextual frames and rhetorical techniques to explore these issues in more depth, using examples from texts to demonstrate how this works in practice.

Analytical framework

Conger's dual categorisation of framing (see Chapter 5) and rhetorical techniques can help us to examine the idea that, "there is a language of leadership that can be learned by using certain techniques and practices" (Conger, 1991: 32). First we examine the concept of framing as a useful device to help us understand how leaders embed ideas in language that connect with the listener's emotional, psychological and intellectual value set. Next we look at the specific rhetorical techniques employed in the contextual frame, such as pronoun use, metaphors (see Chapter 3), stories (see Chapter 4) and specific linguistic devices such as alliteration.

Framing

Framing is the way that leaders describe the present or future purpose of the group or organization. It is the contextual frame in which specific rhetorical techniques are employed. The frame provides the map for interpreting action, by telling followers what reality looks like and how things are, or will be. Framing a task in a particular way influences our perceptions of its validity and its potential outcomes. For example, one can frame a given difficult situation as a problem or as an opportunity, each of which connotes different mind sets and suggests different behaviours.

Different ways of framing the same issue

We can demonstrate the concept of framing through one of our own research projects, in which GPs (general practitioners) were asked to volunteer to join a programme aimed at changing their own prescribing habits (Musson, 1996). This was a notoriously difficult thing to do and many government initiatives, in the form of guidelines couched in dry, objective and unemotional language, had previously failed to bring about this change. Furthermore, the GPs were aware that this local project would actually cost them time and money to implement, and that there was no financial reward for doing the work. In sum, the message was all that the small research team had to persuade GPs to join, and previous messages (that is, guidelines) had singularly failed. The team concluded that the way the message was framed was crucial to securing their involvement. Several factors emerged as central to the framing of the project:

1 The leader of the project was a GP – so the message was framed as dialogue from one professional to another about what constituted best clinical practice. This appealed to the GPs' sense of developing professional identity.
2 A few enthusiastic and innovative GPs were involved from the beginning, so it was possible to frame the project as an innovators' network from the start.
3 The project literature was couched in language that acknowledged the hectic workload of general practice and provided helpful, if very simple, tips on how to do the necessary tasks in the most efficient and effective way. Innovation became easy to do.
4 Soon it was possible to frame the project as involving 50 per cent of the area's practices and at this point GPs were actively volunteering their practices to join this professional community. The practices outside of the project were considered by other GPs to be uninterested in innovation and therefore indifferent to developing better patient care.
5 The rational and unemotional language of guidelines had previously failed to frame the objectives and outcomes in ways that appealed to the GPs' professional identity and sense of community. Neither did these guidelines acknowledge the difficulties of doing innovative work in high-pressure environments.

Framing then, is about being culturally literate and using this cultural literacy to interpret reality for others, to motivate and inspire a group or an organization about its present or future state. An example from the business world used by Conger (1991: 33) is Steven Jobs talking to staff about the future of his then new computer company, *NEXT*. Jobs constructed and framed the strategic goal of the company as, "revolutionising the educational system of a nation." He did not frame the strategy in the more common language (for this genre – see Chapter 5) of increasing the number of computers sold, or enhancing computer specifications, or expanding into different markets, or achieving a certain annual growth rate. Instead, Jobs framed the strategic goal of the company as an activity that would reform the whole of the US educational system. This societal contribution frame, capable of changing the educational landscape, was designed to encourage and inspire the *NEXT* workers to greater levels of organizational achievement (Conger, 1991).

Values and beliefs underpin meaningful framing

For a frame to be successful, it must be made up of values and beliefs, or **mechanical guts** (Conger, 1991: 34) that connect with the listeners' understanding, their own cultural literacy. Amplifying certain values in this way means that the interpretation of an issue, event or process comes to be seen as an extension of these values. A classic and distinctive example is Martin Luther King's "I have a dream" speech in which values and beliefs relevant to white Americans underpinned King's language about the plight of black Americans.

Jeff Bezos at Amazon.com framed his vision for *Amazon* as an extension of his idealism about customer culture and family values. Describing his vision for *Amazon*, he compares the company to Sony and the need to have a:

> mission that's bigger than ourselves ... [Sony] wanted to make Japan synonymous with quality rather than cheap copies. And they succeeded brilliantly. Our mission is to create a new level of expectation in customers, which will cause all companies to raise their level. And if we can do that, that would be truly meaningful. That'll be something we can tell our grandchildren about. That's the difference between a mission and a job. If it's a job, then you won't have stories to tell your grandchildren. (*Observer Magazine*, 11.2.2001)

Here Bezos is not talking simply about his company selling more consumer goods, as we might expect. Rather, he frames the mission around the desire to raise customer service expectations throughout the world (an obviously desirable state – who could argue with such a view?). What is more, he couches this in the symbolic frame of stories (see Chapter 4) worthy of being passed down through family generations – something to be proud of and, crucially, the defining characteristic between just a job and a mission. In this way, he very effectively links family traditions and values with ideas about how best to do business. In this extract, the two spheres of activity are linked symbolically and practically. We must note here though, that we are not suggesting that rhetorical skills can ever be a panacea for material business problems.

Also, we cannot know whether leaders are purposeful in these linguistic activities, or even whether they understand the impact of their linguistic choices. Neither can we know for certain how others receive their language. But we do know that an increasing number of writers attach central importance to a leader's communicative ability (Argyris and Schön, 1978; Kotter, 1982; Weick, 1995). Others see a constructionist approach as the key to understanding how a leader's ideals might persuade others (Grint, 1997; Watson, 2001b).

The framing of the leader's message, or the interpretation of the organization's purpose or mission, including the attendant values and beliefs, is the first step in the effective communication of meaning. But in a way this is only the skeleton or framework upon which the message rests. A critical distinguishing factor between a message being successfully or unsuccessfully remembered and endorsed involves the specific rhetorical techniques employed by the speaker. These provide the expressive flesh for the strategic frame. In the next section we look more closely at some of these techniques and at the way they have been employed by some leaders.

Rhetorical techniques

Rhetorical techniques provide the vivid supporting linguistic evidence that validates the frame of the message. These techniques usually generate symbolic rather than literal meanings, in much the same way that framing (re)produces the values and beliefs under-pinning the strategy. Some of these techniques have been discussed in more depth in other chapters – see, for example, Chapter 3 on the role of metaphor and Chapter 4 on storytelling. But we briefly discuss below what we take to be the major rhetorical tech-niques used by leaders that can enable the symbolic content of their message to have a profound impact.

Pronouns   First, we look at how pronouns are used to shed light on how collective identities are constructed, responsibility attributed and adversarial relationships produced and maintained.

Consider the following three sentences:

It has been found necessary to increase interest rates
We have found it necessary to increase interest rates
I have found it necessary to increase interest rates

- Who is **it** in the first sentence and what does using the term **it** achieve?
- What meaning does the pronoun **we** in the second example generate?
- What meaning is generated by the pronoun **I** in the last example?

Clearly, using the pronoun **I** can have only one meaning. The person making the state-ment is attributing the thought, belief or action to themselves and taking responsibility for this. The pronoun **we** can be used to dilute this sense of accountability, since some-times it is not possible to tell who **we** is without more detail. In instances where a leader may wish to avoid individual responsibility but where there is no group identity to mask this, speakers may have to resort to other linguistic forms such as hiding behind the organizational or institutional role, as Richard Nixon was said to do in the Watergate affair (see the feature below).

The institutional voice – or transforming the topic

Lerman conducted an analysis of interviews carried out with President Nixon during the Watergate scandal. She found that whenever the topic became "too difficult for Nixon to explain" he would "transform" the conversation onto another plane, and talk about "The President" rather than "I." Lerman argued that this strategy allowed Nixon to disassociate himself from the train of events (Lerman, 1985).

We the authors

We write throughout this book as **we**, not as Laurie, or Susanne, or Gill, or even **I** even though we each took specific responsibility for writing individual chapters.

● Why should this be the case?
● What do we achieve by doing so?

The pronoun **we** can be used to produce a collective rather than singular identity, to imbue a statement or a claim with solidarity. In his book entitled *New Labour, New Language*? Norman Fairclough (2000) looks at how **we** is apparently used in two very different ways in New Labour discourse. The first **we** is used to refer exclusively to the Labour Government – "we are committed to one-nation politics." The second **we** is used to refer inclusively to the British people as a whole – "we must be the best" (2000: 35). Fairclough notes though, that the meanings attributed to the different "we's are often highly ambiguous, so that it is sometimes very difficult to know whether the we is meant inclusively or exclusively" (2000: 36). He argues that this ambivalence is "politically advantageous for a government that wants to represent itself as speaking for a whole nation ... in a divided society" (2000: 36/7). The point is that in both instances **we** (or **us**) generates a collective identity and fosters a sense of community. But, as we pointed out in Chapter 2, meanings are always relational, and **we** makes no real sense unless it automatically generates an idea of **them** – in other words, the **not us** people. Pronouns such as **we** or **us** generate a sense of collective **in-group** identity, precisely because they draw on subliminal (and sometimes not so subliminal) ideas about **them**. Symbolic meanings about **us** and **not us** (or **them**) are central to group identities and can be used by leaders to try to generate commitment and unity to the collective identity.

Them and us – us and them

In Margaret Thatcher's speech to the Conservative Party after the Falklands Invasion she successfully uses **us/we** and **them** to differentiate between:

British people [us] who had to be threatened by foreign soldiers [them] and British territory had to be invaded and then – why then – the response was incomparable. Yet why does it need a war to bring out our qualities and reassert our pride? Why do we have to be invaded before we throw aside our selfish aims and begin to work together as only we can work and achieve as only we can achieve?

But less than 500 words further in to her speech, the **us** and **them** has changed to denote the British people [still us] and the Aslef leaders [now them] a "tiny group who decided to use its undoubted power for what? – to delay Britain's recovery, which all our people long to see." Clearly, according to Margaret Thatcher, the Aslef leaders do not represent their workers and are not part of **all our people**, but belong to that other group of **them**. The Aslef workers are at once succinctly and creatively aligned with Argentinean invaders, and therefore alienated from the people they represent and the wider British workforce. (See Barnett and Busby, 1982 for a complete transcript of this speech.)

Pronouns, then, create identities, structure meanings and (re)produce symbolic relationships.

The importance of names   Similarly, the names we give to objects, events, processes and people influence the way we think about them. Names encode certain attributes, values and ideas; they take control of the world in a particular way. This can be clearly seen in the oft-quoted examples of **terrorist** and **freedom fighter** being used to denote the same person, but from different meaning spaces. The act of naming is an act of taking dominance of the world, it provides a point of identity. But it is not enough to assume that others will decode – make meaning about names – in exactly the same way as the encoder anticipated, as we pointed out in previous chapters and Chapter 2 specifically. The example below shows how the decoding process can be different to what was intended.

The naming of companies

Jeff Bezos who founded Amazon.com wanted to call the company Abracadabra.com to reflect the idea that customers could expect magical service, but his lawyer had heard this over the phone as 'cadaver.com,' after which it didn't seem like such a good idea.

(Continued)

- Why not?
- Do you think that Amazon.com would have been more or less successful as Abracadabra.com?

Leaders might create different identities for employees simply by naming them differently, providing of course that the employees share that view of themselves. For example, employees who think of themselves as handbag makers are different to those who consider themselves leather crafters who happen to make handbags. The specificity of the handbag makers' point of identity restricts their horizons as well as their employers. They are less likely to be able to adapt to changes in the marketplace than those handbag makers who think of themselves as leather crafters. This is why some organizations pay close attention to the language they use in everyday discourse. *Xerox*, for instance, defines itself as *The Document Company*. Presumably a document company can build the machinery to make photocopies, but it is not conceptually restricted to do so. Increasing the variety, complexity and subtlety of the language has the potential to change the way employees think about what they do.

Leaders constructing employees

The following excerpts were all taken from the texts of chairman's statements in company reports in an article by Gowler and Legge (1986).

1 "high opinion of the calibre" – "spirit and commitment" – "high morale and determination" – "war time spirit"
2 "employees ... working together represent a national asset" – "staff ... help to develop and direct community projects"
3 "plan to cut back manned steel-making capacity" – "our workforce has been slimmed"
4 "reduction in the number of employees ... causes personal suffering"
5 "local employees are led astray by leaders of external bodies"

- Gowler and Legge identified several different images of employees. Amongst these were employee as public servant, employee as victim, employee as hero, employee as statistic and potential liability, the invisible employee and employee as public servant.
- Can you match any of the statements to the images?
- Why are you able to do this?

Metaphors   We have already seen in Chapter 3 how the metaphors that people use structure certain meanings, how they emphasise certain aspects of a particular domain and shroud other features.

Codifying meanings through metaphors

In the presidential war on bureaucracy in the US, President Carter's Aide described career bureaucrats as "buried in the bowels of democracy." The response from the President of the American Society for Public Administration [a sort of trade union for career bureaucrats in the US] was, "Now I am not a doctor but I know a four letter word for what is typically buried in bowels."

- Try to think of an alternative decoding of the statement made by Carter's Aide.
- Is it actually possible to think of a positive meaning? If not, why not?

Adapted from Gowler and Legge (1986)

Certain metaphors seem to appear more often than others in the talk of leaders. These include metaphors about the family, winning against all odds as in the David and Goliath story and religious symbolism (see discussion of myth in Chapter 2). The first of these is very prevalent in the talk and writing of Anita Roddick (1991). For example, "From the start we ran the company as if we were all one big extended family," "you have to be a mother figure" and "*Ben and Jerry's* ice cream company of Vermont, which is like a brother to *The Body Shop*" (1991: 17) is representative of Roddick's language drawing on metaphors and concepts of the family. These comments symbolically place the organization in the family domain, and draw on the cultural values embodied in family relationships to describe the organization and the way it is led.

In the same vein, and as Conger (1991) notes, Lee Iaccoca, the then Chief Executive of *Chrysler*, in his successful call for government loans to help *Chrysler* in its turnaround, drew on the metaphor of *Chrysler* being "an amalgam of little guys" rather than a multi-million pound company. This metaphor echoes the David and Goliath theme, but he then draws an analogy to the family –

> it wasn't the loans that saved us ... it was the hundreds of millions of dollars given up by everybody involved. It was like a family getting together and saying 'We've got a loan from our rich uncle and now we're going to prove that we can pay him back.' (Conger, 1991: 39)

In all, these metaphors appeal to fundamental American beliefs about the sanctity of small business, individualism, the family and free enterprise. These symbolic messages are confirmed when Iaccoca goes on to ask, "Would free enterprise really be saved if Chrysler failed?" (Conger, 1991: 39).

Mary Kay Ash, founder of an American based cosmetics company, draws upon Christian values as a central metaphor for her company's mission. But she too brings in ideas about family values and attendant beliefs, in her assertion that, "Our company motto is: God first, family second, business third." Note that business is last, not first as you might expect, in this tripartite list. Whether this reflects reality or not is of course open to question. But as Conger (1991) notes, Mary Kay Ash continually draws links to these values – even to the most mundane of company activities – linking the inability of the

Romans to conquer Christians because of their weekly meetings to weekly unit meetings held in the company.

The kind of metaphors and analogies described above, which promote themes about the family, the big guy/little guy struggle, and religious beliefs, work because the listener or reader can immediately recognise and identify with such culturally ingrained values and beliefs. They immediately engage the listener or reader in the common place, but nevertheless highly symbolic, arena of family relationships, religious idealism and struggling against the odds. These themes make such cultural sense to most people that they would not dream of challenging the implicit assumptions on which they are based. They are therefore very powerful symbolic mechanisms with which to engage an audience emotionally and intellectually.

Metaphors in use

1 Winston Churchill coined a famous metaphor when he described the barrier separating Eastern Europe from Western Europe as "an iron curtain."
2 Margaret Thatcher was famously described as "an iron fist in a velvet glove."
3 Ann Morrison talked about "the glass ceiling."

- Why do you think these metaphors work so well?
- What is it about them that made them instantly effective?
- Why do people continue to use them?

Some metaphoric phrases are very short, consisting of only two or three words, as in the box above, whilst others are woven into longer texts such as stories. We have looked at how stories work to convey certain meanings in Chapter 4. You could say that some of the metaphors that we have talked about in this section from the talk of Anita Roddick, Lee Iaccoca and Mary Kay Ash were part of longer stories. But below we look specifically at one or two stories that demonstrate how leaders use stories to convey vividly the values and behaviours that they want to promote in their organizations.

Stories Stories convey certain attitudes and values and are an effective and persuasive way of communicating ideas about how people in an organization can (and should) make sense and behave. By reconstructing events and actions into a sequential plot we make sense of organizational life – or perhaps more accurately, that organizational sense is made for us by stories which become legends in a given organization. Leaders often use stories to show employees how best to think, feel and behave in the organization, and equally importantly how **not** to think, feel or behave. This has been described as an attempt to manage the hearts and minds of employees (Kunda, 1992).

In her book, *Body And Soul*, Anita Roddick (1991) recounts the story of how in the very early days of what was to become *The Body Shop* empire, she and her husband, Gordon, met with bankers to try to persuade them to finance the building of a new warehouse and office complex. They met around the "single table" in *The Body Shop* office, which was simply a partitioned section of the "bursting at the seams" warehouse, to demonstrate the problems of space and give the bankers a presentation about the company. In the middle of this rather formal and very serious event:

> The door burst open and in walked my mum, heaving an enormous laundry basket. She banged it down on the table and proceeded to fold clothing in front of us loudly complaining about the state of Gordon's shirts and the number of buttons that she now had to sew on. Gordon and I took one look at the faces of the Bankers, which were now frozen with embarrassment, and started to shriek with laughter. They could not understand what we found so funny. (1991: 99)

By simply recounting this story Roddick clearly articulates several cultural values of the organization: the family orientation and values, freedom of speech, value of humour and lack of formal procedures and hierarchy, to name a few. These values, embodied in the story, tell people outside the organization what it is like to work in it, and perhaps more importantly, tell employees about the central values that they are expected to adopt at work.

Of course, this story may not be interpreted in the monolithic way that we have implied here, a point that is often ignored in the leadership literature. People are active makers of meaning, not passive receivers, so there may be other polyphonic interpretations that are equally meaningful. But to suggest that all interpretations are equally powerful is to ignore the power relationships that exist in organizations. Furthermore, there may be other stories, or behaviours, whose central message conflicts with the values manifest in a particular story promulgated by a leader.

The power of stories

This story, about the leader of an organization who walked on the table, was told to us by a student in an MBA class. Apparently, at a time when the Scandinavian company was desperately in need of an injection of cash to finance a new and innovative product, this man had gone to a meeting with financial backers to persuade them to put money into the company. The amount he was asking for was huge and, after a long and protracted discussion, the financiers declared themselves unable to fund the project – "It simply cannot be done," they announced. The leader, who was also the founder and at that time was at least 80 years old, rose from the table in complete silence, took off his shoes and socks, climbed onto a chair and onto the long board table, and proceeded to walk the full length of the table twice. He then, still in complete silence, got down from the table onto the chair, sat down and replaced his shoes and socks. He then broke the rather tense silence by saying simply, "anything can be done," at which point the financiers changed their minds and backed the project. This story was always told to new recruits in the organization during their induction.

- What message does this story convey?
- Do you think it is true? Does it matter if it isn't?
- How would you characterise the organization in this story?

In *Ikea*, the story of the founder, Ingvar Kamprad, a very poor boy growing up in Sweden, who, due to his own entrepreneurial efforts, becomes the leader of an international company, works as a unifying symbol, which (hopefully) integrates and holds people together within the global company. As Salzer-Mörling (1998) notes, within the *Ikea* world the saga is widely spread. It ranges from very lengthy detailed stories that tell of the complexities, setbacks and utter determination of Kamprad, recounted in training sessions and a published booklet, to short, simply stated informal versions, such as, "You know, Ikea is so big today that it all started by him selling matches" (Salzer-Mörling, 1998: 113). Sharing this common understanding, even via the very brief shorthand version of "His way!" (Boje, 1995: 1000), is part of the collective *Ikea* world. The story shows how business is to be done, effort expended and how rags to riches can become reality, even in today's corporate world.

Stories then, provide a framework in which people can make sense of their worlds. People construct these narrative accounts as part of the sense making process. In fact, some writers would argue that we cannot make sense without stories (Baumeister and Newman, 1994). Leaders in organizations may or may not engage in the storytelling process in a conscious attempt to manipulate their employees, but it seems to be the case that successful leaders tend to be effective at telling stories which connect with people's everyday experiences and resonate with their values and beliefs (Conger, 1991).

Leaders who can persuade also seem able to develop their skill – or maybe the skill is 'natural' to them – in other rhetorical techniques such as repetition, rhythm and alliteration. We look briefly at these in the next section.

Other rhetorical techniques

In this section we highlight some of the other factors that make speech and writing more effective in holding an audience's attention and being remembered – both of which are important aspects of the meaning making process.

Alliteration is where two or more adjacent words or syllables begin with the same consonant. This linguistic device gives more strength and resonance to what is being said. Politicians often use this to strengthen the point they are making – "The Falklands Factor" (Margaret Thatcher), "You can't play politics with people's jobs" (Neil Kinnock) – but so do business leaders – "Speed, simplicity, and self confidence" (Jack Welch, CEO of *General Electric*), "the last force for freedom" (Steven Jobs at *NEXT*). The effect of the alliteration is to hammer home the point being made much more forcefully.

Repetition and Rhythm, along with alliteration, tend to strengthen the force of what is being said or written, and make a stronger claim for attention. They also ensure more accurate recall of the spoken word. Martin Luther King was a master of repetition and rhythm as his "I have a dream" speech demonstrates. He begins seven consecutive sentences with the progressively louder phrase, "Let freedom ring" and finishes the seventh sentence with the same phrase. As Conger notes, this creates a "song-like crescendo much like the combination of a symphony and a Negro spiritual" (1991: 42). This not only captivates his audience, maximising attention, but it also builds up emotional commitment to the message.

In the previous sections we have largely looked at examples taken from the talk of official leaders in organizations, usually operating in formal situations in their formal roles. We have noted that the corporate saga or story tends to be a monologue, or universalising story (Salzer-Mörling, 1998). We want to turn now to the more informal aspects of organizational life and look more specifically at small talk, or informal talk, and the power inherent in such talk to reflect, constitute and develop shared understandings of the organizational world.

Leadership and small talk

We have left this section until last for two reasons. First, we think that this is a neglected area in the arena of meaning making and managerial leadership, both empirically and theoretically (with a few exceptions that we note later). Secondly, we think that despite all the emphasis on the formal aspects of leadership, it is probably in the small talk arena that real leadership influence prevails.

Small talk carries people's emotions, shapes their ambitions and promotes or disparages them (Silverman and Jones, 1976). It is here, in this informal arena, in these kinds of "corridor" conversations that most ideals, norms and rules emerge and are fostered and circulated throughout organizations (Gustafsson, 1994 cited in Sjostrand et al., 2000: 8), stabilising the expectations of organizational members. This is why Boden (1994) describes small talk and informal talk as the "life-blood" of organizations. Through this kind of fragmented but continuous talk, a shared construction emerges about what has happened in the past, what is currently happening and what will happen in the future (Watson, 2001b). This intersubjective talk evolves into a shared "descriptive sediment" (2001b: 11) that describes the organization's past, present and future.

Sederberg (1984) suggests that the people who can describe and define circumstances in ways that are convincing for others, so that others accept this as the way things have been, are, or will be, are the real leaders in organizations. Clearly, people in power positions usually have the right to talk and produce texts that provide shared meanings, and these are often managerial leaders. But anybody who can influence the organizational agenda by directing and deciding what gets talked about, when and how, also possesses this power. In some cases small talk becomes public talk, supporting and confirming the formal structures of the organization. But sometimes the opposite is true, and small talk becomes the mechanism through which formal talk is challenged and subverted, even changed and revised.

Arenas of small talk

The following are a few arenas in which we have found instances of small talk about issues, situations, individuals and processes that have impacted significantly on formal organizational agendas:

1 Over coffee or at the bar.
2 During a car journey.
3 At the local gym.
4 On the golf course.
5 During social meals outside of work situations.

(Continued)

- Can you think of other arenas where this might happen?
- Who is likely to have access to these arenas?
- Who is likely to be excluded?
- What does this say about formal leadership and decision making in organizations?

As Sjostrand et al. (2001) point out, understanding the significance of small talk invites us to explore in more depth the different arenas where leadership is informally constructed, (re)produced and exercised (2001: 12), and the discursive mechanisms through which this is achieved. Watson (2001b) did this to great effect, and highlighted the chaotic and often contradictory worlds of managers and leaders, and the central role of small talk in their working lives. Theorising managerial leadership then, should include analysis of discursive activity – formal and informal – recognising that small talk exists everywhere and in all organizations. Organizations are arenas of diverse activities, behaviours and understandings, and it may be in the process of small talk that norms are formed and used to navigate these colliding, overlapping and sometimes contradictory processes and practices of meaning making.

Leadership, meaning making and hegemony

We conclude this chapter with some discussion about the **hegemonic processes** that go towards making a leader effective, capable of shaping and framing the prevailing discourses of an organization in a way that promotes particular attitudes and behaviours, which people **adopt willingly**. We have talked earlier about the potential for different meanings to be made by followers who are not passive receivers of information, but make meaning for themselves. What is it then that persuades followers? Why is it that some leaders, formal or otherwise, are able to convince others of their views; that they have the right to make the rules and that these rules are, ultimately, in the best interest of the followers. Gramsci (1986) called these **processes of hegemony** – the ability of some groups (or individuals) – usually those with the greatest economic or cultural capital in an organization – to have a greater opportunity to promote their ideas to a wider audience, and to convince those people to accept their claim to power. Discursive ability is a central part of that cultural capital and must therefore play a vital role in the process.

Hegemony

The central point to Antonio Gramsci's (1986) notion of **hegemony** is that people are not normally forced to concede power or control to another group or groups; rather, they are convinced that their best interests will be served by that other group being in power, or that one group is naturally superior (as in the "great men" theories of leadership, for example). They become convinced that:

- The dominant group's interests are the same as their interests; or
- It is in their interest for the dominant group to be in power; or
- The dominant group deserves to rule because of their 'natural' superiority.

Gramsci put forward the view that hegemony is produced and reproduced through cultural institutions, such as the education system, religious groups or the family. People acquire **cultural identities** through these institutions, some of which are more powerful than others, and these cultural identities carry with them certain norms of behaviour. People's identities are 'produced' by these hegemonic processes, which are, in turn, (re)produced in the talk in and around these institutions.

Key question

Is an effective leader one that can engage in processes that re(produce) **hegemony**? That is, the willing acceptance of a person or a group's ideological beliefs as being the same as or fitting with one's own so that these beliefs become representative of the **main forces which make up the organization and embodied in its routines and practices**.

A political example of hegemonic processes in action might be Margaret Thatcher and her talk about the British economy in terms of housekeeping and the money in her purse – "I cannot spend more on my housekeeping than I have in my purse." This statement works because everybody can understand this common sense view of personal financial management BUT it also allows the principles of not spending more than you have in your purse to become embodied in the economic strategy of the UK.

- Why does this make such common (cultural) sense?
- Why might it not make economic sense?
- Do you think that a male leader would have/could have used such a metaphor so effectively? If not, why not?

In fact, Gramsci (1986) argues that hegemonic processes work precisely because people are not usually **forced** to concede power or control to another group, rather that they believe that their own interests are best served by that other group being in power, or that the other group is naturally superior. In either of these scenarios, discursive ability, or the ability to construct new kinds of common sense, must account for some of that belief, and must therefore be essential to effective leadership.

But perhaps more importantly, the beliefs and values embedded in the talk of leaders come to be seen as the 'right' (and only) way to think, feel and behave in the organization. Furthermore, they come to represent the organization, and become embodied in the activity of the organization, so that they form the base from which all organizational processes and practices come to be judged. During the last decade or so, leaders in organizations may have come to rely more heavily on hegemonic processes because of the emphasis on empowerment, both in the literature and in practice. If leaders have lost some of the material controls that used to prevail in organizations (because of the cuts in middle management as a result of down sizing, for example), then these more subtle forms of control, embodied in hegemonic talk, might be even more central to a leader's ability to maintain power and, ultimately, control.

Summary

In this chapter we have used the context of leadership to discuss concepts examined in previous chapters about the role of language in meaning making. We have briefly reviewed past and current theories about leadership, and put forward the view that effective leadership involves the management of meaning. We have demonstrated how leaders make meaning through discursive activity, arguing that leadership is a language game. Specifically, we have used examples from the texts of formal leaders in the business and political arenas, to explore how leaders might frame their talk about an organization's past, present and future state in a way that can make it meaningful for others. We have also provided examples from the texts of leaders to situate a variety of rhetorical techniques such as story telling, pronoun use and metaphoric language, to show how leaders might connect with and persuade others, through and in their talk. In addition, we have cautioned against the idea that followers are passive receivers of information. Rather, we have tried to show how followers might decode a leader's texts according to some central cultural values. But of course, the decoding process might take many forms, as we have highlighted in Chapter 2.

Finally, we introduced the view that small talk might be the lifeblood of an organization, to highlight the idea that leaders may be found in many areas of the organization, and not simply those people occupying the formal leadership roles. In line with this view, we put forward the idea that successful leaders are those people who engage others in hegemonic processes, persuading them of their 'right' to lead, the 'fit' of their ideas with their own, and having those ideas form the bedrock of organizational processes and practices. We have highlighted the role of discursive activity in that process.

Recommended reading

There are several key texts that talk about leadership and social constructionism. Keith Grint argues in *Fuzzy Management: Contemporary Ideas and Practices at Work* (1997) that it is leadership processes and practices that are critical, not leadership roles, and that leadership is systematically present throughout the organization, and not just at the top of the hierarchy. Grint argues forcefully that to understand this "deep leadership" we need to take a constructionist approach. Paul Bate directly addresses the relationship between leadership and language in his book *Strategies for Cultural Change* (1994). He provides a very stimulating debate and an interesting read about the nature of leadership and language, using data from his considerable work with the then British Rail management.

Focusing more on people in formal leadership roles, Pondy (1978) wrote a seminal text on leadership and language. His chapter, "Leadership is a Language Game," in M.W. McCall and M.M. Lombardo (eds), *Leadership: Where Else Can We Go?*, looks at how leaders establish credibility through language, and is a very interesting and informative read. Similarly, Jay Conger (1998) has written on the art of leadership and the role of language, and specifically persuasion. His article in the *Harvard Business Review*, on "The Necessary Art of Persuasion" is a good read. From a practitioner perspective the writings of Caroselli (2000), which can be accessed on the website of www.Luminguild.com, (accessed on 1.2.2001) provides tips and ideas about the rhetorical characteristics of effective leaders.

A relatively new book by Sjostrand et al. (2000) *Invisible Management: The Social Construction of Leadership* looks in some depth at various aspects of leadership, and is very informative about the idea of small talk and leadership roles. A fuller discussion of hegemony and the relationship of this concept to identity can be found in Schirato and Yell's (2000) *Communication and Culture*, a very accessible and learned read about a range of theoretical approaches to the study of communication generally.

For conceptual analysis and data, Norman Fairclough's (2000) *New Labour, New Language?* is illuminating, and Macarthur's compendium of *The Penguin Book of Speeches* (1999) is packed with easily accessible data on formal speeches.

CHAPTER NINE

Meaning Making in the Electronic Age

In this chapter we do not aim for a comprehensive discussion of the impact of new communication technologies on organizational life. The scope of such a huge subject area is well beyond the boundaries of this book. However, we felt it was necessary to include a chapter on what we call meaning making in the electronic age for several reasons. First, language is clearly central in electronic meaning making; words **are** deeds since words are all there is. In the case of the internet particularly, worlds and selves are actually made and transformed **only** by language. In MUDS (Multi-User Domains) for example, reality is clearly socially constructed, and as Turkle (1997) discovered, analysing this phenomena can help us to more easily understand complex ideas about the construction of reality and meaning making. At least, by thinking about the point that the text is constructed as much by reader or audience as by the author, we hope our readers find this chapter helpful to understanding the meaning making process.

However, there are other strong reasons for doing so given our organizational focus. New technologies such as email have become a central medium of communicating within organizations, impacting on key organizational processes, and therefore merit attention in a text on language and organization. Similarly, these new technologies have given rise to new metaphors of organization – network and virtual organizations for example (Schultze and Orliowski, 2001). In sum, we believe that looking at these contemporary communication media allows us to examine the impact of new technologies on meaning making processes almost as they are developing. Of course, this also means that whatever we write about technology in this chapter will almost certainly be out of date by the time it is published. Nevertheless, we believe that a semiotic approach to the analysis of the electronic age sheds light on the meaning making process in the context of these new media.

Objectives

In this chapter we will:

- discuss the impact of online interactions on the process of meaning making;
- outline the potential and problems of email and internet use;
- consider emoticons and abbreviations in text messaging as new language forms;
- consider the mobile phone as a medium of spatial and temporal flexibility;
- argue that organizational websites are places of identity construction; and
- discuss *PowerPoint* and the relationship between form and content.

Introduction

Analysing the development of new communication technologies means that we can watch new rules about meaning making being made in situ. For example, the continuing debate in many organizations (noted in Chapter 5), often made very public, about what emails can and cannot be used for, and the accessing of the web within work time for private activities. Similarly, we can look at the difference that new communication technologies can make to the way meaning is made. In these ways new technology can reveal the processes involved in meaning making. Just as a chemical indicator reveals things that are there but previously unseen by the naked eye, so new communication technologies can bring to light the processes which we take for granted in meaning making.

Online interaction strips away many of the signs that we rely on to make sense of who we are and who we're interacting with. As we discussed in Chapter 2, we make sense of people and situations through a range of clues, cues and signs outside of actual language use itself. In embodied interactions, such as face to face or over the telephone for example, there are a wealth of cues of varying reliability that indicate our identity and status, and that of others involved in the exchange. Our gestures, clothes, voices, inflection, intonation and even our body shapes signal messages about status, power and group membership, and these in turn indicate what we can expect from each other and how we will anticipate and interpret each other's behaviour (see Chapter 7). All of this is lost online. Language is (at the moment) everything in the online meaning making process. And, like all situations (in that everything always contains its opposite), this has positive and negative potential. We could say, for example, that this has immense emancipatory promise, in that individuals are much more likely to be judged on the merit of their ideas online rather than by their race, ethnicity, class, age or gender categorisation. This is clearly possible, in that anybody can 'be' anything in online communication. However, particularly in organizational contexts, some authors argue that it is at least as likely, and probably even more likely, that traditional status hierarchies are reproduced or even magnified in online communications (Smith and Kollock, 1999).

How extensive is electronic communication?

We are regular users of electronic communication, so much so that when one of us lost our technological capability recently because of hardware problems we were lost without our technological links. We had not realised how much we had come to depend on this method of communication. The extent and range of our usage came as a shock to us. Do you realise how dependent you are on the new communication technologies? Try answering the following questions to find out:

- How many times have you used the internet or email in the last two weeks?
- How many times have you used more conventional forms of communication (land line telephone, letter writing) in the same period?
- The loss of which communication media would most disrupt your everyday life?

Making sense of the electronic environment

The internet, the world wide web or the information highway are the common ways in which we describe and talk about the new communication system that enables us to be in contact in real time, anywhere in the world, with anybody, provided that they have the necessary technical equipment and connections. It is a fantastic communication platform that can give voice to those previously unheard, link very different cultures, create new forms of community and nascent cultures (through the development of MUDS, for example), and where the self can be constructed – in **persona** rather than in **person**. As the ubiquitous *Microsoft* advert implies, "you can be anything, anytime, anywhere." In many ways, this new communication medium is facilitating the building of new rules of interaction, rather than passively applying old rules to a completely new context (see the sections on email and text messaging).

Gender online

People seem to go to great lengths to reproduce stereotypical gender identities online. 'Are you male or female?' is such a commonly asked question that it was long ago abbreviated to 'RUMorF?' in online interactions. Significantly, no such abbreviations are in widespread use for questions concerning age, height, weight, or socio-economic status etc. Gender seems to be the one characteristic of our

(Continued)

embodied lives that is a central feature of interaction throughout the internet (O'Brien, 1999), and people seem to go to great lengths to be 'authentic' from a gender perspective. But, even more interestingly, gender is often reproduced online in more limited and stereotypical ways than in embodied interaction, so that people present themselves as stereotypical ideals. It seems, then, that a world without physical constraints has led to greater homogenisation of identities, rather than new identity forms.

- Why do you think this might be so?
- Do you think online interaction should be an opportunity to perform a variety of fabricated roles and identities?
- What does this say about real people?

Interestingly, all three ways of describing this phenomenon – the internet, world wide web and information highway – are metaphorical (see Chapter 3), drawing on ideas of this new communication medium as a network or web, of roads or of fibres and filaments. We (the authors) do not know whether this in any way represents the material reality of what the internet or the web actually looks like, and we do not need to know to be able to use it effectively. But understanding it this way gives us a frame (crucially, already known to us) on which to hang our understanding. We understand what highways and webs look like and the basic properties that enable them to connect different locations and nodes. It is not therefore difficult for us to think that we understand how the internet actually works, because we liken it to these common objects and imbue it with their characteristics. This is how metaphors work, as we explained in Chapter 3. Thus, webs of meaning woven through metaphor continue to be central, even in the electronic age.

Similarly, we can already understand our computer screens because we draw on already known concepts such as a **desktop** with **files** and **folders**. In fact, the whole software package that many of us use is called *Office*, a concept with which we, like millions of others, are very familiar. These familiar concepts act as metaphors for the unfamiliar, and so this very familiarity enables us to understand a very unfamiliar object, and the way it might work for us. But of course, this familiar understanding also constrains, because just as we are able to understand this new phenomena through old concepts like files and folders, we will also see and experience this new technology in terms of the limits and restrictions of those old concepts. Files and folders can get full, for example, but this concept of fullness hardly applies to computer capacity in the same way. Similarly, links between concrete material files, such as correspondence, are hard to devise and maintain, yet we are told that links between computer files are very easy to activate. But none of us use this facility routinely, because the experience that we trigger or draw on by using the sign 'file' tells us that this is a messy and difficult task. Again, this is another example of how everything contains its opposite in the meaning making process. Just as the familiarity of the sign makes us feel secure and facilitates our understanding of a new concept, so we will apply the constraints inherent in that sign to the new phenomena – we will understand the new in terms of the old (see Chapter 3).

Computers and the writing process

As I write these words, I keep shuffling the text on my computer screen. Once I would have had to literally cut and paste. Now I call it cut and paste. Once I would have thought of it as editing. Now with computer software, moving sentences and paragraphs about is just part of writing. This is one reason I now remain much longer at my computer than I used to at my paper-writing tablet or typewriter. When I want to write and I don't have a computer around, I tend to wait until I do. In fact, I feel I *must* wait until I do. (Turkle, 1997: 29)

● Why do you think Turkle feels like this?
● Why might it be harder to turn away from a computer screen than a piece of paper?

Home pages and **windows** are other good examples of how we make meaning by drawing on already recognizable concepts, concepts that are sometimes so familiar that we are barely conscious of the ideas and assumptions that underpin them. Calling one's computer space a homepage and filling it with virtual objects and links, which correspond to one's interests, reproduces something akin to our homes. Except, of course, these homepages are not exactly the same as our homes, in that we live **through** a collection of icons scattered about the computer network rather than **in** a collection of rooms materially located in a single space. This is a fundamental difference, since the homepage becomes a single entity only through our efforts – we produce different aspects of the self that go together to make up the whole. Turkle (1997) sums this point up very well when she describes homepages as, "real estate metaphors for the self" whose décor is "post-modern" in that "its different rooms with different styles are located on computers all over the world" (1997: 259). Homepages are not really like our homes then, even though we understand them through the traces of meaning connected with the material reality of our homes.

We make use of the concept of windows in a similar fashion. By using the window metaphor we understand our computer screens in terms of something as familiar as a window. But thinking about the reality of windows as a computer concept raises another issue. Interestingly, when we look at our computer screens we don't necessarily think that we're looking **through** a three dimensional window, rather than **at** a two dimensional piece of paper. As Johnson (1997) points out, the more we use computer windows, the more the illusion of looking out onto data space wears off. We come to see and think of them as flat documents – perhaps drawing on the paper metaphor rather than the window metaphor, a possibility which Johnson overlooks. But, drawing on the work of Derrida, Johnson does draw our attention to the idea of **dead** metaphors (see Chapter 3). He suggests that when we look at computer windows as pieces of paper rather than as portals, it is because the, "luster of the original metaphor has worn off, become literalised … the familiarity of the terms has erased their rhetorical value, like a coin whose face is rubbed out from wear and tear, transforming it from currency to simple metal" (1997: 87). Johnson suggests that because we no longer think of our virtual windows as analogues of the real-world version, we lose some of the revealing capacity of the original metaphor, and this of course impacts on the way we actually use the virtual window.

The point is that desktops, homepages and windows are all examples of how we make sense of the new, through images and concepts of the old – how we apply our existing consciousness to understanding the unfamiliar. This metaphorical language allows us to express something for which no words have yet been invented (see Chapter 3), but at the same time we are constrained to use only those metaphors that reflect our own habits, or structures, or ways of thinking about the world.

An intercultural experience – or the power of the *Microsoft* jingle

Whilst attending an academic conference in China in 1996, we were invited to visit the home of a colleague and friend who worked at the prestigious University of Beijing. She lived alone in a one-roomed flat on campus in a residential block reserved for staff. We entered the building eager and inquisitive to see how Chinese academics lived. We were immediately shocked and dismayed at the squalid conditions, so far removed from our own home environments (and indeed the rather sumptuous surroundings of the 'Western' Hotel in Beijing where we were staying). To reach the flat we went up a dark and dismal staircase, which opened onto a large but equally gloomy and dank landing, all of which had clearly never been painted or decorated in any way. On one side of this grim and cheerless communal area were the very primitive cooking facilities shared by all the families on this floor – perhaps ten in total. On the other side were the equally austere, and shared, washing and bathing facilities. To our western eyes all of this looked bleak, forbidding and deeply depressing, but our host showed no sign of feeling this way. On the contrary, she had told us over lunch how lucky she was to have this flat to herself when most of the twelve feet square rooms opening directly off the landing housed families of two and three people. As she opened the door to her room – the one area in which she had any privacy at all – we were equally astonished at the amazing array of computer technology, so at odds with the primitive communal facilities on the shared landing. The state of the art computer, printer and scanner easily surpassed our own rather old fashioned technology. As she proudly switched on the computer, we heard the familiar jingle of windows loading. We realised then, that although we were in an extremely unfamiliar environment, experiencing the alien lifestyle of a very different culture on the other side of the world, the jingle was an instantly recognisable connection to our own very different lives in England. That this apparently nondescript, even mildly irritating jingle could provide such a memorable link to our own everyday existences demonstrates its ubiquitous nature as a **sign** (see Chapter 2). For us, in this strange context that we found ourselves, it performed a reassuring role, providing familiarity in the unfamiliar, and thereby laying bare its universality.

Electronic mail

Electronic mail or email as it is more commonly known, is perhaps the most widely used aspect of the new communication technologies. It is easy to search the web for **netiquette** and find numerous sites with titles such as (the do's and dont's of online communication) "The Ten Commandments of Email" or "10 Tips for Great Email". Notice the biblical metaphor which lends strength and gravitas to the advice. Why should we need this kind of guidance when we do not need similar direction to use say, a mobile phone? The answer lies in the swift rise of email as a prime communication medium in terms of speed and range. It is an extremely cost-effective and functionally efficient form of data transfer, more so than the telephone or conventional letter writing. In a very short space of time, email has become a business necessity and an increasingly important way for family and friends to stay in close contact. But it seems that this very functionality – speed and range – has given rise to new rules for using this medium. It is commonplace, for example, for senders and receivers of email to be much more relaxed in their attitudes to spelling and grammar, even in formal emails between businesses. The guidance sites usually demonstrate the new rules of this **netiquette** as the following examples show:

- Email messages differ from traditional business and personal letters in terms of brevity.
- Email messages are short and get to the point quickly.
- Everyone is on a first name basis in the world of email and titles are seldom used.
- Because of the conversational nature of email it's ok to use humour and expressive verbs and adjectives.
- Because many email systems don't read underlining or boldface, you can use CAPITAL letters for emphasis, but this should be done with caution because it can be interpreted as shouting.

These ideas raise some interesting issues and questions – not least about the origin of these rules. How have these rules of interaction (or any other come to that) come to be established as appropriate? Why should it be fitting to be more informal, adopt a conversational approach, and ignore conventional rules of polite interaction such as formal terms of address in email interactions? Perhaps, as we indicated earlier, part of the answer lies in the very speed of the medium, likening email interactions to conversations, rather than the more formal exchange of letters, for example, thus making conversational rules more apt, even for a written medium. Perhaps this apparently spontaneous medium also signals the relaxation of formal rules in western society in general. And maybe it also owes something to its roots in academia. Academics were the first group to use email on a regular basis, and the culture of the academic community has always had an egalitarian bent (at least on the surface). So perhaps this more informal approach to email has its roots in many factors including the functionality of the medium, the wider historical context and the specific cultural context of the initial users. Certainly, it is changing the way people communicate on many levels.

Managers' preferences for different types of communication

In a survey of 371 managers looking at media preferences for different types of communications (Markus, 1994), 83 per cent stated email was preferable 'to communicate many things to many people' whereas only two per cent thought face to face meetings were a better approach. However, when asked their preferences for expressing emotions of feelings, 70 per cent preferred face to face as opposed to seven per cent who would use email as their preferred option.

- Why do you think we choose one form of language over another in certain situations?
- Which form of communication do you prefer, and in what circumstances?

When we think about the many cultural and social contexts that are connected by the email medium, especially in relation to our point above about the nature of the email rules that have developed, and that English tends to be the common language of email (see Chapter 6), we are confronted with another interesting issue. What if these diverse, but now linked, communities have different norms embedded in patterns of interaction? We know, for example, that the countries of the Far East tend to have a much more formal approach towards interaction than many Western countries. What is the effect of the ubiquitous email rules on these cultural patterns of interaction? What is the likely outcome for the more formal interactional patterns, and what is the impact of that change for the culture of these societies more generally? Of course, we cannot answer these questions with any degree of certainty, but they are issues worth thinking about (see Chapter 6 for more background).

Email – a functional tool, a social device or big brother?

A colleague, Jayne, told us about the following dilemma created by different ideas about appropriate use of email.

A friend of mine is, like me, a subscriber to AOL as a service provider. He has activated a 'buddy-list' (which anyone can do), to which he has added my name. Now, whenever I go 'on-line' he can see this and he tends to immediately write a brief message to me such as 'Hi? Busy? Are you in 2night?' This makes me feel *really* uneasy.

- Why do you think Jayne feels uneasy?
- Do the two people have different 'protocols' of email behaviour? If so, how might you describe them?
- What would you do about this problem if you were Jayne?

Looking at organizations specifically, email can be thought of as part of the unmanaged organizational space, that part of the organization that has not, as yet, been subjected to prescribed organizational control mechanisms. Many companies have not yet formalised their approach to employees using email, and web access, outside of the formal requirements of the job. Indeed, it would be hard to see how this could be achieved with any degree of certainty and accuracy where employees use these technologies as part of their work. This is especially the case when the technologies are central to a key shift that is taking place around work more generally. An implication of the emergence of new metaphors to describe organizations such as network and virtual (Schultze and Orliowski, 2001), is that many people are now enabled, entirely through the use of new technologies such as email and the internet, to work anywhere and at any time (Tietze and Musson, 2001). This is a key factor in the move from people working solely at the workplace and working more from home, for example. This trend is likely to grow rather than come to an end, not least because of the potential savings for companies in not providing expensive office space, the increasing financial and environmental cost (and danger?) of travel, and the social and psychological benefits that people who work from home generally report.

Online interaction

- Do you think that traditional hierarchies are likely to be reproduced in online communication when people work from home?
- How/why/when might this be the case?
- What are the 'signs' that are likely to enable/prevent this happening?

For many people in many companies, email and internet use occupy what we might describe as the shadowland between the organization and the individual's interests. These boundaries are never really clearly marked, however hard they can appear and feel to a worker or an organization. It is, for example, always possible to *think* about activities other than work, even in the most constraining work contexts. But email and internet use enable a more interactive approach to this boundary – it is possible for many employees to use these for private as well as company interactions. Furthermore, they appear much more difficult to control and police than say telephone use. However, it would be naïve to think that this is impossible. As Zuboff points out, communication and information systems "can automatically and continuously record almost anything their designers want to capture" (1988: 322). Such systems can be used as control mechanisms, as well as having liberating potential. In the end, it is likely to be the authority structure that will determine how these systems are used.

When delete does *not* mean obliterate

Even though control issues about email use do not appear to have been resolved in many organizations, it is worth remembering that the delete button for email does not actually mean **erase**, **remove** or **scrub out** as a thesaurus might suggest. Emails, it seems, are never really obliterated, merely stored in some huge filing cabinet in the sky (notice the metaphor) for retrieval at any time.

● Do you think that most people realise that it is possible to retrieve emails even when they've apparently been deleted?
● Similarly, emails can be forwarded to anybody else with great ease.
● What are the implications of these factors for organizational control?

Email, then, like other electronic means of communication (or indeed communication more generally), can be used as a subversive or a liberating tool. The central factor in determining how this is played out is clearly one of power: for example, who has the power in organizations to determine what is proper and appropriate use.

Emoticons, abbreviations and new words

Emoticons (or **smileys**) are a set of new signs that were principally designed to show emotions through icons. These icons can represent various emotional states, or they can act as a shorthand for frequently used words and phrases, and they are commonly used in email and text messaging. They perform two related functions; first they are a kind of abbreviation to avoid having to laboriously and repeatedly type conventional words or phrases, and to enable us to express emotions that cannot be conveyed in email and text messaging. 'Talking' via email or text messaging omits those aspects of communication that are 'said' through facial expressions, voice tone, and body language in general. They are interesting to us for several reasons.

Some emoticons (smileys) in common use

:-)	Standard smiley (joking; satisfied)	(-_-)	Secret smile
:->	Sarcasm	:-@	Screaming; swearing
:-*	Kissing	:-D	Laughing
:-(	Sad	X(	Fed up; angry
:C	Very sad	:o|	Bored
:-/	Sceptical	:'-)	Happy tear
[ ]	A hug	<->	Ouch!
:-( )	Shouting	OoO	Surprised

From a semiotic perspective (see Chapter 2), we can see how this new sign set has developed into a whole new language. And just like other languages, this new sign system is capable of creating a huge number of meanings from a rather small number of alphanumeric characters. It is possible to download pages of these new signs from websites that also explain their meaning, and these sites often request that new Emoticons or smileys are submitted for publication on the site. This last factor is a clear sign that this form of communication is fairly embryonic, and that clear rules have not yet been established around the grammar or vocabulary of the system.

Technology as the medium of change in language

In his book *Language and the Internet*, David Crystal points out that technology has always been the main source of new vocabulary entering the English language, whether from the industrial revolution or developments in medicine and science. But the current speed of change in vocabulary is unprecedented, matching the speed of the internet.

> In the past it would have taken years for a word to become common currency; these days a word can make it into the dictionary in a few months ... the main impact of the internet lies not in the number of extra words that have come in, but in the speed with which they are spread. (Crystal, 2001)

As the poet TS Eliot declared many decades ago:

> For last year's words belong to last year's language
> And next year's words await another voice

- What do you think TS Eliot meant by this?
- Can you think of any examples of new words, or words that belong to another era?

The views of Eliot and Crystal on how new words and changing interpretations of existing ones are linked to changes in society, are echoed in the way conventional ideas about grammar can also be changed by new technologies. The common abbreviations, sometimes described as **vowel dessication** (vwls-r-4-wmps), used particularly in text messaging are eroding traditional ideas about the immutability of grammatical rules. For example, the famous Shakespearian phrase can be reduced to 2b or nt 2b. Indeed, u r sd to b pst it if u dnt use u in ur emails & txts. Furthermore, if we consider email to be a fast form of communication, then we have to look at text messaging as communication of lightening speed. Both of these points are important when we think that the younger generations are probably much more at ease using text messaging and email than other conventional communication media such as writing with pen and paper. Meanings, then, are being made in radically different forms through structures that were once considered fixed, but are clearly capable of change.

English in the digital age

What do you think the following **Weblish** terms mean?

F2F	GAL	Geek out
Gubbish/rubbage	History	Prolly
Thx	Trep	Vanilla

If you don't know, you can have a look at the following sites:
netlingo.com
webopedia.internet.com
hotwired.lycos.com/hardwired/wiredstyle
hotwired.lycos.com/special/ene

The mobile telephone as a medium of spatial and temporal flexibility

Do you know anyone who does not possess a mobile telephone? Probably not, unless they are very small children or very old adults, and even then they might still use this ubiquitous form of communication. Ten years ago very few people had access to this technology but now it is an ever-present phenomenon. We include it in our discussion here because of its omnipresent nature and the related use of text messaging. The text message is central to the way people communicate and make meaning with mobile phones and the rewriting of grammatical rules that we outlined above (mainly through vowel dessication) is being played out through this medium, perhaps even more so than through email. Also, and perhaps more importantly, the technology enables spatial and temporal flexibility, as do all technologies which create virtual worlds. It is possible to email someone from anywhere in the world and for that person to *not* know exactly when you are doing so or from which location. Laptop computers make this spatial and temporal flexibility even easier. It is also possible to use a mobile phone for email communication, although we have found few examples of people doing so currently.

Technology and change

As Zuboff commented over a decade ago, "Computer-based technologies are not neutral; they embody essential characteristics that are bound to alter the nature of work within our factories and offices, and among workers, professionals and managers" (1988: 7).

- What do you think Zuboff meant by this?
- What are the essential characteristics of the mobile telephone that can change the nature of work?

The spatial and temporal dimensions of the mobile phone when used as a medium for conversation are what interest us here. We believe that these dimensions are important because the conversation is in real time and we can actually hear the other person speak, and we can make assumptions about where they are speaking *from*. Drawing on common understandings built up around landline telephones (again interpreting the new in terms of the old) we make sense of the new technology according to our default assumptions (Kittay, 1987; see Chapter 3) about the old. This may be because the mobile and landline phone technologies perform exactly the same function, even though they have very different temporal and spatial characteristics. We tend to assume that somebody is in a particular material environment in the absence of other information to the contrary, and we can use mobile telephony to exploit this assumption. We use a story from Pantelli's (2001) work here to demonstrate our point.

Spatial flexibility

Pantelli (2001) recounts the story of a female entrepreneur, Pat, on holiday in France. Having taken over the management of a particularly complex customer case at short notice she updated herself on the problems through faxes sent to the hotel from her consultancy company in the UK. She then rang the client on her mobile phone using a local cemetery as an open-air office (due to excellent reception combined with the availability of convenient flat surfaces!), and proceeded to have a very serious business negotiation with the client. Only when she returned to the UK did she reveal to the client that she had been overseas during their telephone discussions, but she did not disclose her actual location in the cemetery.

- What role did the mobile phone play in Pat's negotiations?
- Where do you think the client thought that Pat was, and why?
- Would it have mattered if the client had known her location? Why, or why not?
- Would you have interrupted your holiday in such a way?

The mobile phone then can enable spatial and temporal flexibility; it is possible to speak to anybody at any time and in any place in the world (with a few exceptions). We can make meaning through this spatially and temporally unbounded medium in ways that can exploit this flexibility and suit our broader purposes.

Organizational websites

Our discussion so far has focused mainly on the web or the internet as a new space within which new communicative practices have emerged. One important organizational aspect of this is the company website, which even the smallest of business ventures sees as essential. This new genre of communication is often simply seen as a marketing opportunity with enormous potential (Armstrong and Hagel, 1996), but it addresses complex audiences both within and outside the organization. Employees, shareholders, customers, competitors and others with the potential to join these groups can access these sites and will seek to make sense of them in potentially different ways. The company website then can be seen as the place whereby different discourses might come together and be deployed (see Chapter 5) in order to create a specific company identity capable of managing and developing these different internal and external relationships, with existing and prospective diverse groups.

Stories are often the medium through which this company identity is made coherent and preserved (see Chapter 4). The *Ikea* and *The Body shop* websites, for example, tell the 'official' stories of how the companies grew from their lowly beginnings into the commercial giants of today, largely through the efforts of their transformational leaders (see Chapter 8). The stories disseminate many key ideas and themes considered central to the past and future success of the companies, including those of daring to think differently, doing business differently and the struggle of the little company (David) against the corporate giants (Goliath). One function of these websites, through the official stories they tell, is to act as depositories of meaning to counteract the increasingly fragmented and diverse organizational worlds as the companies become major global players. The stories are the medium through which the various audiences are encouraged to make the same coherent and believable sense of a diverse set of realities.

Very little research work has been done in this area, even though the selection and manipulation of usually already existing company material provides an opportunity to explore how companies create particular meanings and identities involving specific discourses. It is possible, for example, to examine company websites for discourses of ethical or social responsibility, particularly since these discourses reflect a public concern that many businesses are beginning to feel impelled to address (Fineman, 1998; Kernisky, 1997). How they address these issues, the words they use, the signs they draw upon, the discourses they deploy, and eventually the identities they construct should inform the debate about meaning making in organizations. As Tsoukas (1999) points out in his discussion of the conflict between Shell and Greenpeace in the North Sea, the website functions as an arena in which companies are increasingly competing in discursive space, where winning the 'argument' is central.

Analysing a company website

Choose a company website and, using the techniques outlined so far in this book, analyse the site to see what meanings are being encoded, through which mechanisms, and to what effect:

1 What are the key signs and symbols, visual and written? What do they connote?
2 What stories are being told? What are the themes? Why are these themes being used?
3 What imagery is deployed? Are there vivid metaphors? What are the connotations of these? Is the language mainly rational and metonymic?

4 What discourses are being drawn upon? Why might the company consider these important?

5 How is the leader constructed, and to what effect?

- Do you think that you have decoded the site as the encoders intended? If not, why might that be?
- If you have your own website, think about how you have encoded your own meanings to construct your identity online and how this might be decoded by others.

PowerPoint – the relationship between form and content

Finally, we look in this last section at a software package for making presentations, because we believe that the discussion demonstrates some fundamental points about the power of technology to structure our thought processes and meaning making practices. *PowerPoint* is the ubiquitous presentation software package that can be found on millions of computers around the world. Ian Parker argues in an article about the history of *PowerPoint* in *The New Yorker* magazine (28 May 2001), that it is not simply a software **tool** that enables us to make presentations. Rather, it is a social instrument, much like a car or a suit of clothes, or even a new nose or body part courtesy of a plastic surgeon, which we carry around with us and by which we are judged and judge ourselves. From this perspective, Parker suggests that the *PowerPoint* package has turned "middle managers into bullet-point dandies ... and there are tracts of corporate America where to appear without *PowerPoint* would be unwelcome and vaguely pretentious, like wearing no shoes" (2001: 76). This latter view resonates with us, working in an academic environment where to not use *PowerPoint* for lectures is seen as rather luddite, and/or a sign of seniority and privilege. Perhaps particularly in a business school context, *PowerPoint* can be said to give one power, or conversely not to use it at all can be used to signify that one is a 'real' academic. (Incidentally the spell check on the software package used to write this chapter recognises that *PowerPoint* has two capital Ps, but does not recognise the word luddite at all!)

Whilst Parker's argument might be mildly amusing and echo some truth for others and us, his central point is much more relevant to our discussion about the process of meaning making. Parker suggests that *PowerPoint* has a much more insidious effect than that outlined above. He believes that it actually influences the way we think, editing our ideas and structuring our thoughts. Because the software organises information for us hierarchically – into headings and bullet points, even if we choose not to use the much more directive AutoContent Wizards – we cannot escape the inherent AutoContent spirit of *PowerPoint*. This fundamentally influences our thinking and organizes our thoughts. So, Parker powerfully argues, in boardrooms, industrial plants and lecture theatres around the world, people are communicating without paragraphs or pronouns: rather, the "world is condensed into a few upbeat slides with seven or so words on a line, seven or so lines on a slide" (2001: 78). Perhaps more importantly though, people are beginning to use this software package to organise events in their social and family lives. It has migrated from

PowerPoint

- Make your first point here
- Followed by the second
- Third
- Fourth
- Fifth etc.
- Don't put too many words on the slide otherwise the audience will be unable to read it and
- They may spend too much time and energy trying to do so rather than listen to you!

This is a PowerPoint slide created by using a template.

- Try to imagine a presentation on where a slide like this might be inappropriate.
- Would it be helpful to you to use a slide like this to tell a story?
- Could a comedian give a good performance using such a slide?
- Do **you** feel that the structure of the slide might change the way you think?

Figure 9.1   PowerPoint

the business world into the private domain. For example, Parker tells the story of an American mother who used the programme to produce a presentation to persuade her daughters to clean their rooms and do their chores. Similarly, he tells of it being used to provide background stories and photographs at a wedding reception, and in church ceremonies more generally.

We think that Parker has a point when he says that "in the glow of a *PowerPoint* show, the world is condensed, simplified, and smoothed over – yet bright and hyper-real – like the cityscape background in a *PlayStation* motor race" (2001: 78). The medium becomes the message. Crucially, the software package encourages us to believe that information is **all** there is, and that process – the art of the storyteller or rhetorician – is overshadowed, if not obliterated, in the course of presenting. *PowerPoint* then, is an example of a technology that reduces the complexity of the world, in this instance to a series of bullet points, and in its wake can subtly change our way of thinking about the world itself, and how it is to be a human in it.

Summary

In this chapter we have looked at the process of meaning making within the context of the electronic environment. We have discussed how we make sense of new concepts and communication media in terms of already familiar ideas and understandings, usually through the use of metaphor. Desktops, homepages and windows are all examples of how we make sense of the new, through images and concepts of the old – how we apply our existing consciousness to understanding the unfamiliar. We have seen how this can both enable and constrain our understanding.

New communication media such as electronic mail give rise to new communicative practices through which new rules for meaning making, grammatical, lexical and functional, emerge. These new electronic media can change the way people communicate and work on many levels, including spatial and temporal dimensions. We have also seen how new metaphors to describe organizations, such as virtual or network organizations, have occurred as a result of these new technologies, and how these reflect and influence the material reality of the way people work.

The electronic environment has enabled a new semiotic sign system of emoticons to develop, which we need to learn if we want to be fluent in this new 'language,' primarily because the non-verbal aspects of communication can be lost on line. This new sign system, and the vowel dessication of text messaging, is subject to the same encoding and decoding processes of meaning making as all other languages.

Organizations have a public presence in the electronic environment through organizational websites. We have seen how these can be used to generate certain company identities, through the deployment of different discourses and stories, whereby various diverse audiences are encouraged to make sense of the company in a coherent way.

Finally, we have examined the relationship between form and content through a discussion of the ubiquitous use of the software package, *PowerPoint*. *PowerPoint* can reduce the complexity of the world to a series of bullet points, overshadowing if not obliterating rhetorical practices. Through this discussion we have seen how technology has the power to structure our thought processes and communicative practices, changing our ideas about the world and how it functions.

Recommended reading

Sherry Turkle's book *Life on the Screen: Identity in the Age of the Internet* (1997) looks at the wonders and dangers of virtual interactions from a psychological perspective. She argues that we come to see ourselves differently through new technology, that we enter into identity-transforming relationships with our own selves and others through the new communication media. Turkle's analysis of the self as a fluid, multiple entity is underpinned by the work of French poststructuralists such as Lacan, Foucault and Deleuze. It's a very good and learned read.

Steven Johnson's 1997 book *Interface Culture: How New Technology Transforms the Way We Create and Communicate* is a fascinating examination of how interfaces through which we control information – buttons, graphics and words on the screen – influence our daily lives. This is an absorbing look at how technology has transformed society and the directions it may take us in the future.

Communities in Cyberspace, edited by Marc Smith and Peter Kollock (1999), is a collection organized into four main sections: identity, social order and control, community structure and dynamics, and collective action. This book looks at how the idea of community is being challenged and rewritten by online interactions.

From an organizational perspective, although not directly addressing the issue of language, Shoshana Zuboff's *In the Age of the Smart Machine: The Future of Work and Power* (1988) is a classic text. Zuboff looks at the impact of computerisation in the workplace, the concomitant transformation in work patterns and the wider philosophical and social significance. Staying with the organizational perspective, Schultze and Orliowski (2001) in their article "Metaphors of Virtuality: Shaping an Emergent Reality" show how metaphors largely derived from the domain of computer science have been used in the practitioner literature on virtual organizing. They examine the implications of this for the social understanding and enactment of virtuality.

Conclusion

This book contributes to the understanding of meaning making processes: what they are and how they work, in and outside of organizations, so as to understand better human behaviour within structural contexts. This is our central theme and chapter-by-chapter we have introduced different slants on this thesis, showing meaning as being emergent in (and reflective of) a system of relationships, as processual, social, unstable and never fixed. From this perspective, meaning is, so to speak, in a perpetual process of becoming. We have tried to write a book that speaks to the naïve reader in a language that they can easily understand. Our major aim has been to translate the ideas and practical application of a very complex and difficult subject, between the very different worldviews of people like ourselves – academics, with language, skills and concepts not normally used outside of our established cultures (or webs of meaning) – and the naïve reader. But we had a further aim which we hope this book can go some way to achieving: to shift meaning making perspectives from the marginal and largely silent periphery of organization studies into the din of centre stage.

In the introduction to this book you were asked to think about the role and power of words and language when we asked you to consider the English saying that, 'sticks and stones can break my bones, but words can never hurt me.' We asked you to do this to initiate the process of reflection on what words/language actually **do** in the construction of reality(ies), rather than seeing them as 'mere messengers from the kingdom of reality' (Gergen, 1989: 11). Understanding that language **does** things is the first step in understanding meaning making: **how** meaning making happens, and **why** certain meanings are made in certain circumstances is central to understanding how organizations work.

In Chapter 1 we focused on language, meaning and the construction of social reality, using the webs of meaning metaphor to reflect our view that people are both suspended in webs of meanings, but · that they also actively spin those webs through their engagement with the social world. We explained that the bedrock of our position is an interpretive perspective on the social world, and that this entails giving up one's own position as final, ultimate and absolute, and thus relaxing one's grip on certainty. We acknowledged the discomfort, confusion and even worry that this can cause for individuals, but also the new possibilities that such a stance can open up. In this chapter we presented a case study about Judith, the disillusioned night nurse and aspiring entrepreneur. The case study was written to invite some deeper reflection on organizational/structural factors and how one person can and does act within those, and thereby create new realities. This **acting** is done through uttering words and sentences that express emotions and values (dissatisfaction, disillusion, exhaustion, hope), and words are also used to buy the nursing home, negotiate the contract, gather an understanding of the employed staff and so on. Words and language were used symbolically as well as the means through which **material** reality was shaped; indeed the two go together in the process of meaning making.

In Chapter 2 we focused on semiology, and its relevance to organization studies, both as a framework for understanding language, but also other kinds of cultural texts, such as buildings, adverts and myths. We discussed the view that everything around us – language, artefacts, even behaviour – is a sign, generating cultural meaning, and that the relationship between the sign and its meaning is arbitrary, and that this process happens largely at a subconscious level. In this chapter we also considered the view that signs and symbols do not derive their meanings in isolation, but through their relationships with other signs and symbols. This semiological approach illuminates the symbolic nature of organizational life, and forms the theoretical base for the following chapters.

In Chapter 3 we looked at the role of tropes (rhetorical figures, or figures of speech) in generating meaning. We showed how language is full of all kinds of rhetorical figures, but we focused specifically on metaphor. We discussed both the generative function of metaphor in providing new ways of reframing organizations, and the value of examining metaphors-in-use in organizations so as to yield deeper insights into emotional realities and organizational value systems.

We looked at stories and narratives in Chapter 4, and the rise in popularity of these little narratives as topics of study, in the context of supposedly declining metanarratives. We discussed the different ideas about what stories are, and what storytelling entails, and we introduced some stories from our own research data to show how some functions and features of storytelling are polysemic, and again are expressive of emotional realities and values. We also showed how stories could be used as mediums of social control, as well as a means to understand and theorize better organizational meaning making processes. This discussion generated questions about the provenance of certain stories, and why some were heard and others suppressed, raising issues of power and manipulation.

These themes were also raised in Chapter 5, where we used the concepts of genre and discourse – form and content respectively – as framing devices to explore the cultural knowledge that people use to make sense of, and act upon, cultural texts and social contexts. We rejected a wholly deterministic view of genres and discourses, and whilst not underestimating the power of discourse in particular, or the dominance of certain interpretations, we argued that people can – and do – read against the grain, to reconstruct discourses according to their particular life experiences and circumstances. We see both genres and discourses then, as neither static nor wholly deterministic, since both are reproduced and transformed through social practice, but we do not underestimate the role of power in this process.

Neither do we underestimate the role of power in meaning making across cultures, which is the subject of Chapter 6. In this chapter we viewed cultures as webs of meaning making, and again explored the role of language in creating, sustaining and transforming social realities, through a discussion of linguistic determinism, linguistic relativity and the role of non-verbal communication. We looked specifically at the role of English as the lingua franca of intercultural encounters and business communication generally, and discussed the idea that ethnocentrism is the main barrier to intercultural communication.

In Chapter 7 we looked at gender as a significant strand of the meaning webs that cultures create. We viewed gender as an ongoing social process constructed at the levels of society, organization, interpersonal interaction and the individual, seeing gender as situated within specific communities of practice and wider structures of opportunity and constraint, reproduced, challenged and changed through interaction. To deepen and broaden our understanding we examined the historically separate but closely associated ideas about gender coming from linguistics and organization studies, exploring points of overlap and convergence. Looking at organizations specifically, we highlighted the need to attend to how and why masculinity and femininity are constituted by organizational actors, discursively and through other sign systems, and the implication of these strands for understanding and action within the meaning web.

In Chapter 8 we looked at the leadership process as another strand of the web of meaning, seeing leadership as a language game, through which influence and persuasion is generated. In this chapter we looked specifically at the linguistic processes and rhetorical techniques used by many formal leaders, applying many of the concepts discussed in previous chapters, to deconstruct leaders' talk to see how they encode new meanings and rework old ones into new kinds of common sense, thus tapping into processes of hegemony. We also cautioned against the idea of followers as passive receivers, rather we highlighted that the decoding process might take many forms and cannot be taken for granted. We also pointed out that the small talk arena of organizations is where much leadership influence prevails and thus leaders can be found throughout the organization, not simply in formal roles.

In our final chapter, we looked at the process of meaning making in the electronic environment. We demonstrated the value of a semiotic approach in deconstructing how we make sense of the new through already familiar ideas and understandings, showing how these existing concepts both enable and constrain. We discussed how electronic media can change the way people communicate and work on many levels, including the development of new metaphors of organization, new languages, changing grammars, and the construction of company identities. We also discussed the implications of the temporal and spatial flexibility of the electronic environment.

Changing worlds

Whilst we have been writing meanings have changed. Of course, meanings are always changing, as we have stressed throughout this book, but people have argued, and will no doubt continue to argue, that the events of 11 September 2001 have changed the world fundamentally and forever. Certainly this seems so for many of us in the West. Commentators have argued that we live our lives largely protected from the vagaries suffered directly (and sometimes constantly) by many people living in other parts of the world – war, famine, large scale economic ruin – to name a few. Furthermore, these commentators argue that we have taken for granted many of our values and ideals – and the institutions that house them – as right, proper and unassailable. It has shocked many of us to find that this is not so, and led to outrage, trepidation and fear of worse things to come. Yet, we cannot argue with the fact that many more people have died in other disasters, natural or entirely of human origin, prior to the tragedy of 11 September 2001. It is the nearness of the tragedy, both spatial and temporal, and the challenge to our own ways that has shaken us so.

In the Introduction and Chapter 1 we stressed the constructedness of the social world and the inherent 'relative' position in this stance: signs have no absolute point of reference, but their meaning is constituted in and through the relationship they have with other signs. Their meaning can only be understood within the wider system (or context). This position could be viewed as problematic in so far as values, morality or meaning systems are shown to be contingent upon, and valid only within, their particular cultural/structural contexts. Outside of these contexts they lose their legitimacy. In Chapter 6 on Intercultural Communication, for example, we introduced the notion of ethnocentrism with the help of a reader's letter on her experience of living in Singapore. The writer of the letter was judging life in Singapore from the point of view of a Western citizen, finding the "other" culture alien and inferior. The letter writer reflected on her experience from an absolute point of view – all other practices, values or beliefs were assessed from this position. In our view, this is dangerous and contributes to the continuation of conflict, blame and resentment both within and outside of organizations. But we acknowledge that this leaves us with a difficult problem. How is one supposed to make judgements about right or wrong, about how to act and what to believe across different (cultural) contexts? Has this become impossible? We believe not, but we also believe that these processes need to start with reflections on how standards and points of reference in general, and specifically our own, become imbued with meaning.

For us, living in a **relative** world implies two fundamental propositions:

First: That there are no absolute standards or points of reference from which to comprehend or judge the 'others' existence: there is no neutral ground.
Second: That standards or points of reference are relative to each other: they are connected.

The first proposition, if taken on its own, might resonate with allusions of moral nihilism or an anything goes philosophy (Feyerabend, 1975). However, proposition two stresses the **connectedness** of points of reference. Taken together, the two propositions constitute a position that denies the existence of absolute, once and for all standards, but sees the beginning of a moral stance embedded in the attempt to understand the very connectedness of different points of reference, or meaning systems. In this vein, absolutism in thought and action is rejected (there can be no infinite justice), rather, we must try to understand the complexities of meaning systems, and their interconnectedness. Language such as 'black and white,' and 'who is not with us is against us' does not fall into this position. These binary opposites help to maintain cultural disharmony, because as we have said repeatedly, language **does** things.

On the notion of **justice**, we believe that principled justice is possible and that it entails the willingness and ability to "imagine what it is like to be someone other than yourself [...this] is at the core of our humanity. It is the essence of compassion, and it is the beginning of morality" (McEwan, 2001). It seems to us that such an act of imagination implies a sense of connectedness, through the awareness of simultaneous **difference** ('I am not you') and '**commonality**' ('I am like you'). This dualism asks us to work from a basis where we recognize, understand and value similarities as well as differences. But we do not see this as a simple task, because similarities are sometimes hard to find, and this often supports our belief in our own position as the true one. Except, "truth must always be understood in terms of how it is made, for whom, and at what time it is 'true'" (Fiske, 1987: 256). This clearly represents a challenge to our preconceptions, taken for granted ideas and beliefs about the nature of the social world, expressed in and through our language.

We believe that the biggest challenge for the twenty-first century is to find ways to live together on this globe and to find ways to talk about the *connectedness of lives and cultures*. For us the application of semiology to our lives, to organizational and social settings, and to our consultancy and teaching practice, supplies a discursive resource to do so.

References

Ackroyd, S. and Thompson, P. (1999) *Organizational Misbehaviour.* London: Sage.

Agar, M. (1994) *Language Shock. Understanding the Culture of Conversation.* New York: Morrow and Company Inc.

Akin, G. and Schultheiss, E. (1990) "Jazz Bands and Missionaries: OD Through Stories and Metaphors," *Journal of Managerial Psychology,* 5(4): 12–18.

Alexander, M. (1996) *The Myth at the Heart of the Brand. ESOMAR Publication Series,* 203: 109–124.

Alexander, M., Burt, M., Collinson, A. (1995) "Big Talk, Small Talk: BT's Strategic Use of Semiotics in Planning its Current Advertising," paper presented to The Market Research Society Conference, London.

Alvesson, M. (1994) "The play of metaphor," in J. Hassard and M. Parker (eds), *Postmodernism and Organisations.* London: Sage. pp. 114–131.

Alvesson, M. and Billing, Y. (1997) *Understanding Gender and Organizations.* London: Sage.

Alvesson, M. and Willmott, H. (eds) (1992) *Critical Management Studies.* London: Sage.

Argyris, D. and Schön, D. (1978) *Organizational Learning: A Theory of Action Perspective.* Reading, MA: Addison-Wesley.

Armstrong, A. and Hagel, J. (1996) "The Real Value of On-line Communities," *Harvard Business Review,* May–June: 134–141.

Baldry, C., Bain, P. and Taylor, P. (1998) "Bright Satanic Offices: Intensification, Control and Team Taylorism," In Thompson, P. and C. Warhurst, (eds), *Workplaces of the Future.* London: Macmillan. pp. 163–183.

Banerjee, N. (2001) "Some 'Bullies' Seek Ways to Soften Up," *The New York Times,* 10 August: C1.

Barker, P. (1998) *Another World.* New York: Picador.

Barley, S. (1991) "Semiotics and the Study of Occupational and Organizational Culture," in P.J. Frost, L.F. Moore, M.R. Louis, C.C. Lundberg, J. Martin (eds), *Reframing Organizational Culture.* London: Sage. pp. 356–371.

Barley, S. (1983) "Semiotics and the Study of Occupational and Organizational Cultures," *Administrative Science Quarterly,* 28: 393–413.

Barnett, A. and Busby, A. (1982) *Non Brittania; Why Parliament Waged its Falklands War.* Londres: Allison and Busby.

Barrett, F.J. and Cooperrider, D.L. (1990) "Generative Metaphor Intervention: A New Behaviourial Approach to Working with Systems Divided by Conflict and Caught in Defensive Perception," *Journal of Applied Behavioural Science,* 26(2): 219–239.

Barthes, R. (1973) *Mythologies.* London: Paladin. (1st edn, 1957)

Bate, P. (1994) *Strategies for Cultural Change.* Oxford: Butterworth-Heinemann.

Baumeister, R.F. and Newman, L.S. (1994) "How Stories Make Sense of Personal Experiences: Motives that Shape Autobiographical Narratives," *Personality and School Psychology Bulletin*, 20(5): 676–690.

Benjamin, W. (1968) "The Storyteller: Reflections on the Works of Nikolai Leskov," in H. Arendt (ed.), *Walter Benjamin: Illuminations*. London: Jonathan Cape.

Beston, A. (2001) "Earrings Against Sexism," *The New Zealand Herald*, Story ID.198046, 3 July 2001.

Boden, D. (1994) *The Business of Talk*. Cambridge: Blackwell.

Boje, D. (1991) "The Storytelling Organization: A Study of Story Performance in An Office-Supply Firm," *Administrative Science Quarterly*, 36: 106–126.

Boje, D. (1994) "Organizational Storytelling. The Struggles of Pre-modern, Modern and Postmodern Organizational Learning Discourses," *Management Learning*, 25(3): 433–461.

Boje, D. (1995) "Stories of the Storytelling Organization: a Postmodern Analysis of Disney as Tamar-Land," *Academy of Management Journal*, 38(4): 997–1035.

Boje, D. (2001) *Narrative Methods for Organizational and Communication Research*. London: Sage.

Boje, D. and Dehenney, R.F. (1993) *Managing in the Postmodern World: American's Revolution against Exploitation*. Dubuque, IO: Kendall-Hunt.

Bowles, M.L. (1989) "Myth, Meaning and Work Organization," *Organization Studies*, 10(3): 405–421.

Boyce, M. (1995) "Collective Centring and Collective Sense-making in the Stories and Storytelling of One Organization," *Organization Studies*, 16(1): 107–137.

Boyce, M. (1996) "Organizational Story and Storytelling: a Critical Review," *Journal of Organizational Change Management*, 9(5): 9–26.

Brown, A. (1998) *Organizational Culture*. London: Pitman Publishing.

Brown, M.H. (1992) "That Reminds me of a Story. Speech Action in Organizational Socialization," *The Western Journal of Speech Communication*, 49(Winter): 27–42.

Burr, V. (1995) *An Invitation to Social Constructionism*. London: Routledge.

Burrell, G. and Morgan, G. (1979) *Sociological Paradigms and Organizational Analysis*. Aldershot: Arena.

Cameron, D. (1985) *Feminism and Linguistic Theory*. New York: St. Martins Press Inc.

Cameron, D. (1992) *Feminism and Liguistic Theory*. 2nd edn. London: MacMillan.

Cameron, D. (2000) *Good to Talk? Living and Working in a Communication Culture*. Lond. Sage.

Caroselli, M. (2000) "Language of Leaders," *Executive Excellence*, 17(5): 12.

Chandler, D. *Semiotics for Beginners*. http://www.aber.ac.uk/~dgc/semiotic.html, accessed 3 April 2001.

Chen, G. and Chung, J. (1994) "The Impact of Confucianism on Organizational Communication," *Communication Quarterly*, 42(2): 93–105.

Chia, R. (2000) "Discourse Analysis as Organizational Analysis," *Organization*, 7(3): 513–518.

Choo, C.W. (1998) *The Knowing Organization. How Organizations use Information to Construct Meaning, Create Knowledge and Make Decisions*. Oxford: Oxford University Press.

Clark, T. and Salaman, G. (1996) "Telling Tales: Consultancy as the Art of Story Telling," in D. Grant and C. Oswick (eds), *Metaphor and Organization*. London: Sage. pp. 168–184.

Cm2250 (1993) *Realising Our Potential: A Strategy for Science, Engineering and Technology*. London: HMSO.

Coates, J. (1998) *Language and Gender: A Reader*. Oxford: Blackwell Publishers.

Cobley, P. and Jansz, L. (1997) *Semiotics for Beginners*. Cambridge: Icon Books.

Cockburn, C. (1991) *In the Way of Women*. London: MacMillan.

Cohen, L. (1997) *Women's Move from Employment to Self-Employment: Making Sense of the Transition*. Unpublished PhD thesis, Sheffield Hallam University.

Cohen, L. and Mallon, M. (1999) "The Transition from Organizational Employment to Self-Employment: Perceptions of Boundarylessness," *Work, Employment and Society*, 13(2): 329–352.

Cohen, L. and Musson, G. (2000) "Entrepreneurial Identities: Reflections From Two Case Studies," *Organization*, 7(1): 30–48.

Cohen, L., Duberley, J., McAuley, J. (1999a) "Fueling Discovery or Monitoring Productivity: Research Scientists Changing Perceptions of Management," *Organization*, 6(3): 473–498.

Cohen, L., Duberley, J., McAuley, J. (1999b) "The Purpose and Process of Science: Contrasting Understandings in UK Research Establishments," *R&D Management*, 29(3): 233–245.

Cohen, M.D., March, J.G. and Olsen, J.R. (1972) "A Garbage Can Model of Organizational Choice," *Administrative Science Quarterly*, 17(1): 1–25.

Collier, M.J. and Thomas, M. (1988) "Cultural Identity and Intercultural Communication," in W. Gudykunst and S. Ting-Toomey (eds), *Culture and Interpersonal Communication*. Newbury Park: Sage.

Collinson, D.L. (1988) "Engineering Humour. Masculinity, Joking and Conflict in Shop Floor Relations," *Organization Studies*, 9(2): 181–199.

Conger, J.A. (1991) "Inspiring Others: The Language of Leadership," *Academy of Management Executive*, 5(1): 31–45.

Conger, J.A. (1998) "The Necessary Art of Persuasion," *Harvard Business Review*, 76(3): 84–95.

Crawford, H. (1995) *Talking Difference: On Gender and Language*. London: Sage.

Crystal, D. (2001) *Language and the Internet*. Cambridge: Cambridge University Press.

Culler, J. (1986) *Saussure*, 2nd edn. London: Fontana.

Czarniawska, B. (1992) *Exploring Complex Organizations. A Cultural Perspective*. London: Sage.

Czarniawska, B. (1997) *Narrating the Organization. Dramas of Institutional Identity*. Chicago and London: University of Chicago Press.

Czarniawska, B. (2000) *Writing Management. Organization Theory as a Literary Genre*. Oxford: Oxford University Press.

Czarniawska-Joerges, B. and Joerges, B. (1990) "Linguistic Artifacts at the Service of Organizational Control," in P. Gagliardi (ed.), *Symbols and Artifacts: Views from the Corporate Landscape*. Berlin: Walter de Gruyter. pp. 339–361.

Davenport, T.H. and Prusak, L. (1998) *Working Knowledge. How Organizations Manage What They Know*. Harvard: Harvard Business School Press.

Davidson, D. and Cooper, G. (1992) *Shattering the Glass Ceiling*. London: Paul Chapman.

Davies, C. (1995) *Gender and the Predicament in Nursing*. Milton Keynes: Open University Press.

Davison, C. (1994) "Creating a High Performance International Team," *Journal of Management Development*, 13(2): 181–190.

Deal, T.E. and Kennedy, A.A. (1988) *Corporate Cultures. The Rites and Rituals of Corporate Life*. Reading, MA: Addison Wesley.

de Beauvoir, S. (1972/1989) *The Second Sex*, trans. H.M. Porshley. New York: Vintage.

Denby, J. (2001) *Corazon*. London: HarperCollins.

Derrida, J. (1978) *Writing and Difference*. London: Routledge.

Donnelon, A. (1996) *Team Talk*. Boston: Harvard University Press.

Du Gay, P. (1991) "Enterprise Culture and the Ideology of Excellence," *New Formations*, 13 (Spring): 45–61.

Eckert, P. and McConnell-Ginet, S. (1992) "Think Practically and Look Locally: Language and Gender as Community-Based Practice," *Annual Review of Anthropology*, 21: 461–490.

Eisenberg, E.M. and Riley, P. (2001) "Organizational Culture," in F.M. Jablin and L.L. Putnam (eds), *The New Handbook of Organizational Communication. Advances in Theory, Research and Method*. London: Sage. pp. 291–322.

Eleman, P. (1975) "The Universal Smile," *Psychology Today*, 9: 35–38.

Ezard, J. (2001) "Needless Battle Caused by Uncommon Language," *The Guardian*, 14 April 2001.

Fairclough, N. (1992) *Discourse and Social Change*. London: Polity.

Fairclough, N. (2000) *New Labour, New Language?* London: Routledge.

Feyerabend, P. (1975) *Against Method*. London: New Left Books.

Fineman, S. (1998) "The Natural Environment, Organization and Ethics," in A. Parker (ed.), *Ethics and Organizations*. London: Sage. pp. 238–252.

Fisher, W.R. (1984) "Narration as a Human Communication Paradigm. The Case of Public Moral Argument," *Communication Monographs*, 51: 1–22.

Fisher, W.R. (1987) *Human Communication as Narrator. Toward a Philosophy of Reason, Value and Action*. Columbia, SC: University of South Carolina Press.

Fishman, P. (1983) "Interaction: The Work Women Do," in Barrie Thorne, Cheris Kramarae and Nancy Henley (eds), *Language, Gender and Society*. Rowley, MA: Newbury House. pp. 103–119.

Fiske, J. (1982) *Introduction to Communication Studies*. London: Routledge.

Fiske, J. (1987) "British Cultural Studies and Television," in R.C. Allen (ed.), *Channels of Discourse*. Chapel Hill, NC: The University of North Carolina Press.

Foucault, M. (1972) *The Archeology of Knowledge*. London: Tavistock Publications.

Foucault, M. (1979) *Discipline and Punish: The Birth of the Prison*. Harmondsworth: Penguin Books.

Foucault, M. (1981) *The History of Sexuality, Vol 1*. Harmondsworth: Penguin Books.

Foucault, M. (1984) "The Order of Discourse," in M. Shapiro (ed.), *Language and Politics*. Oxford: Basil Blackwell.

Gabriel, Y. (1993) "Organizational Nostalgia: Reflections on the Golden Age," in S. Fineman (ed.), *Emotion in Organization*. London: Sage.

Gabriel, Y. (1995) "The Unmanaged Organization: Stories, Fantasies and Subjectivity," *Organization Studies*, 16(3): 477–501.

Gabriel, Y. (1998a) "Same Old Story or Changing Story? Folklore, Modern and Postmodern Mutations," in D. Grant, T. Keenoy and C. Oswick (eds), *Discourse and Organization*. London: Sage.

Gabriel, Y. (1998b) "The Use of Stories," in G. Symon and C. Cassell (eds), *Qualitative Methods and Analysis in Organizational Research*. London: Sage.

Gabriel, Y. (2000) *Storytelling in Organizations. Facts, Fictions and Fantasies*. Oxford: Oxford University Press.

Gabriel, Y. and Lang, T. (1995) *The Unmanageable Consumer: Contemporary Consumption and its Fragmentation*. London: Sage.

Gamble, W. (2001) "The Making of the Christine Rankin Legend," *The New Zealand Herald*, Story ID. 203838, 4 August. Accessed on the Internet, 18 October 2001.

Geertz, C. (1973) *The Interpretation of Cultures*. New York: Basic Books.

Geertz, C. (2000) *Available Light. Anthropological Reflections on Philosophical Topics*. Princeton: Princeton University Press.

Gergen, K.J. (1989) "Organization Theory in the Postmodern Era," paper presented to the *Rethinking Organization* Conference, University of Lancaster.

Gergen, K. (1992) "Organization Theory in a Postmodern Area" in M. Reed and M. Hughes (eds), *Rethinking Organizations. New Directions in Organization Theory and Analysis*. London: Sage. pp. 207–226.

Gergen, K. (1999) *Invitation to Social Construction*. London: Sage.

Gherardi, S. (1995) *Gender, Symbolism and Organizational Cultures*. London: Sage.

Gowler, D. and Legge, K. (1986) "Images of Employees in Company Reports: Do Company Chairmen View their Most Valuable Asset as Valuable?," *Personnel Review*, 15(5): 9–18.

Gramsci, A. (1986) *Selections from Prison Notebooks* (ed. & trans. Q. Hoare and G. Smith). London: New Left Books.

Grant, D. and Oswick, C. (1996) *Metaphor and Organization*. London: Sage.

Grant, D., Keenoy, T. and Oswick, C. (eds) (1998) *Discourse and Organization*. London: Sage.

Gray, J. (1992) *Men Are From Mars, Women Are From Venus: A Practical Guide for Improving Communication and Getting What You Want in Your Relationship*. New York: Harper Collins.

Green, E. and Cassell, C.M. (1996) "Women Managers, Gendered Cultural Processes and Organizational Change," *Gender, Work and Organization*, 3(3): 168–178.

Grint, K. (1997) *Fuzzy Management: Contemporary Ideas and Practices at Work*. Oxford: OUP.

Gudykunst, W.B. (1998) *Bridging Differences. Effective Intergroup Communication*. London: Sage.

Guirdham, M. (1998) *Communicating Across Cultures*. London: Macmillan.

Gumperz, J. (ed.) (1982) *Language and Social Identity*. Cambridge: Cambridge University Press.

Guy, V. and Matlock, J. (1993) *The New International Manager. An Action Guide for Cross-cultural Business*. London: Kogan Ltd.

Halford, S. and Leonard, P. (2001) *Gender, Power and Organizations*. Basingstoke: Palgrave.

Hall, E.T. (1956) *Beyond Culture*. New York: Doubleday.

Halliday, M.A.K. (1978) *Language as Social Semiotic*. London: Edward Arnold.

Hansen, C.D. and Kahnweiler, W.M. (1993) "Storytelling: An Instrument for Understanding the Dynamics of Corporate Relationships," *Human Relations*, 46(12): 391–409.

Hanson, J. (1995) "English is as English does," *THES*, 7 July: 19.

Harlow, E., Hearn, J. and Parkin, W. (1995) "Gendered Noise: Organizations and the Silence and Din or Domination," in C. Itzin and J. Newman (eds), *Gender, Culture and Organizational Change*. London: Routledge.

Hatch, M.J. (1997) *Organization Theory. Modern, Symbolic and Postmodern Perspectives*. Oxford: Oxford University Press.

Hatch, M.J. and Ehrlich, S.B. (1993) "Spontaneous Humour as an Indicator of Paradox and Ambiguity in Organizations," *Organization Studies*, 14: 505–526.

Hayward, S. (1996) *Key Concepts in Cinema Studies*. London: Routledge.

Hearn, J. (1985) "Men's Sexuality at Work," in A. Metcalf and H. Humphries (eds), *The Sexuality of Men*. London: Pluto Press.

Hodge, R. and Kress, G. (1988) *Social Semiotics*. London: Polity.

Hodge, R. and Kress, G. (1993) *Language as Ideology*. 2nd edn. London: Routledge.

Hoffman, E. (1989) *Lost in Translation. A Life in a New Language*. London: Minerva.

Hofstede, G. (1984) *Culture's Consequences*. London: Sage.

Hofstede, G. (1991) *Culture and Organizations: Software of the Mind*. London: McGrawHill.

Hofstede, G. (1993) "Cultural constraints in management theories," *Executive*, 7: 81–94.

Hofstede, G. (1999) "The Universal and the Specific in 21st Century Global Management," *Organizational Dynamics*, 28(1): 34–49.

Hofstede, G. (2001) *Culture's Consequences. Comparing Values, Behaviours, Institutions and Organizations Across Nations*. London: Sage.

Hofstede, G. and Bond, M.H. (1988) "The Confucius Connection. From Cultural Roots to Economic Growth," *Organizational Dynamics*, 16(4): 16–21.

Höpfl, H. (1993) "The Making of the Corporate Acolyte. Some Thoughts on Charismatic Leadership and the Reality of Organizational Commitment," *Journal of Management Studies*, 29(1): 23–33.

Hornby, N. (2001) *How to be Good*. London: Viking.

Hosking, D.M. (1997) "Organizing, Leadership and Skilful Process," in K. Grint (ed.), *Leadership: Classical, Contemporary and Critical Approaches*. Oxford: Oxford University Press.

Huczynski, A. and Buchanan, D. (2001) *Organizational Behaviour. An Introductory Text*. 4th edn. Harlow: Prentice Hall.

Isaacs, W. (1993) "Taking Flight: Dialogue, Collective Thinking and Organizational Learning," *Organizational Dynamics*, 21(3): 24–39.

Isaacs, W. (1999) *Dialogue and the Art of Thinking Together*. New York: Currency.

Itzin, C. and Newman, J. (eds) (1995) *Gender, Culture and Organizational Change: Putting Theory into Practice*. London: Routledge.

Jackson, N. and Carter, P. (2000) *Rethinking Organisational Behaviour*. Harlow: Pearson Education.

Johnson, S. (1997) *Interface Culture: How New Technology Transforms the Way We Create and Communicate*. San Francisco: Harper.

Johnson, U. and Woodilla, J. (1999) "The Ironic Freedom or How Irony Facilitates the Construction of Multiple Organizational Realities," paper presented at *Aesthetics II*, Boston Institute of Higher Education Conference.

Kandola, R. and Fullerton, J. (1998) *Managing the Mosaic: Diversity in Action*. London: Institute of Personnel and Development.

Kanter, R.M. (1977) *Men and Women of the Corporation*. New York: Basic Books.

Keenoy, T., Oswick, C. and Grant, D. (1997) "Organizational Discourses: Text and Context," *Organization*, 4(2): 147–158.

Keeny, T., Oswick, C. and Grant, D. (2000) "Discourses, Epistemology and Organization: A Discursive Footnote," *Organization*, 7(3): 542–544.

Kernisky, D.A. (1997) "Proactive Crisis Management and Ethical Discourse: Dow Chemical's Issues Management Bulletins 1979–1990," *Journal of Business Ethics*, 16(8): 843–853.

Kets de Vries, M. (1991) "Leaders Who Make a Difference", *European Management Journal*, 14(5): 486–93.

Kittay, F.E. (1987) *Metaphor. Its Cognitive Force and Linguistic Structure*. Oxford: Clarendon Press.

Knights, D. (1992) "Changing Spaces: The Disruptive Impact of a New Epistemological Location for the Study of Management," *Academy of Management Review*, 17(3): 514–524.

Knights, D. and Morgan, G. (1991) "Corporate Strategy, Organizations, and Subjectivity: A Critique," *Organization Studies*, 12(2): 251–273.

Knights, D. and Wilmott, H. (1992) "Conceptualising Leadership Processes: A Study of Senior Managers in a Financial Services Company," *Journal of Management Studies*, 29(6): 761–782.

Kotter, J. (1982) *The General Managers*. New York: The Free Press.

Kress, G. (1985) *Linguistic Processes in Socio-Cultural Practice*. Geelong: Deakin University Press.

Kristeva, J. (1979) *Desire in Language*.Trs. Thomas Gora, Alice Jardine and Leon S. Roudiez. Oxford: Basil Blackwell.

Kunda, G. (1992) *Engineering Culture: Control and Commitment in a High Tech Company*. Philadelphia: Temple University Press.

Kundera, M. (1984) *The Unbearable Lightness of Being*. Tr. M.H. Heim. London: Faber and Faber.

Lakoff, G. and Johnson, M. (1980) *Metaphors We Live By*. Chicago: University of Chicago Press.

Lakoff, R. (1973) *Language and Woman's Place*. New York: Harper and Row.

Lakoff, R.I. (1975) *Language and Women's Place*. New York: Harper & Row.

Layder, D. (1994) *Understanding Social Theory*. London: Sage.

Lerman, C.L. (1985) "Media Analysis of a Presidential Speech," in T.A. Van Dijk (ed.), *Discourse and Communication*. Berlin & London: De Gruyter.

Levi-Strauss, C. (1969) *The Raw and the Cooked*. London: Cape.

Lilley, S.J. and Platt, G.M. (1997) "Correspondents' Images of Martin Luther King Jr: An Interpretive Theory of Movement Leadership," in K. Grint (ed.), *Leadership: A Reader*. Oxford: OUP.

Linstead, S. (1985) "Jokers Wild: The Importance of Humour in the Maintenance of Organisational Culture," *Sociological Review*, 33(4): 741–767.

Lodge, D. (2001) *Thinks*. London: Secker and Warburg.

Lyotard, J.F. (1979/1986) *The Postmodern Condition: A Report on Knowledge*. Manchester: Manchester University Press.

Macarthur, B. (1999) *The Penguin Book of Twentieth Century Speeches*. London: Penguin.

Mallon, M. and Cohen, L. (2001) "My Brilliant Career? Using Stories as a Methodological Tool in Careers Research," *International Studies of Management and Organization*, 31(2): 48–68.

Maltz, D. and Borker, R. (1982) "A Cultural Approach to Male–Female Miscommunication," in J. Coates (ed.), *Language and Gender: A Reader*. Oxford: Blackwell.

Mangham, I. and Overington, M.A. (1983) "Dramatism and the Theatrical Metaphor," in G. Morgan (ed.), *Beyond Method*. London: Sage.

Mangham, I.L. and Overington, M.A. (1987) *Organizations as Theatre: A Social Psychology of Dramatic Appearances*. Chichester: John Wiley and Sons.

Markus, M.L. (1994) "Electronic Mail as the Medium of Managerial Choice," *Organization Science*, 5(4): 138–154.

Marshak, R.J. (1993) "Managing the Metaphors of Change," *Organizational Dynamics*, 22(1): 144–156.

Marshak, R.J. (1996) "Metaphors, Metaphor Fields and Organizational Change," in D. Grant and C. Oswick (eds), *Metaphor and Organization*. London: Sage. pp. 147–165.

Martin, J. (1982) "Stories and Scripts in Organizational Settings," in A. Hastord and A. Isen (eds), *Cognitive and Social Psychology*. New York: Elsevier-North Holland.

Martin, J., Feldman, M.S., Hatch, M.J. and Sitkin, S.B. (1983) "The Uniqueness Paradox in Organizational Stories," *Administrative Science Quarterly*, 28: 438–453.

McEwan, I. (2001) "Only Love and then Oblivion. Love was all they had to set against their murderers". *The Guardian*, 15 September.

Morgan, G. (1986) *Images of Organization*. London: Sage.

Morgan, G. (1993) *Imagination. The Art of Creative Management*. London: Sage.

Morgen, S. (1994) "Personalizing Personnel Decisions in Feminist Organizational Theory and Practice," *Human Relations*, 47(6): 665–684.

Mullins, L.J. (1994) *Management and Organizational Behaviour.* 3rd edn. London: Pitman Publishing.

Mullins, L.J. (1999) *Management and Organisational Behaviour.* .5th edn. London: Pitman Publishing.

Mumby, D K. and Clair, R. (1997) "Organizational Discourse," in T.A. Van Dijk (ed.), *Discourse as Structure and Process*. Vol 2. London: Sage.

Musson, G. (1994) *Managing Change in Primary Care.* Unpublished PhD Thesis. University of Sheffield.

Musson, G. (1995) *"The FACTS Project: Interim Evaluation Report of the FACTS Aspirin Programme,"* a Sheffield Business School Publication.

Musson, G. (1996) *Qualitative Evaluation of the FACTS Aspirin Programme*. Sheffield Hallam University.

Musson, G. and Cohen, L. (1999) "Understanding Language Processes: a Neglected Skill in the Management Curriculum," *Management Learning*, 30(1): 27–42.

Nippert-Eng, C.E. (1996) *Home and Work*. Chicago: University of Chicago Press.

O'Brien, J. (1999) "Writing in the Body: Gender (Re)production in Online Interaction," in M.A. Smith and P. Kollock (eds), *Communities in Cyberspace*. London: Routledge.

O'Cathain, A., Musson, G. and Munro, J. (1998) "Shifting Services From Secondary to Primary Care: What do the Agencies Involved see as the Barriers?" *Journal of Health Services Research and Policy,* 4(3): 154–160.

Ortony, A. (1975) "Why Metaphors are Necessary and Not Just Nice," *Educational Theory*, 25(1): 45–53.

Ortony, A. (ed.) (1993) *Metaphor and Thought*. 2nd edn. Cambridge: Cambridge University Press.

Oswick, C. and Grant, D. (eds) (1996) *Organizational Development and Metaphorical Explorations*. London: Pitman Publishing.

Oswick, C. and Montgomery, J. (1999) "Images of an Organisation: The Use of Metaphor in a Multinational Company," *Journal of Organizational Change*, 12(6): 501–523.

Oswick, C., Keenoy, T. and Grant, D. (1997) "Managerial Discourses: Words Speak Louder Than Actions?," *Journal of Applied Management Studies*, 6(1): 5–12.

Palmer, I. and Dunford, R. (1996a) "Metaphors in Popular Management Discourse. The Case of Corporate Restructuring," in D. Grant and C. Oswick (eds), *Metaphor and Organisation*. London: Sage. pp. 95–109.

Palmer, I. and Dunford, R. (1996b) "Conflicting Uses of Metaphors: Reconceptualising their Use in the Field of Organizational Change," *Academy of Management Review*, 21(3): 691–706.

Pantelli, N. (2001) "Impressions and Boundaries in Virtual Work Spaces. Managing Boundaries in Orgs Sub Theme 20," 17th EGOS Colloquium, Lyon, France.

Parker, I. (2001) "Absolute PowerPoint: Can a Software Package Edit our Thoughts?," *The New Yorker*, 28 May 2001.

Parker, M. (2000) "The Less Important Sideshow: The Limits of Epistemology in Organizational Analysis," *Organization*, 7(3): 519–523.

Peters, T. and Austin, N. (1986) *A Passion for Excellence. The Leadership Difference.* London: Fontana.

Peters, T.S. and Waterman, R.H. (1982) *In Search of Excellence*. New York: Harper & Row.

Phillips, N. and Brown, A. (1998) *Organizational Culture*. 2nd edn. London: Financial Times-Pitman.

Phillips, N. and Hardy, C. (1997) "Managing Multiple Identities: Discourse, Legitimacy and Resources in the UK Refugee System," *Organization*, 14(2): 159–185.

Pierce, C.S. (1958) *Collected Papers, 1931–1958*. Cambridge, MA: Harvard University Press.

Pinder, C.C. and Bourgeois, V.W. (1983) "Controlling Tropes in Administrative Sciences," *Administrative Science Quarterly*, 27(4): 641–652.

Polkinhorne, D.E. (1987) *Narrative Knowing and the Human Sciences*. Albany, NY: State University of New York Press.

Pondy, L. (1978) "Leadership is a Language Game," in M.W. McCall and M.M. Lombardo (eds), *Leadership: Where Else Can We Go?* Durham, NC: Duke University Press.

Potter, J. (1997) "Discourse Analysis as a Way of Analysing Naturally Occurring Talk," in D. Silverman (ed.), *Qualitative Research: Theory, Method and Practice*. London: Sage.

Prasad, P. and Mills, A.J. (1997) "From Showcase to Shadow: Understanding the Dilemmas of Managing Workplace Diversity," in P. Prasad, A.J. Mills, M. Elmes and A. Prasad (eds), *Managing the Organizational Melting Pot: Dilemmas of Workplace Diversity*. Thousand Oaks, CA: Sage.

Pritchard, C. and Wilmott, H. (1997) "Just How Managed is the University?," *Organization Studies*, 18(2): 187–217.

Putnam, L.L. (1982) "Paradigms for Organizational Communication Research," *Western Journal of Speech Communication*, 46: 192–206.

Putnam, L.L. (1983) "The Interpretive Perspective. An Alternative to Functionalism," in L.L. Putnam and M.E. Pacanowsky (eds), *Communication and Organizations. An Interpretive Approach*. London: Sage.

Reed, M. (1998) "Organizational Analysis as Discourse Analysis: A Critique," in D. Grant, T. Keenoy and C. Oswick (eds), *Discourse and Organization*. London: Sage.

Reed, M. (1990) "From Paradigms to Images: The Paradigm Warrior Turns Post-modernist Guru," *Personnel Review*, 19: 35–40.

Reed, M. (2000) "The Limits of Discourse Analysis in Organizational Analysis," *Organization*, 7(3): 524–530.

Roddick. A. (1991) *Body and Soul*. London: Random House.

Rollinson, D., Broadfield, A. and Edwards, D.J. (1998) *Organisational Behaviour and Analysis. An Integrated Approach*. Harlow: Addison-Wesley.

Rorty, R. (1989) *Contingency, Irony and Solidarity*. Cambridge: Cambridge University Press.

Roy, D. (1960) "Banana Time: Job Satisfaction and Informal Interaction," *Human Organization*, 18(2): 156–168.

Sackman, S. (1989) "The Role of Metaphor in Organization Transformation," *Human Relations*, 42(6): 463–485.

Salzer-Mörling, M. (1998) "As God Created the Earth. A Saga that Makes Sense?," in D. Grant, T. Keenoy and C. Oswick (eds), *Discourse and Organization*. London: Sage. pp. 104–118.

Samovar, Ł.A. and Porter, R.E. (eds) (2000) *Intercultural Communication. A Reader*. Belmont, CA: Wadsworth.

Samovar, L.A. and Porter, R.E. (2001) *Communication Between Cultures*. 4th edn. Belmont, CA: Wadsworth.

Sapir, E. (1949) *Selected Writings*. Ed. D.G. Mandelbaum. Berkeley and Los Angeles: University of California Press.

Saussure, F. de (1974) *Course in General Linguistics*. Ed. J. Culler, Tr. W. Baskin. London: Fontana. (1st edn, 1915)

Savage, M. and Witz, A. (eds) (1992) *Gender and Bureaucracy*. Oxford: Blackwell.

Schein, E. (1993) "On Dialogue, Culture and Organizational Learning," *Organizational Dynamics*, 22(2): 40–51.

Schein, E. (2000) "Sense and Nonsense about Culture and Climate," in N.M. Ashkanary, C.P. Wilderom and M.F. Peteresons (eds), *Handbook of Organizational Culture and Climate*. London: Sage. pp. xxiii–xxxi.

Schirato, T. and Yell, S. (2000) *Communication and Culture*. London: Sage.

Schneider, S. and Barsoux, J.L. (1997) *Managing Across Cultures*. Hemel Hempstead: Prentice Hall.

Schön, D. (1993) "Generative Metaphor: A Perspective on Problem-setting in Social Policy," in A. Ortony (ed.), *Metaphor and Thought*. 2nd edn. Cambridge: Cambridge University Press. pp. 137–163.

Schultze, U. and Orliowski, W. (2001) "Metaphors of Virtuality: Shaping an Emergent Reality," *Information and Organization*, 11: 45–77.

Sederberg, P. (1984) *The Politics of Meaning: Power and Explanation in the Construction of Social Reality*. Tucson, Arizona: University of Arizona Press.

Sennett, R. (1998) *The Corrosion of Character: The Personal Consequences of Work in the New Capitalism*. New York: W.W. Norton & Co.

Sewell, G. (1998) "The Discipline of Team: The Control of Team-Based Industrial Work Through Electronic and Peer Surveillance," *Administrative Science Quarterly*, 43: 397–428.

Shaw, G., Brown, R. and Bromiley, P. (1998) "Strategic Stories. How 3M is Rewriting Business Planning," *Harvard Business Review*, May–June: 41–50.

Sheppard, D.L. (1989) "Organizations, Power and Sexuality: The Image and Self Image of Women Managers," in J. Hearn, D.L. Sheppard, P. Tancred-Sherif and G. Burrell (eds), *The Sexuality of Organizations*. London: Sage.

Silverman, P. and Jones, J. (1976) *Organizational Work: The Language of Grading/The Grading of Language*. London: MacMillan.

Sims, D., Gabriel, Y. and Fineman, S. (1993) *Organizing and Organizations*. London: Sage.

Sinclair, J. (1994) "Reacting to what?," *Journal of Organizational Change Management*, 7(5): 32–40.

Singelis, T. (1994) "Nonverbal Communication and Intercultural Interactions," in W.R. Brislin and T. Tomoko (eds), *Improving Intercultural Communications*. London: Sage.

Sjostrand, S., Sandberg, J. and Tyrstrup, M. (2000) *Invisible Management: The Social Construction of Leadership*. London: Thomson Learning.

Smith, M.A. and Kollock, P. (eds) (1999) *Communities in Cyberspace*. London: Routledge.

Sogon, S. and Mascutaine, M. (1989) "Identification of Emotion from Body Movements: A Cross-cultural Study of Americans and Japanese," *Psychological Reports*, 65: 35–46.

Spender, D. (1980) *Man Made Language*. London: Routledge and Kegan Paul.

Srivastva, S. and Barrett, F. (1988) "The Transforming Nature of Metaphor in Group Development: A Study in Group Theory," *Human Relations*, 4(1): 31–64.

Stohl, C. (2001) "Globalizing Organizational Communication," in F.M. Jablin and L.L. Putnam (eds), *The New Handbook of Organizational Communication. Advances in Theory, Research and Method*. London: Sage. pp. 323–375.

Sumner, W.G. (1940) *Folkways*. Boston: Ginnand.

Tannen, D. (1990) *You Just Don't Understand: Women and Men in Conversation*. New York: William Morrow, Ballantine.

Tannen, D. (1994) *Talking 9 to 5*. London: Virago.

Tannen, D. (1995) "The Power of Talk: Who Gets Heard and Why," *Harvard Business Review*, September–October.

Tannen, D. (1996) *Gender and Discourse*. Oxford: Oxford University Press.

Tayeb, M.H. (1996) *The Management of the Multicultural Workforce*. Chichester: John Wiley.

Taylor, S.S.(1999) "Making Sense of Revolutionary Change: Differences in Members' Stories," *Journal of Organizational Change Management*, 12(6): 524–539.

Tietze, S. (1998) "*The Role of Language in the Process of Creating Meaning in a Professional Organisation*," unpublished PhD dissertation, Sheffield Hallam University.

Tietze, S. (2000) "'Time is Money' and 'Life is a Game': Metaphors of the Market Place in Organisational and Individual Sense-making," *The International Journal of Applied Management*, 1(3): 3–18.

Tietze, S. (2002) "Intercultural communication … begins at home," *The International Journal of Applied Management*, 3(2): 3–12.

Tietze, S. and Musson, G. (2001) "Working from Home: Managing Guilt," *Organisation and People*, 9(1): 34–39.

Tinker, T. (1986) "Metaphor or Reification: Are Radical Humanists Really Libertarian Anarchists?," *Journal of Management Studies*, 23: 363–384.

Townley, B. (1994) *Reframing Human Resource Management*. London: Sage.

Troemel-Ploetz, S. (1998) "Selling the Apolitical," in J. Coates (ed.), *Language and Gender: A Reader*. London: Blackwell.

Trompenaars, F. (1993) *Riding the Waves of Culture. Understanding Cultural Diversity in Business*. London: Nicolas Brealey Publishing.

Tsoukas, H. (1991) "The Missing Link: A Transformational View of Metaphoric Organization Science," *Academy of Management Review*, 16(3): 566–585.

Tsoukas, H. (1999) "David and Goliath in the Risk Society: Making Sense of the Conflict between Shell and Greenpeace in the North Sea," *Organization*, 6(3): 499–528.

Turkle, S. (1997) *Life on the Screen: Identity in the Age of the Internet*. New York: Simon & Schuster.

Watson, T. (1995a) "Rhetoric, Discourse and Argument in Organizational Sense Making: A reflexive tale," *Organization Studies*, 16(5): 805–821.

Watson, T.J. (1995b) *Sociology. Work. Industry*. London: Routledge.

Watson, T. (2000) "Discourse and Organization," *Human Relations*, 53(4): 559–573.

Watson, T. (2001a) "Ethnographic Fiction Science: Making Sense of Managerial Work and Organisational Research Processes with Caroline and Terry," *Organization*, 7(3): 489–510.

Watson, T. (2001b) *In Search of Management: Culture, Chaos and Control in Managerial Work*. Revised edn. London: Routledge.

Weick, K. (1995b) *Sensemaking in Organization*. London: Sage.

West, C. and Zimmerman, D. (1983) "Small Insults: A Study of Interruptions in Cross-sex Conversations Between Unacquainted Persons," in Barrie Thorne, Cheris Kramarae and Nancy Henley (eds), *Language, Gender and Society*. Rowley, MA: Newbury House. pp. 103–119.

Westwood, R. and Linstead, S. (eds) (2001) *The Language of Organization*. London: Sage.

Whorf, B.L. (1956) *Language, Thought and Reality*. Cambridge, MA: MIT Press.

Wilkins, A.L. (1978) *"Organizational Stories as Expressions of Management Philosophy: Implications for Social Control in Organizations,"* unpublished PhD thesis, Stanford University, Palo Alto, CA, USA.

Wilkins, A.L. (1984) "The Creation of Company Cultures: The Role of Stories in Human Resource Systems," *Organizational Dynamics*, 12(3): 24–38.

Wilkins, A.L. and Martin, J. (1979) *"Organizational Legends,"* Research Paper no. 521, Stanford University Research Paper series, Palo Alto, CA, Stanford University.

Wilkins, A.L. and Thompson, M.P. (1991) "On Getting the Story Crooked (and Straight)," *Journal of Organizational Change Management*, 4(3): 18–26.

Wilkinson, B. (1996) "Culture, Institution and Business in East Asia," *Organization Studies*, 17(3): 421–447.

Williamson, J. (1978) *Decoding Advertisements: Ideology and Meaning in Advertising*. London: Boyars.

Wilson, F. (1995) *Organizational Behaviour and Gender*. London: McGraw-Hill.

Yen Mah, A. (1997) *Falling Leaves*. London: Penguin Books.

Yukl, G. (1989) "Managerial Leadership: A Review of Theory and Research," *Journal of Management*, 15(2): 251–289.

Zimmerman, D.H. and West, C. (1975) "Sex Roles, Interruptions, and Silences in Conversation," in B. Thorne and N. Henley (eds), *Language and Sex: Difference and Dominance*. Rowley: Newbury House, pp. 105–109.

Zuboff, S. (1988) *In the Age of the Smart Machine: The Future of Work and Power*. Oxford: Heinemann Professional.

Index

Index by Margaret Binns